THE EDUCATION OF A
DESIGN ENTREPRENEUR

Edited by Steven HELLER

RESS
K

D1318975

This book is dedicated to Nicolas Heller, future author.

07   06   05   04   03   02   5   4   3   2   1

Published by Allworth Press
An imprint of Allworth Communications
10 East 23rd Street, New York, NY 10010

Book design by James Victore, James Victore, Inc.
Interior page design by Jennifer Moore, James Victore, Inc.
Page composition/typography by Sharp Des!gns, Inc., Lansing, MI

ISBN: 1-58115-221–3

Library of Congress Cataloging-in-Publication Data
Education of a design entrepreneur / edited by Steven Heller.
p. cm.
Includes index.
ISBN 1-58115-221-3
1. Graphic arts—Marketing. 2. Sales promotion. I. Heller, Steven.
NC1001.6 .E35 2002
741.6'023'73—dc21
2001007896

Printed in Canada

TABLE OF CONTENTS

vii **ACKNOWLEDGMENTS**

viii PREFACE: **SO YOU WANT TO BE YOUR OWN BOSS**
by Steven HELLER

x INTRODUCTION: **AUTHORSHIP IN THE DIGITAL AGE—
YOU'RE NOT JUST A DESIGNER ANYMORE, OR ARE YOU?**
by Steven HELLER

CHAPTER 1: THE ENTREPRENEURIAL LIFE

2 **HOW HARD CAN THIS BE, YOU ASK?**
by David C. BAKER

4 **THE EDUCATION OF A DESIGN "ENTREMETTEUR"**
by Véronique VIENNE

8 **HOW TO TEACH ENTREPRENEURIALISM (NOT)**
by Ellen SHAPIRO

12 **BIRTH OF AN IDEA: OR, HOW I LEARNED TO
BE OBSERVANT AND LEAVE THE REST TO FATE**
by David VOGLER

18 **MAKING MY OWN MAGAZINE**
by Daniel NADEL

CHAPTER 2: TECHNOLOGY, INFORMATION, EDUCATION

23 **ENTREPRENEUR BY CIRCUMSTANCE**
with Clement MOK

31 **ANIMATED PROPERTIES**
with Peter GIRARDI

35 **OWNERSHIP ABOVE ALL**
with David SMALL

39 **EXPERIENCING EXPERIENCE**
with Edwin SCHLOSSBERG

43 **INFORMATION IS MY GAME**
with Richard Saul WURMAN

49 **MAPMAKER, MAKE ME A MAP**
with Stephan VAN DAM

55 **GROUP THINK**
with David M. KELLEY

59 **IMPROVING EVERYDAY LIFE**
with Yves BEHAR

65 **PRODUCTS OF NEED**
with Ellen SHAPIRO

CHAPTER 3: TOYS, GAMES, GIZMOS

73 **MAKING HAY FROM PLAY**
with Eric ZIMMERMAN

79 **SERIOUS PLAY**
with Byron GLASER and Sandra HIGASHI

85 **POWERED BY THE LIGHT**
with Richard MCGUIRE

93 **THE BIGGEST GAME**
with Forrest RICHARDSON

97 **FOOD THAT DOES NOT SPOIL**
with Saxton FREYMANN

103 **COMMUNICATING WITH EVERY PERSON ON EARTH**
with Maira KALMAN

107 **DESKTOP MONUMENTS**
with Constantin BOYM

CHAPTER 4: MAGAZINES, BOOKS, PERFORMANCE

113 **NESTING MAGAZINES**
with Joseph HOLZMAN

119   **NOT JUST A MAGAZINE ANYMORE**
with Josh GLENN and Anthony LEONE

127   **AN EXPRESSIVE JOURNAL**
with Hans Dieter RICHERT

131   **A MAGAZINE OF HIS OWN**
with Marty NEUMEIER

137   **WEBZINE ON DELINE**
with Mel BYARS

141   **BOOK AS PERFORMANCE**
with Warren LEHRER

149   **STORYTELLING IS EVERYTHING**
with Gary BASEMAN

CHAPTER 5: ART, WRITING, OBSESSION

157   **SPIRITUAL, OBSESSIVE, SACRED**
with Marshall ARISMAN

161   **DESIGN À CLEF**
with Chip KIDD

167   **BLONDES SELL MORE BOOKS**
with Natalia ILYIN

CHAPTER 6: FURNITURE, CLOTHES, ACCESSORIES

173   **MATERIALS AND THE BODY**
with John MAEDA

177   **MAVERICKS IN THE RAG TRADE**
with Michael Patrick CRONAN and Karin HIBMA

181   **NAME ON THE MARQUEE**
with Jay VIGON

185   **CLOTHES FOR THE STREET**
with Gary BENZEL and Todd ST. JOHN

189   **FROM A LONG LINE OF MERCHANTS**
with Sandy CHILEWICH

CHAPTER 7: NOVELTIES, SPECIALTIES, GIFTS

195 **CANDY MAN**
with Seymour CHWAST

199 **ANIMAL MAGNETISM**
with Alexander ISLEY

203 **THE ROLE OF TASTEMAKER**
with David SALANITRO

209 **MAKING LOTS OF PEOPLE HAPPY**
with Remo GUIFFRÉ

215 **HOUSE OF CARDS**
with Margaret and John MARTINEZ

CHAPTER 8: TYPE, GRAPHICS, DESIGN

221 **REVOLUTIONARY TYPES**
with Rudy VANDERLANS

229 **THE HEYDAY OF COMMERCIAL ART**
with Rich ROAT

233 **TYPECAST BUSINESS**
with Erik VAN BLOKLAND

237 **AN ELEMENTAL BUSINESS**
with Mies HORA

241 **AT HOME IN VIRTUAL SPACE**
with Marlene MCCARTY

247 **MAKING MAGIC**
with David LAI

251 **LABORATORY OF POP**
with Joshua BERGER

255 **HAPPY EXPERIMENTS**
with Stefan SAGMEISTER

ACKNOWLEDGMENTS

Everyone has a creative strength that, if nurtured, could change the course of his or her life. The designers interviewed for this book have found numerous ways to expand upon their basic talents and carve out careers without precedent. I want to thank each one of the interviewees for generously sharing those careers with me—the successes and failures. Without their cooperation, there would be no book.

I also want to thank Lita Talarico, my cochair of the M.F.A. Design department at the School of Visual Arts. Together we have developed a program for encouraging the designer as author/entrepreneur. Without her collaboration, I could not have pursued this approach to design education.

Thanks also to Silas Rhodes, chairman, and David Rhodes, president, of the School of Visual Arts for believing in the idea that designers have the potential to develop their own products and ideas. Their support of the M.F.A. program has been invaluable.

This book could not have taken shape without the oversight of Nicole Potter, editor; Jamie Kijowski, associate editor; Kate Lothman and Liz Van Hoose, editorial assistants; and Tad Crawford, publisher, of Allworth Press.

And last, but not least, thanks to James Victore for creating a beautiful cover and intelligent interior design for this book.

—STEVEN HELLER, *EDITOR*

SO YOU WANT TO BE YOUR OWN BOSS

by Steven HELLER

Graphic design students are taught to dispense their expertise to clients. Hands-on dispensing of expertise is the essence of a profession that, since its nascence as an offshoot of the late–nineteenth-century printing industry, has framed, packaged, and organized ideas, products, and information. However, the best graphic designers are not simply pairs of hands. Rather than follow predigested formats and timeworn formulas, they push the limits of type and image, creating unique icons that sometimes become artifacts of popular culture. Designers may be "problem-solvers" rather than self-initiators, but the act of invention is no less acute.

So, given their ability to create original and novel objects, why do so many graphic designers remain service providers? With such creative aptitude, doesn't it make sense that designers should also be content producers, attending to their own muses, at least once in their lives?

They should *and* they do. Many graphic designers have flirted with some kind of entrepreneurship, and others have become very successful at it. Actually, it's a two-way street: Some entrepreneurs have even practiced graphic design in order to retain more control of the overall look of their wares. These two trends are decidedly on the rise, because the personal computer, like no other technology before it, has put the means of production in the designer's hands. Moreover, graphic design is better recognized as a valuable asset in the creation, production, and manufacture of a total product.

This book is the first to examine the evolution of the designer as entrepreneur (or author). And I refer specifically to designers involved in the origination, production, and fabrication of products from books to toys, films to fashions, furniture to accessories, and countless other self-motivated ideas. I began by exploring graphic design as the foundation for entrepreneurial pursuit, but ultimately included many other design disciplines from which entrepreneurs emerge.

Although only a few design and art schools actually teach designers how to be entrepreneurs, I have made this book one in the Allworth Press "Education of . . ." series, because I believe that schools should not only encourage students to apply their formal training and aesthetic instincts towards self-generated projects, but to develop academic standards so that entrepreneurialism and authorship are routinely components of curricula on the undergraduate and graduate levels. This does not suggest that every design student is meant to be an entrepreneur—it does take fortitude and stamina to run a business—but it means that the option is viable for those who have what is demanded.

The Education of a Design Entrepreneur is not exactly formatted along the lines of the other "Education of . . ." books. For example, there are no sample syllabi, because there are almost none to be found. Instead, and in addition to essays on the process of being an entrepreneur, I have interviewed over forty design entrepreneurs to better understand what enabled them to create their respective products and how, in turn, they market their wares. Their responses are unique to their respective goals, and each offers different insights into a personal quest to make things that will satisfy both ego and economy.

Many of the designers included in *The Education of a Design Entrepreneur* have proven successes, but some have met failure. Many have found welcoming audiences, but for some, the process has been more difficult than imagined. Some have transformed themselves from full-time designers into full-time cottage industries and beyond. But above all, the lesson to be learned from this book is that design entrepreneurship is a viable activity, as long as one has the talent and guts.

AUTHORSHIP IN THE DIGITAL AGE— YOU'RE NOT JUST A DESIGNER ANYMORE, OR ARE YOU?

by Steven HELLER

Part One

Graphic designers are faced with important choices these days. If you didn't already know it, we are in the digital loop. We can either move other people's words and pictures around on a computer screen, or make words and pictures express our own ideas. With our design skills, we routinely make other people's notions come to life, so why not our own?

It may not have been a viable option a decade ago. In fact, before the digital revolution changed the professional ground rules, we were content collaborating with (in the best situations) or serving so-called content creators. Today, graphic designers have the opportunity to be authors in the metaphoric and practical senses of the word. Our ability to package, organize, and aestheticize through the manipulation of type, image, and decoration is a foundation for more inclusive control of an entire creative process. Want to publish a book? Any designer can be a packager, producer, or editor in the desktop environment. And owing to Internet publishing and distributing, an e-book is potentially a breeze. Want to launch a retail shop? With less bureaucratic interference than it takes to open a storefront, a Web site can be launched to fulfill many desires.

Okay, a graphic designer cannot become an author or entrepreneur just by pressing a button—it does take considerable savvy *and* a great idea—but the digital world invites the ambitious to expand on their expertise or passion into realms other than typographical or Photoshop servitude. And while every business venture has inherent risks, designers are in a better position now than ever to take steps that will lead towards independence—creative, monetary, or otherwise.

Nonetheless, the digital environment poses certain roadblocks for the auteur. As it is in film, auteurship is bracketed by integral collaborations. It is certainly easier to be the sole creator when faced with paper and pen, or even with Quark, than in the multimedia realm. The creator relies on technical support to bring ideas to life and the expertise of others to transform notions into gems worthy of the medium. But ultimately, this model is not that different from traditional authorship. In book publishing, for example, the writer is supported by editors who read copy for content, proof copy for sense, and check copy for facts. Often, the editor truly shapes and molds. Are these collaborators authors, too? Routinely, they are simply part of the process. Regardless of writing ability, the main idea stems from the author of record.

There are many possibilities for authorship, yet no formulas. The first thing, however, is that juggling is essential. Charles Spencer Andersen did not give up his design studio when he founded the CSA Archive. Tibor and Maira Kalman did not fold M&Co. when M&Co. Labs, the subsidiary that produced its popular watches, earned a modicum of success. Authorship can be something of a sideline that grows (or doesn't) into a profit center, but it won't happen overnight. Which is to say that one's design business should, at the outset at least, support any entrepreneurial pursuits. The business of business may be business, but the business of design authorship is charting new territory. In the beginning, it is good enough to simply create something that is one's own idea.

Funny Garbage, the New York multimedia design firm known for creating Web sites and CD-ROMs for high-visibility brands, recently launched a small subsidiary called Funny Garbage Books. Paradoxically, it used its success in the digital realm to create a print product. Being a book packager is not being an author, but it is being an entrepreneur who decides on what content will be published. The first book on their initial list is a collection of comic drawings by Gary Panter, which has nothing whatsoever to do with the Web. Nonetheless, it was born of its creators' art and design passions. But it is one thing to get a very handsomely designed and produced volume into print and another to sell it. FG used its organizational infrastructure to produce the volume, but it must now learn about the publishing industry from the bottom to get the book into the market and sustain viablity.

To be a designer-entrepreneur ultimately means learning new skills that, as mere designers, we did not need to know. Most designers, after all, become designers to play with form. Our fundamental concerns are more or less artistic, e.g., finding the perfect typeface to highlight a pristine layout. Most of us can spend the day noodling away, repositioning a word by a quarter of a point left or right. Business issues are left to the bean counters. But in the new, holistic practice of authorship and entrepreneurship, these concerns must not be ignored or set aside.

Three years ago, I created an M.F.A. Design program at the School of Visual Arts, New York, devoted to "authorpreneurship." The overriding difference between this and other advanced degree study programs is that students are "trained" to be content creators. And trained is an apt word, because our students are former professionals who, for the most part, never conceived of conceiving their own intellectual property. In a sense, they must be reprogrammed to think of themselves as integral creators. But they also must be made aware that their products are not developed within the vacuum of an academy. Instead, under real-life simulations, they must first (in year one) explore and find what it is that they have to offer (and capitalize on it), and second (in year two), invent a product that will be promoted, developed, and marketed to a defined audience (whomever that may be). They are encouraged to use their design skills (and each student has very different abilities) to frame, package, and structure their ideas. But design is the vessel, not the end.

Given the prevailing fashions, most students focus on the Internet as their epicenter, but invariably, after reflection, it is only a component of larger ideas. With the rise and fall of dot.coms, the designer-authorpreneur must realize that it is axiomatic that the trendier the trend, the less the need over time. Web sites are good vehicles for transmitting and distributing ideas, but for the Web to be a viable end in itself requires much luck. Nonetheless, it can be a necessary hub of commerce. SVA students are, therefore, creating magazines, books, retail products, film, and video that use the Web for promotion and sales, but look to other media for the end product.

Whatever is produced, and however it is accomplished, designers in the digital age must be open to the redefinition of their roles. The graphic design paradigm from as recently as a decade ago is no longer exclusive. Although not everyone can be an author or entrepreneur—not every designer wants to or can create unique products—pushing type or an image around on a PC or Palm Pilot display will yield fewer rewards. Then it will be time to give authorship a chance.

Part Two

One of my students who bought the author concept hook, line, and Flash has devoted himself to doing an M.F.A. thesis project that involves developing the concept, design, and content for an ambitious Web site. I cannot tell you the title or specifics of the project, because the intellectual property lawyer on our faculty insists that students make us agree to nondisclosure pacts. Since the work is now in development and has not yet been awarded a copyright or patent, my lips are sealed. What I can say, however, is that if it works, this will not be a huge dot.com profit center, but it could be an invaluable asset to graphic design pedagogy as both tool and resource. It has, therefore, become intellectually rigorous and incredibly elaborate—perhaps too elaborate for a single person to handle.

The project began modestly enough as a site that compiled various book essays and magazine articles. Originally, it was going be a Web digest and reference outlet, something along the lines of artsandletters.com, featuring a variety of scholarly and journalistic writing. The student is taking sole responsibility for accumulating, excerpting, indexing, and publishing this body of work and also the hands-on design of the site. For the final thesis, he is required to create a home page that links to various pages, each on a subtopic, and then build supplementary visual content around these existing entities using various means. He must also provide an interactive component for users' commentary, such as "response" pop-up screens. The idea is viable if the outside writers agree to his terms, which includes nonexclusive rights to publish their work in full without a fee—he cannot afford at this time to pay them for subsidiary rights. He has received positive response from some of the "content providers" on his wish list, but a few rightfully want compensation for what amounts to unlimited distribution of their work.

The royalty issue was his first major obstacle. The "Kinko's Law" stipulates that permission must be obtained from a copyright holder for any published material that is copied and distributed apart from the original venue (i.e., books or magazines). Some writers routinely suspend fees; nonetheless, others are sticklers for the small honorarium. Given the prospect of losing important content, however, the student decided to develop a venue, not unlike Contentville.com, now defunct, that gives terse summaries of all texts, while the entire work is available for a nominal fee. This required that he investigate online methods of releasing information and "shopping cart" options. He subsequently learned that it would be quite difficult, because these services require cash reserves. His alternative was to summarize some texts and link to the authors' sites or other resource sites. He felt that this compromises the idea to make a wide range of materials directly available, and yet for now, linking is the only acceptable solution.

This glitch caused him to do further research of other sites on the Web, where he found similar archival and distribution services. Although his material would be different, and while improving on an existing idea is perfectly fine, the student concluded that his first idea was not good enough. He, therefore, decided to expand the parameters to include original material that he will author—a virtuous goal with inherently profound challenges that proved to be his second obstacle.

It is one thing to be a warehouse (and the Web is perfect for that), another to be a retail store. Or using another analogy, it is comparatively easy to write or edit a single book, but taxing to shepherd a multivolume encyclopedia. The pressures in terms of time, energy, intelligence—oh yes, and stress—decidedly increase. This is where the sole-authorship paradigm is put to the test. In addition to assembling and writing the content—and writing in such a way that the audience will enjoy rather than feel obligated to read—the issue of maintenance is paramount. If the student found financial underwriting (which, incidentally, is encouraged but improbable), then he could hire an editor, designer, tech wonk, etc. But as a student project, this must be a bare-bones operation—though a highly sophisticated one. The students in this M.F.A. program are encouraged to make their thesis as unique and viable as possible, which often involves projecting their work five years into the future. But for the prototype, the student was rightly convinced that this project would not stand a chance in the marketplace if he did not launch it with all the value-additives he now proposed. The faculty advisors agreed. So, the question is how to make it work.

You might ask why this student did not team up with other students? Catch 22: The M.F.A. Design program promotes individual authorship. We do not restrict the use of outside assistance, including commissioning freelancers. But at least for now, we prohibit joint authorship. The challenge is to do it alone, which, in the digital medium, increases the obstacles.

The upside and downside of digital authorship, as well as the computer's seduction, is the belief that one can do almost anything on the desktop. Our students are taught the benefits of collaboration, yet we believe that to truly master the authorial product, they must have hands-on knowledge of all the components that lead to the success or failure of their thesis. In this case, the student made a decision to expand his fundamental idea to a theoretically solid place, but that severely challenged its overall functionality.

Obstacles arose in direct proportion to the student's increased ambition. The thesis advisory committee (which includes three or more "thesis faculty"—we employ five thesis teachers addressing different aspects of the work, business, concept, and technology) set the minimum standards. The students, however, must set their own high standards, so once this student announced his new direction, the additional goals became integral to his final requirements. Not only do the technological demands expand (more screens, more links, more visual FX), but his own knowledge base is duly challenged. So far, most of our students come from a print background with some training on the Web. This student had been in the corporate communications area, but had taken a few HTML classes before applying to our program. During his first M.F.A. year, he took HTML and Flash—enough to know the capacity of the technology, but not enough to be expert. He also took a course that taught him to graph and manage content. These skills had to be increased over time, which meant a lot of remedial work was necessary. Still, he would have benefited from more help from a dedicated tech person.

While he is on terra firma when acting as a compiler or editor of existing material, the development of original content requires more experience and greater understanding—perhaps more than he can acquire in two semesters, the allotted thesis preparation time. Good compilations require considerable research and reading, but being a confident writer takes experience. He entered this process without extensive knowledge of his theme, and over time, he voraciously accumulated some of what he needed.

While this is a valuable acquisition, his knowledge is tertiary in parts. Therefore, how to parlay his weakness into strength is his biggest challenge.

He is adamant that he will be the sole author, because he came out of a background where every element of design was more or less predetermined. He has developed two overall design prototypes, which are navigationally sound and typographically handsome (without being overly stylized). The essays and articles are being accumulated, and he's uncovered more resources than he initially expected to find. He is also devising a way to add some original materials through interviews and reportage that introduce voices of others who possess some of the missing pieces, which takes some of the onus off his lack of knowledge. He is also determining how many or few bells and whistles are needed to give the site extra impact—given his time constraints, he will probably forego the unnecessary Flash animations in favor of more conservative GIFs. Some things are coming together nicely, while others could be greatly enhanced by more collaboration and better management.

This is indeed a learning process for the student *and* those of us who administer and teach in the program. It is one thing to espouse authorship (a few of our print-based authors have been fairly successful) and another to put it into practice in the real world. It's still another to develop an authorial voice in the digital environment on one's own. The goal for this student is to get the proper funding to launch his site. He says he'll do it himself if he cannot raise the money. But the ambitious nature of this undertaking makes it imperative that he link up with a partnering institution. I wish I could tell you what this is (I could be sued and my Ferrari repossessed). If it never sees the light of day (other than its intranet test launch), it will be a loss to the design community. But if the student can make the pieces work together and find others with additional strengths, educators will definitely find it valuable.

THE ENTREPRENEURIAL LIFE

HOW HARD CAN THIS BE, YOU ASK?

by David C. BAKER

The design business has seldom been about the client or about the client's client. It's been about the thing designed, whether an annual report, marketing support brochure, or corporate identity. In other words, the frequent result of design efforts is collateral; it doesn't have much intrinsic value, but instead points to something else that does, like a company or a product the brochure illustrates.

This supporting role has not provided the enduring satisfaction that many designers have longed for, and it has inserted clients and their clients as necessary evils to the design process. And while designers pursue the business of design, they secretly (or not so secretly) long to bypass the client and create a product that is designed, excited in the process by the more enduring results of their labor. So, instead of creating a brochure that effectively sells a chair that effectively lines the client's pockets, they create the chair instead. This chair, though, isn't so much about money as it is about control and influence. "Control" because the pursuit of design is hampered by client vagaries, and "influence" because the designer is leaving his or her mark on society with an object that can be pointed to.

Most designers start a business that does design because they love the creative process and because they want to exert as much control over that process as possible. Underneath the motivation is the movement to make a business out of a personal love. This is not good.

The minute you start a business, you begin to move away from your two loves— creativity and control—unless you do it right.

For instance, you love creating products and you are tired of others making money off your efforts. You decide to create your own product, unfettered by silly clients. "How hard can this be?" you ask. The answer is right around the corner, as hundreds of designers discover.

The safer approach is to intentionally separate the business from your personal pursuits. Create the chair, but don't assume you'll get rich from it. Make several copies, and give them away at family reunions.

The minute you depend on creativity for a living, you cede control to somebody else's judgment (the client) and somebody else's assistance (the employee). This is obvious as it relates to a graphic design business. You don't get paid until you get approval (the client), and you don't get plum assignments unless you have a support staff larger than yourself (the employee). The former tends to knock the distinctive edges of your work, and the latter proves distracting because of the management demands on your time.

So, you create a product that eliminates the need for both, forgetting that there are still clients (those who will buy your products) and dependents (those who will manage the manufacturing, marketing, and distribution processes).

We all long to do design without client interference—better yet, without clients at all. This pushes us to create products as an outlet for our creativity with fewer constraints than we are experiencing at the moment. A better approach is to "get a life" and go back to the things we enjoy doing without the tainting affects of money. This is something that you can do without clients.

The alternative is to prostitute your business to provide creative stimulation. I'm not saying that you shouldn't pursue the creation of products, but rather that you do it for the right reasons. If you do it to slake that creative thirst, you'll fool yourself about the complexity of the process and fail as a result, underestimating the importance of planning the manufacturing, marketing, and distribution of your product. But if you treat it as a business, you'll do your homework, find the right partners, and design the product with an eye toward commercial success, not creative stimulation. But as you can see from this last description, success means an inevitable ceding of control and creativity, the very things that prompted the pursuit in the first place.

You need a creative life unrelated to making money. Once those urges are satisfied, you can insert the sullying qualities of money into the equation and make smart decisions. Who better to create incredible products than designers? Against that obvious reality, how is it that so few ideas make it to the marketplace?

The world of making money doesn't belong to those with good ideas. It belongs to those who know how to take their ideas to the marketplace.

DAVID C. BAKER is the principal of ReCourses, Inc., a management consulting firm that works with public relations, advertising, interactive, and design firms. He is also the editor of *Persuading*, a monthly journal addressed to the same market. He speaks and writes widely for an international audience on the business side of creativity.

THE EDUCATION OF A DESIGN "ENTREMETTEUR"

by Véronique VIENNE

Without taking her eyes off me, she reaches toward her desk. The upper right-hand drawer glides silently. Her expression is so inscrutable, one would think she is about to perform a mercy killing. But instead of a revolver, the head of human resources extracts a box of tissues from some secret compartment and pushes it across the polished teak surface toward me.

"Sorry," she whispers. "We are restructuring your department. We have to let you go."

I am fired.

Called to her office for what I had assumed was a routine staff salary review, I was totally unprepared. Now, I realize that I am disheveled and that I don't have my lipstick on. In my book of etiquette, handing an employee the pink slip without giving her time to put her lipstick on is tantamount to police brutality. No, I don't need a tissue, thank you. I am pissed. I am mad. I am experiencing déjà vu.

A veteran of corporate downsizing, I should have known better. Designers are always the first ones to be "transitioned" when a company needs repositioning as a result of yet another bottom-line-inspired merger and acquisition. By now, it's almost routine: One day, new management calls everyone in your department to the conference room for the usual pep talk—yada, yada, yada. Beware: If the newcomers seem truly eager to "reassure you that your job is secure," your days on the payroll are most likely numbered. Instead of reading the signs, though, you probably cling to your illusions: You are a valuable asset to the company, your team has met all its financial objectives, *and* you've never gone over budget. However, all your diligence and hard work counts for nothing when figure-crunchers have decided it's time to swing the axe in order to hype their third-quarter earnings.

Eventually, I got the message. I had to become my own boss.

For designers, it's relatively easy to set up a small studio. Because the initial investment is low compared to that of a hairdresser or a caterer, for instance (your chances of being sued for using the wrong typeface are pretty minimal), you don't even need a business plan. You can just lease $15,000 worth of electronic equipment, design a cool business card, hire an accountant, and you are ready to open shop. Chances are, your first clients are friends of friends who don't expect you to write a detailed proposal, let alone sign a nondisclosure agreement. Before you know it, every month, you are billing twice as much as your old take-home salary. Being a design entrepreneur? It's a cinch!

Tax time will be a rude awakening. As will the day the printer switches the cyan and the magenta plate on a rush job, and a client calls in a panic because there is no date on the invitation you designed for their big fund-raising gala next week. The first time something of the sort happened to me—my client's logo was printed upside down on the back of a brochure—I was so mortified, I briefly considered jumping under an oncoming subway train.

So, you learn to factor in time and money for (1) a copyeditor, (2) a fact-checker, (3) a production manager, and (4) a lawyer. Instead of an intern to answer your phone—or a welfare mother, in my case—you hire someone with a marketing degree. The next thing you know, you are reading *Managing Brand Equity* by David Aaker and *The Conquest of Cool* by Thomas Frank. In your car, you listen to Tom Peters' seminar tapes. And—good grief—you now take prospective clients to expensive lunches.

This phase of the process can be a lot of fun. I know I enjoyed it. I became second to none in proposal writing. I learned to pontificate about the difference between strategic and tactical thinking. And I perfected the fine art of tracking product attributes versus product perceptions on graphs and charts of my own making.

Unfortunately, not everyone shared my enthusiasm for corporate-speak. When discussing a project with designers, I was chagrined to notice their reluctance to embrace my innovative marketing approach. Illustrators listened in dubious silence as I described in glowing terms what the client had in mind. And photographers no longer dealt directly with me—I had to negotiate assignments through their agent.

Eventually, it dawned on me that I was no longer designing—I was managing design projects for my clients.

It's not enough to own your business—as your client list grows, if you want to remain a bona fide design entrepreneur, you also have to be able to own up to the work you do in the name of profit. If you don't, you become what the French call an "entremetteur"—a go-between, a mediator, a procurer, and at times, a pimp.

Suffice it to say that sooner or later, if your business is successful, you will be faced with disagreeable dilemmas. Like when you are asked to help reposition a sugar-loaded soft drink as a healthy sports beverage. Sell cheap underwear as luxury items. Or mount an advertising campaign to convince kids that your client *really* cares about the environment. Don't worry, though. Whatever you decide, no one needs to know. So much of the work you do for your clients is confidential—and you don't sign your work, do you?

In this country, you never see the name of a design studio or an advertising agency on a package, a poster, an ad, a piece of junk mail, or even a fancy brochure. Paul Rand, who insisted he be allowed to apply his hand-scrolled signature on his posters and book jackets, was a notable exception in the field. Famous photographers—Bruce Weber, Helmut Newton, Richard Avedon, even Irving Penn—don't get to sign their advertising campaigns. And only insiders know who designed the Nike logo, who masterminds the Calvin Klein image, or who came up with the semitranslucent aesthetic of the iMac computer.

This arrangement, which conveniently blurs the boundaries between art and commerce for all parties involved, is most beneficial to clients who buy from designers the right to their design production and can thus claim creative ownership of both the ideas and their execution.

In the rare instances when people are credited for their creative input, like in the case of Target promoting Michael Graves, it can have dire consequences for the designer's prestige—cheapening both his name and his work. "Who designed that shoddy Target kettle with a bird whistle?" asked a friend of mine recently. "Was it Philippe Stark, Frank Gehry, or that other guy, Michael Graves?"

And how about the struggling artists who contributed to the now celebrated Absolut Vodka advertising campaign? Sure, they got paid handsomely for their work, but they never got fully credited in *The Absolut Book* that reproduces their work.

Fair enough. You cannot expect to retain authorship of your work if you sell clients all rights to your intellectual property. What you can do, though, is try to hold on to the cultural content of the work you do by building up your image independently of your professional identity. By writing books about your ideas. By creating and distributing small editions of your personal designs. By teaching at a local art school. By organizing seminars on topics that interest you. Or you can set aside one afternoon a week to paint, draw, take acting lessons—whatever helps you discover new talents or improve existing skills. While the courts are considering the complex implications of copyright laws in the new economy, you can develop a noncommercial identity and become someone who can't be bought. Tibor Kalman did it. So can you.

Of course, it will cost you.

My career as a design entrepreneur took a financial downturn when I realized that I could do with writing what I couldn't do with designing. With words, I could create a rich body of visual imagery—and retain full authorship of it. Of course, as an unknown writer, I found myself at the bottom of the food chain, sometimes getting paid as little as twenty-five cents a word or less. But with my name now printed on the page, I am able to take full credit—and full responsibility—for the content I am providing.

Although I do plenty of "work-for-hire" writing, selling it to clients without restrictions, in the same way a designer sells his services, I can also, in many instances, license my words for a limited amount of time, and with some limited control on how it is presented. Granted, I don't have total creative freedom, but I can still be part of the design community. Most important, I now get to have lunch with all my peers—the same people I used to bore with my marketing jargon—and not once during the meal do they hear me talk about "image territory," "branding equity," or "trade leverage."

A friend of mine, a successful designer I respect, recently sold his thriving design consultancy to a large international advertising concern. Not only did he get to laugh all the way to the bank, but he also remained under contract to run his company for the next couple of years. Of course, some of his loyal employees had to be "transitioned," to avoid "redundancy"—a mildly unpleasant affair, considering that he had nurtured his staff like a father for the last fifteen years. A week after the deal was sealed, he got a phone call from someone he had never met who introduced himself as the CFO of the company that now owned him. "I heard that your presentation with the client yesterday was very good," said the man. "You are doing a great job, congratulations!!!"

For a minute, my friend thought he was going to get sick. "With that one patronizing remark," he explained, "the CFO made it clear that I was no longer the boss. It was devastating."

That's the problem with all of us designers: Deep down, we are incurable idealists. We are artists—we hate to sell out. Some of us are not even sure we like commerce all that much. Instead of rejoicing each time the cash register rings, we sulk, because the measure of our success, ultimately, is the success of our clients.

Or at least that's what our clients would like us to believe.

We know better. The real measure of our success is how much fun we have when designing.

VÉRONIQUE VIENNE is the author of short essays on culture and lifestyle and has written *The Art of Doing Nothing, The Art of Imperfection,* **and** *The Art of Growing Up,* **published by Clarkson Potter in 1998, 1999, and 2000. Also available is a collection of her design essays,** *Something to Be Desired,* **published by** *Graphis* **in 2001.**

HOW TO TEACH ENTREPRENEURIALISM (NOT)

by Ellen SHAPIRO

If you did what I do, right now, you'd be sitting at a table in a poorly lit hotel ballroom waiting for your next visitor. When she arrives—it will most certainly be a she, most teachers are—you'll stand up and demonstrate Alphagram Learning Materials . . . with feeling, as if you were doing it for the very first time, and as if your life depended on it (because in a way, it does).

Like Estée Lauder "touching" women and making them customers for life by stroking creams on their faces, you'll go through your moves. The first thing you'll do is point out how the visual cues in Alphagram icons help students make lasting sound-symbol associations. Then, if she shows interest, you'll show how easy it is to change sound-spellings with Alphagram Word Maker cards—for example, adding a silent *e* to a three-letter word ("mop") to make the vowel long ("mope"). And if she's impressed, exclaiming, "I've been looking for something like that for years," you might go on to demonstrate how the numbered arrows of Alphagram Tracing Letters can help disgraphic students form correct cursive letters.

Even after you've carefully demonstrated all the products and answered all her questions, she still might walk away and buy from another publisher, that big company with a huge booth whose materials look really ugly. ("Name recognition," your consultants say, when you express amazement at how teachers could keep buying that stuff when yours is right there and obviously so much better.) But wait! It looks as if she's going stay and become a customer! In which case, you'll ring up her order, put her purchases and receipt into an "Alphagram, The Better Way to Teach the ABC's" shopping bag (clear plastic, better to show the covers and colors), thank her with a big smile, and tell her she can call any time with questions. You will do all this lovingly and wholeheartedly, without irony, because you want to make her (and the other teachers at her school) customers for life, and because you truly believe in these products and know they will help children, especially children with learning disabilities, learn to read, spell, and write.

Sometimes, like now, no one will visit your table for long stretches of empty minutes (all the teachers are in workshop sessions). At other times, you'll be overwhelmed by people grabbing products and shoving money and credit cards at you.

To be honest, you spend only six or so days a year doing this, being a "vendor" at literacy conferences. Your other days as a design entrepreneur are filled with such tasks as trying to find out what teachers, schools, and districts will be looking for next year, testing prototypes, negotiating with wholesalers, creating links for your Web site, dealing with inventory issues ("What do you mean, you don't know where the truck is?"), and making sure orders are taken correctly and cartons are packed and shipped properly.

All of the above and much more will be done during hours that could supposedly be spent designing lucrative, award-winning corporate identity programs and annual reports. Why? You are driven. And because every publisher to whom you showed your prototypes (including the big company with the huge booth) just didn't get it and turned you down. You were stubborn. You saw there weren't any well designed materials that would work for kids like your son, who had difficulty learning to read. And you just knew that—unlike all your previous goofy product concepts—this one was really good and would sell. So, you decided to go into the publishing business yourself. It was like some powerful invisible hand was pulling you along. And here you are. In four years, it's become a success, more or less.

Now, suppose other graphic designers were interested in not devoting their entire careers promoting or packaging other people's ideas and wanted to become design entrepreneurs themselves. Could you teach them how to do it?

That's a question I've been grappling with for two years while attempting to help the M.F.A. design students at New York's School of Visual Arts develop their own prototype products and create the business plans with which to sell them.

Each project starts just about the same way: The student makes an oral presentation to the class, and I think, "That sounds beautiful, but who will buy it?" Then, week by week, the student works through the process of refining the product, defining the market, determining how to reach buyers—and putting all this into a document that will clearly communicate to a potential investor or partner what the product will do, why it is a good idea, and how it can be profitable.

This kind of teaching takes a lot of one-on-one consultation. Class members as a group have a tendency to criticize something they don't understand or, more often, unrealistically and enthusiastically applaud weak ideas. I've found that the best way to be of assistance is to meet with each student several times individually, giving him or her the opportunity to present concepts orally, visually, and in writing. I probe, evaluate, suggest, ask for alternatives. "All my friends like it" is an easy way out that will probably lead to failure. A competitive analysis with realistic numbers is difficult, but necessary. In the hopes of making their presentations stronger, students often conveniently ignore other products in the category. Then I, the unsympathetic teacher, am in the unenviable position of pointing out that a Yahoo search turned up 7,345 other, similar concepts. After each round of being refined, shaped, sharpened, the product is again presented to the class.

No matter what the product—it could be a publication, Web site, store, line of consumer products intended to be sold in existing stores, method for delivering services, or even a work of performance art—I have found that it will have the best chances for success if:

✤ The idea truly comes from the heart and personal experience. Without that insight and passion, it's nearly impossible to see it through.
✤ The product is original and meets a real, measurable market need.
✤ The audience can be reached on a limited budget.

This usually means no fantasy projects that would require national TV and magazine advertising. No launches of new beverages or mass-audience magazines or search engines. In fact, a watchword of my class is that the target market cannot be "everybody." But if students can define a niche audience—be it Korean-American parents, snowboarders, travelers to Puerto Rico, or owners of small dogs in New York City—they'll probably be able to find and reach them. They can advertise in special-interest magazines. They can use local radio and cable TV. They can buy lists and get messages directly into mailboxes. And if they can prove to a bank or venture capitalist that the product can be sold for more than it will cost to run the company, manufacture the product, and reach the audience—they're in business. Then, all they have to do is persevere relentlessly . . . and do it with feeling. And do it with a business head, not just a design head. Read the *Wall Street Journal*, I exhort the students, not just the design magazines. (Today's lead *WSJ* article, for example, is about a company called Bid4Assets Inc. that's selling off the hardware left behind by last year's sure things, eToys and Pets.com. That's sobering.) I also tell them to get rid of those layered images and illegible type. The purpose of a business plan is to get people excited about a product, so make sure they can read it.

Often, a student product is not something conventional or tangible, but, admirably, an idea for making the world a better place: a way to improve New York's subways or help addicts get off drugs or help people with limited vision conduct their lives. Which makes it even harder to develop and "sell," but even more worthwhile to pursue.

As Al Greenburg, former chairman of the communication design department at Parsons School of Design, used to say, "This is not an exact science." It's much easier to teach, say, cooking. The instructor demonstrates how to make a finished dish, and each student is required to imitate it and create the same appearance and taste experience, perhaps adding some personal touches. I used to think there was nothing tougher than critiquing students' letterheads. But teaching "design entrepreneurialism" is even more challenging. Entrepreneurs learn as they go. They have to experience the process first-hand, figuring out for themselves by trial and error what works and what doesn't.

Not every student project will be a winner, or even get off the ground. Most students end up taking jobs after graduation rather than starting companies. With $1,600-a-month studio apartments, who can blame them? But slowly, persistently, that invisible hand will pull them along, too, and, I think, many of them will choose to trade economic security for an irresistible idea.

ELLEN SHAPIRO, a graphic designer and writer, is the author of the book *Clients and Designers* and coauthor of *Ready, Set, Read!: Skills and Activities That Help Build Confident Readers,* a guide for elementary school teachers.

BIRTH OF AN IDEA: OR, HOW I LEARNED TO BE OBSERVANT AND LEAVE THE REST TO FATE

by David VOGLER

I believe good product solutions begin with observing and fulfilling a vacant niche. My best ideas usually come from a perceived gap in the market intersecting with my abilities and interests. In other words, almost every day, I find myself observing a situation and saying "Gee, wouldn't it be cool if I could make something that does [fill in the blank]."

I try to focus on entertainment products that combine innovation with a touch of subversiveness. In all cases, their common bond is design. In this case, I define design as an overall, intrinsic product concept, not just surface graphics. Such products can take many forms and be expressed in many mediums. And products that mix good communication design with clever audience service fascinate me.

The first step is identifying an unserved customer's need. Once that is clear, the task becomes a matter of fulfilling it with a good design solution. (Yeah, I know, I know. That's a helluva lot easier said than done.) My ideas are almost never born from typical "idea-generating" tools, such as panicked flipping through design annuals, regimented brainstorm sessions, or mass-market "just-add-water" inspiration books. (Admit it, at one point or another, we've all resorted to such embarrassing creative crutches.) For me, I have found that the best design solutions arrive through happy accidents, play, or good old-fashioned emotional turmoil. I'm serious. Here are three product examples that should give you an idea of what I'm talking about.

Product Problem: Make a unique new toy
Design Solution: Nickelodeon's Gak

For many years, people referred to me as the "father of Gak." That's not entirely true. This toy was the result of a team of talented folks at both Nickelodeon and Mattel. I worked at Nickelodeon Consumer Products as the creative director who guided the

© Nickelodeon

franchise through numerous line extensions. More accurately, I guess you could say I was the resident "Godfather of Gak."

What is Gak, you might ask? For those of you who were preteens in the 1990s, you already know the answer. Gak was essentially a blob of florescent goo that became a toy sensation and the physical manifestation of the Nickelodeon brand. Gak was a compound that looked a little like "slime" but had a more rubbery, viscous quality. Gak was messy, silly, funny, and fun. Like the greater Nickelodeon brand, it appealed to both boys and girls at the same time. Gak celebrated a free-form play experience where there was no right or wrong way to interact with it. Best of all, it was universally loved by kids and hated by grown-ups. Packaged in an amorphous "splat-shaped" vessel, Gak made wonderfully rude fart sounds when pressed back into the container's crevices. The toy was so popular with the audience that it sold over eight million units in its first year alone. Not only was Gak a new kind of toy, it was a whole new toy category.

The birth of Gak was the result of two companies sharing a common goal and a happy accident. The time was 1991, and Nickelodeon had decided to get into the toy business by licensing its brand to Mattel. Together, the two companies set out to create a line of "activity toys" that emphasized kid empowerment. When the Nickelodeon executives first visited Mattel, they asked the toy maker to show them "all the ideas the other guys rejected." (Part of the Nick brand philosophy was to embrace ideas that were quirky, unproven, and out of the mainstream. Looking back, I realize that was Nick's hiring policy as well.) That same year, Mattel's chemical engineers had invented a "recipe" for a new, colorful compound, but couldn't find an opportunity to deploy it. As a result, the concept was banished to their version of the "Island of Misfit Toys." When Nick saw this gooey substance, they fell in love with it. Coincidentally, Nickelodeon was running a game show called *Double Dare* that was based on physical challenges and lowbrow, "pie-in-the-face" stunts. Whenever a messy substance was shown splattering a contestant, the show's hyperactive host would occasionally refer to it with the nonsense word "gak."

It was a match made in product heaven: Mattel had the compound, while Nickelodeon had the back story. Together, we took elements that neither company valued and produced a solid design solution. Gak was a product idea born from serendipity.

Product Problem: Make Disney feel cool
Design Solution: D-Toys

After working at Nickelodeon, I moved to Los Angeles and joined Disney Online. For three years, I was the creative director devoted to their subscription Web site called *Disney's Daily Blast.* As you'd expect, it was a site filled with content based on all the traditional Disney characters. However, I soon discovered that the audience (as well as my staff) couldn't stay healthy on a diet consisting of only Disney saccharine. We all desperately needed some edge and diversity.

The business folks at Disney also concluded they needed to capture an "older" audience of kids to stay competitive in the Web marketplace. The problem was, the Disney brand wasn't considered "cool." In fact, when we asked any kid over the age of eight what they thought of Disney, they told us they associated the brand with "being a baby."

With this in mind, I smelled an opportunity brewing and invented a franchise of content called "D-Toys." The idea was devilishly simple: This was to be a line of small "digital toys" that could be an antidote to the warm 'n' fuzzy Disney surroundings. I wanted to provide a home for experimental ideas and diverse illustration styles. The D-Toy franchise became a creative oasis for creating content that didn't follow the rigid Disney mandates.

D-Toys were designed to be small nuggets of interactive fun. They were not exactly games, but rather open-ended toys with no specific play pattern, a little like a Slinky or Play-Doh. They were also intentionally small files, so they didn't require a long download. They required no preconceptions or instructions. They were like a humble prize in a CrackerJack box—fun, fast, and plentiful. Smart design was the glue that held them

all together. Each one celebrated the art of art direction by looking and playing differently than the one that came before. Their consistency was their inconsistency. And that was a paradox that rattled the Mickey Mouse traditionalists.

At first, the Disney brass was skeptical. But they soon acknowledged the value of D-Toys once they began to draw rave reviews and increasing Web traffic. D-Toys was a product solution initially born out of my rebellion against the Disney system. Ironically, this act of creative subversiveness became a big win for the very brand they mocked.

Product Problem: Make online multiuser gaming possible
Design Solution: MULAN from Mutation Labs, Inc.

Recently, I was bitten by the entrepreneurial bug and teamed up with some former colleagues to open a new kind of studio. The mission of our new office is to converge and "mutate" media. It's a boutique company we call "Mutation Labs." The business is actually set up very much like a laboratory. Half of our time is spent servicing select entertainment companies, while the other half is spent inventing our own products and bringing them to market. I'd like to think of us as the "Xerox PARC of new media mischief."

Our lab consists of handpicked talent that blends design, code, and entertainment disciplines. A driving goal of Mutation Labs is the creation of multiplayer interaction on the Internet—specifically, incorporating 3-D elements and multiplayer capabilities.

Last year, Mutation Labs released two successful multiplayer games to the public, Wave Rave and Le Food Frenzy: The Rugrats in Paris Game. Both were created for Nickelodeon and can be played at *www.nick.com*. These games were Shockwave-based and utilized a technology that already has a wide install base amongst Internet users. The technical plumbing behind the scenes that linked players together was third party software called POPX. Unfortunately, POPX wasn't very reliable, and it failed more than it succeeded.

Admittedly, creating a Web technology that links multiple users together has always been a difficult task. In fact, no one has successfully created a solid solution to accomplish this goal. How do we take two or more machines and get them to coexist in the same session? And how do we send messages back and forth fast enough to produce a "twitch" action game instead of a slow, turn-based game like checkers? It isn't easy, but we realized that if someone could crack that nut, we'd enter Web content nirvana.

Essentially, we identified a hole in the market and then worked to fill that need by creating MULAN.

MULAN (Multi-User Lobbying and Networking) is a new kind of software that combines elegant design and clever coding. It enables developers to easily handle grouping, launching, and communication—the three vital elements that make multiuser Internet games possible. It also uses peer-to-peer communication, thus making better use of bandwidth and end-user computers. Best of all, MULAN will allow players' machines to communicate with each other without depending on a central server. I know this all sounds like technobabble, so bear with me. Those of you who stay late in your office each night playing Quake or Tomb Raider will thank me later. MULAN is a product idea that came from our firsthand market observations, our love of games, and our giddy personal desire to build a better mousetrap.

DAVID VOGLER is principal of David Vogler Design. He is a consultant to MTV Networks and is a frequent guest lecturer at the School of Visual Arts and Carnegie Mellon University's Human Computer Interaction Institute. The Web site he's most proud of building is *www.TheManShow.com.*

MAKING MY OWN MAGAZINE

by Daniel NADEL

The *Ganzfeld* is an annual book of design, comics and illustration. It began as a project that three of us—myself, Patrick Smith, and Tim Hodler—made as a vessel for our own work and that of our friends. The first issue, printed in September 2000, was a 6" × 8" paperback, 152 pages long, resembling nothing so much as an academic journal into which were squeezed comics, jokes, pictures, essays, fake essays, and other things. It was a not a 'zine, nor was it exactly a "real" publication. It was impossible to describe, and its package was completely unrelated to its content. It sold dismally. Since then, Patrick and Tim have left, and Peter Buchanan Smith is now an equal partner. I publish and edit; he art directs and edits.

When the first issue was released, somebody told me that distribution is everything. I thought he was silly; he was right. The first issue tanked, because we had very limited distribution and knew nothing about it. I learned that bookstores and distributors in general aren't willing to take a chance on an obscure publication by a bunch of nobodies at $10.95 a pop. We were trying compete in the zine market, but our price was too high and the content neither one thing nor the other. It was not literary, cartoony, or humorous enough to find a genre niche. Furthermore, though our price justified it, our content and scope were unable to compete in the more rarified art market. And without a built-in market, it is very hard to sell anything (unless, of course, you make your own market, but we failed to do so).

Which is not to say I regret it—we made something that made us happy—merely that it happened. But the first issue is also fairly opaque; even our friends said it seemed created mostly to amuse ourselves, something, perhaps, our commercial audience could sense as well. Regardless, I have about a thousand stacked in my apartment, awaiting a cult following. After that first issue, I realized I didn't want to go through that kind of agony again just so some friends and I could have fun. We did that, and to do it again seemed like an easy and uninteresting venture. It seemed essential to expand our vision and really try to make something larger or different or simply better. Not everyone agreed, and thus the departures.

As Peter and I gained momentum in compiling our second issue (which will be in stores soon after this book is published), it became apparent that given our effort and the extraordinary design, drawings, comics, stories, and essays we'd gathered, better distribution was essential. Looking at *2wice* one day, I learned about D.A.P. (Distributed Art Publishers), which immediately seemed a perfect fit. We needed a company that could get us in the right sections and stores, one that knows how to handle the visually eccentric and the somewhat obscure. And since Peter and I were well on our way towards making a 176-page book, and had decided it would be annual, a bookstore, rather than newsstand distribution, was needed.

After some initial contact, I wrote a mission statement that included a paragraph on the market itself, a highlights page, a prospectus for future issues, short biographies of our contributors, and finally, a spec sheet. Then, I asked a publisher friend of mine to overhaul the seven-page proposal to make it that much more professional. We made two dummies, a snappy stationery design, and dropped it off one morning after a brief meeting with my contact there. Two weeks later, they took it, and I was very relieved. Of course, it's not that simple. Sometimes, you have to write and employ a language you'd rather not, make claims you didn't know you believed, to get something through. I reconciled my commercial and artistic aspirations and got on with it. But indeed, the most important part of the whole game is, in fact, distribution.

Whereas the first issue was really three guys doing whatever we wanted, the second gradually gained a real purpose, until one day Peter and I were able to conceive and write a substantial paragraph describing what the *Ganzfeld* is. And so? It's turned into an attempt to, as we say, bridge the gap between comics, illustration, and design. You see, I came to design through comics, and later, children's books: My first knowledge of Rand and Lionni was through their kids' books. And lately, work by *Ganzfeld* contributors such as Maira Kalman and Chris Ware blur all the lines—is it design? Comics? Illustration? The point, we think, is that some of the best visual work being done today cannot be called one or the other, and yet deserves recognition from all. So, why aren't the mediums all just happily interacting?

Anyhow, the *Ganzfeld* is meant to amend that by offering an impeccably designed book containing work by illustrators, fine artists, designers, and cartoonists—work that, in general, diverges from their normal practice. To that end, for example, we asked Nicholas Blechman, Red Grooms, Louise Fili, and Ron Rege, Jr., to make three wallpaper designs each. We are also fascinated by picture stories—not quite comics, not quite illustrated stories, the territory of that rare beast, the illustrator/designer: Paul Cox and

Richard McGuire fit this bill perfectly. And, of course, there are cartoonists, some writing, and even some funny poetry.

The *Ganzfeld*, then, is built as a forum for these various activities to play in and yet be rooted, through writing, design, and taste, in the culture at large. Our goal is not to prove the above, but rather reaffirm it and create a coherent document of it that can sit anywhere in the cultural landscape. Our selections are based on personal taste and quality. Sometimes, we ask someone to do whatever he wants, and sometimes, as the case with the wallpaper, we think of a project and then find just the right artists. It's a long process, including the inevitable cutting process, as we figure out what needs to stay or go to make the book cohesive. This means, for example, one sketchbook feature instead of two, or expanding a series of drawings from three to five, to give it more weight, or cutting a picture story or essay simply because it doesn't succeed, and so on.

Being a design entrepreneur, in our case, means using design as a pot into which we can stew all its related mediums—it stands both as content, an aid to the content, and as its container. The *Ganzfeld* is our vision of one way design can go and a few different things it can do.

DANIEL NADEL is coeditor of the *Ganzfeld* (*www.theganzfeld.com*). His writing has appeared in *Print, Graphis, TRACE: AIGA Journal of Design, Metropolis,* and *The Economist.* He lives in Brooklyn.

TECHNOLOGY, INFORMATION, EDUCATION

2

ENTREPRENEUR BY CIRCUMSTANCE

with Clement MOK, Interactive Guru

A designer, digital pioneer, software publisher/developer, author, and design patent holder, CLEMENT MOK founded multiple successful design-related businesses—Studio Archetype, CMCD, and NetObjects, one of Fortune's 1996 Top 25 Coolest Technology Companies. Most recently, he was the Chief Creative Officer of Sapient, a role he played from 1998 until 2001, when his own business was acquired. Sapient became the first service firm to be listed in the history of the S&P 500's index. Over his twenty-plus years career, he's consulted for clients like Apple, Adobe, E-Trade, IBM, Mayo Clinic, Microsoft, Netscape, Nintendo, QVC, Sony, United Airlines, UPS, and Wells Fargo Bank. As an advocate on design and technology practices, he has received hundreds of design awards from numerous professional organizations and publications. Mok has been involved with the launch of numerous new technologies and companies, including Apple's Macintosh, Herman Miller's Aeron chair, the Microsoft Network, interactive television, broadband applications, Web cast events, expert publishing systems, and major identity programs. Mok is the 2002–2003 president of the American Institute of Graphic Arts.

Would you describe yourself as an entrepreneur?

It's hard for me to imagine the title of entrepreneur on my business card . . . so I don't think it's an accurate description. An entrepreneur is how someone might categorize who I am. I am definitely entrepreneurial. I draw the distinction between entrepreneurial and entrepreneur, because the former refers to a point of view or approach and the latter refers to a state of being. Tibor is entrepreneurial, but I would not call him an entrepreneur . . . The same is true with Philippe Starck, Milton Glaser, and a countless number of designers out there.

When I started my studio thirteen years ago, I considered my firm as a Silicon Valley start-up—not as a design firm. This distinction determined and defined the nature of the work and the kind of clients we were willing to take on. It determined our approach to design and the expectations we have of our clients . . . It was being entrepreneurial. I would describe myself as a designer first, and then, I am an entrepreneur by circumstance.

You have certainly been ahead of the curve in things digital. What do you account for this forward thinking?

What is referred to as foresight has to do with being in the right place at the right time or dumb luck. Being at Apple in the early eighties influenced the way I think about design and technology. Seeing technological advance in development before the rest of world does was an advantage. Understanding the compromises in the development process and making friends with software programmers did not hurt either. My knowledge about digital technology did not come about overnight—after all, I was a high school math flunkie. My understanding of digital technology was through osmosis and being around this stuff longer than anyone else. I was tinkering and working on a Macintosh in 1983. I had direct access to the engineers who were working on the operating system and software applications. This exposure enabled me to see connections and relationships to things that were less than obvious to most people.

Access and proximity were not the only factors. One has to also understand the potential and the significance of the opportunity . . . And this is where the entrepreneurial side of me kicks in.

How did you parlay your knowledge into successful businesses?

Design is about recognizing and seeing patterns. It's about seeing things that to others are not readily visible. It's about giving form to ideas. My design knowledge and skills help translate ideas into accessible business terms. Instead of confronting the client, I've learned to co-opt them into the design development process. I had to learn their terms and their games, but subversively let them come to the conclusion that it was their idea all along.

What is the ratio of your activity between "design" and the "business of design?"

My current ratio between "design" and the "business of design" is zero. But if I restate the answer as a ratio between the "design of a business" and the "business of design," I will have to say it's 100 percent of my time. In fact, this was the only way I was able to justify and sustain my interest in running a business as long as I have.

You have established successful companies. At what point do you know when to start and when to stop, when to take total charge and when to sell off to another?

From the get-go, I've always been interested in learning. The reason I left Apple was because I was no longer learning. It really didn't matter what kind of learning, just as long there was personal growth.

I start things because I am interested in the subject. I am good at helping people understand and visualize the end state—the graphic design skill comes in very handy. The design consulting practice, Clement Mok Designs and Studio Archetype, were created around my interests concerning the ins and outs of Silicon Valley. My fascination there was about the ridiculous and groundless hype technology companies continue to corner themselves in.

CMCD, my royalties-free image publishing company, was created in 1992 out of my interest in media and publishing. I saw the connections and the applications of the photo CD technology with the needs of the design practitioners. Kodak insisted that this was a consumer product and that the vertical niche was difficult to penetrate. The truth of the matter was that they had spent so much money in the development of this that they had to find a way to justify their investment.

I asked Aldus (remember them?) to help me launch this idea, and they procrastinated. After six months, I got tired of waiting and proceeded without truly understanding what I was getting into.

The old "mother of invention" scenario kicks in.

Nine months after entry into the market we were the leader in the category, with significant negative cash flow. I underestimated the capital required to deal with inventory, distribution, and marketing. It nearly bankrupted me and put the design consulting practice in jeopardy. I knew at that point I had to sell the distribution rights to someone else. It meant giving up a lot—control as well as financial considerations. In the end, it was important for me to have the products in the market under proper care. I learned a great deal about media publishing and the dynamics of that industry. In short, that knowledge has served me well as an Internet consultant.

I started NetObjects, the Web site authoring software company, in 1995, because I was frustrated with the tools available for developing designs for Web site. I believed and imagined that a tool like Quark or PageMaker needed to be built for Web development. I was curious about what it was like to design an application from beginning to end. Over the years, I was always part of the development cycle and felt that there was too much compromise. Getting involved in the development of a software application fulfilled that need.

Did you do this on your own?

Having learned the lessons of not mixing the capitalization of a service company with a product company with CMCD, I thought it was important to get this company launched with outside capital. NetObjects was founded with an engineer, a product manager, a marketing guy, and a designer. This was the closest I ever was to being an entrepreneur. For a period of two months, we were trolling for venture dollars to get the company funded. Once we bagged the money, I was back into product development and design mode.

I stayed with NetObjects for over two and a half years. I've learned a great deal about what it was to develop and maintain software products. I also learned about the huge gaps between engineers, marketers, and designers. Most importantly, I've learned the limitations and constraints "design" can play when all we focus on are the things we create. If you don't design the context in which "design" can thrive, it will continue to be an uphill battle. The design of the context and the environment requires skills outside of the domain knowledge of aesthetics and functions. I left NetObjects because I was no longer having an impact in driving the "design" agenda. I was not actively involved in the "design of the business"—I didn't have the skill, nor was I prepared for it. The company went public after I left.

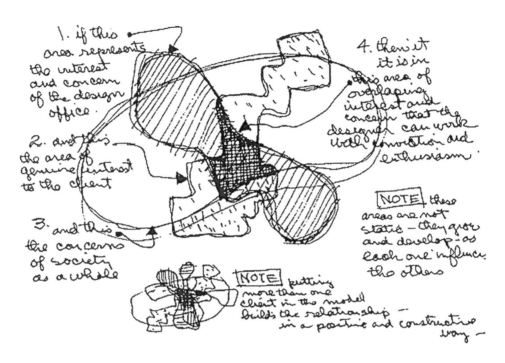

Charles Eames' model of convergence.

Why did you sell your studio to Sapient?

The decision to sell Studio Archetype to Sapient was driven by market conditions and my interest in "designing a business." If you don't succeed, try and try again.

Studio Archetype was involved with the Internet and online services (alpha and beta releases of the Microsoft Network) back in 1995. Providing design services for an exploding market forced us to grow in ways we had not prepared for. We were all of twenty-plus persons in 1994. We grew to thirty-five in 1995, and by 1997, we were over a hundred, with offices in New York and Atlanta. This expansion came as a result of the needs of our clients and the desire to play a bigger role in shaping the growth of the new medium. To accomplish this, one had to be involved with important projects with sizeable audience reach and significant scale. This presented learning opportunities for me and for all involved.

Prior to this decision, I had learned to separate my personal needs from that of the people in the studio and the business. The needs were similar, but they were not the same. Charles Eames' model of the convergence of personal needs, business needs, and social needs (see diagram above) informed how I needed to shape the office.

During this growth period, we were trying to develop depth in our technology practice without much success. What top-notch programmer would work for a design company when dot.com start-ups can give them stock options? By mid-1997, it became apparent many of our clients were asking us to do work that we were technically challenged by—connect and map the transaction to their commerce engine, inventory, and distribution systems. Being technologically agnostic was a liability. Partnerships and outsourcing were virtually impossible. It was at that point I realized that I'd taken the business as far as I personally could. To design the next stage of the business required skills and resources I did not have. Recognition of this limitation—skills and resources that I cannot hire or grow—drove the decision to sell to an appropriate "foster parents."

Your involvement with Sapient is impressive, but why did you resign from the company after putting so much of yourself into it?

With Sapient, I got a chance to "design a business"—transforming it from a system integration technology consulting company to one of the best Internet consulting firms.

It was hard, and it was not an easy journey. Most importantly, I did what I set out to do—that was to design the context and environment in which design can thrive.

My decision to leave has to do with exhaustion and the need to find new challenges. I will continue to play a role at Sapient, but at an arms length as an advisor to the company's development of best practices.

What would you say are the negatives of creating cutting-edge companies?

It takes a certain temperament to create and work within the kinds of companies I create. Change and job obsolescence were built into the business from the get-go. It was by design to push people to grow and learn. I have no regrets for the path I've taken . . . I would do it again the same way in a heartbeat. I believe that if you don't try and push the outer edges, you'll never know what the limits are.

During the business building, did you feel you were missing out on the designing?

I don't really feel like I've not been designing. Designing a business has been deeply gratifying. I don't think you can compare designing a business and practicing communication design the same way. Yes, I miss the practice of the craft, but I don't feel like I am missing out.

What would you say has been your biggest entrepreneurial challenge?

To convince designers to be more entrepreneurial.

Now what?

Take some time off, and then find things to design.

ANIMATED PROPERTIES

with Peter GIRARDI, Executive Creative
Director and Cofounder of Funny Garbage

PETER GIRARDI coined the Funny Garbage name as a child while redesigning
New York City subway cars with graffiti. He had been a creative director at the
Voyager Company, the preeminent producer of CD-ROMs and laser discs, when
he and John Carlin started Funny Garbage in 1996. Currently, Girardi is Funny
Garbage's executive creative director and also serves as an adjunct professor
at the School of Visual Arts. Funny Garbage has received numerous design
awards and has emerged as one of the most sought-after interactive design
firms in a rapidly changing market. The company has a special expertise in animation and built the Cartoon Network Web site from the ground up. Other
clients include HBO, Warner Music Group, VH1, the Experience Music Project in
Seattle, Compaq, The Wolfsonian Museum, and Knoll, Inc.

Why did you start Funny Garbage?

For most of the usual reasons: thinking I knew more than everyone else I'd ever worked
for, thinking I knew what they were doing wrong, and how I could make things better.
It turns out not to be as easy as all that. I wound up respecting my past employers more
than I did when I worked for them. Also, it was for the creative freedom. Freedom to
pick and choose the projects I wanted to do, the projects I could really bring more of
myself to. We started FG at an interesting time for new design companies. Technology
and design were and still are colliding. Something good always turns up if design and
technology battle it out. I wanted to be part of that in a significant way.

Funny Garbage has made its reputation working for high-profile Web
clients, but your goal is to be a content provider. How is this playing out?

It's an interesting balance. The majority of our work is for large media/content companies: AOL Time Warner, Viacom, Cablevision, and Disney. The rest of our work is
mainly for cultural institutions. We never did a lot of work for "start-up" dot.coms.
There really was no "there" there for us. We love content—real assets and meaningful
cultural commodities.

It was natural that when working for these companies, we would start to extend
our relationship past providing design service into providing content ideas. The kind of
content we provide isn't just the typical tangible properties, like animated characters and

other "hard" assets, but also more intangible content, like new forms of user interfaces, software, information visualization. These are also forms of content—structual and formal.

Serving clients and creating ideas are not mutually exclusive, but they can be. How do you balance the two?

I know this is a line that most design companies love to spout, but we have incredibly good, collaborative working relationships with our clients. We don't really have clients that come in for one job and don't come back again. We have long working relationships with clients whose content and work we have a real understanding and passion for. If we're ever in a meeting where we feel uncomfortable about throwing out an idea, or speaking honestly about some aspect of a job, then something's wrong.

How much freedom, say, does Cartoon Network give you producing content?

Lots. We have to follow all the usual standards and practices for kids' content, but other than that, it's a real collaboration between us and Cartoon. Plus, we've worked with them for a long time. We have a good track record. It's more like a creative partnership when producing content for them. It's also important to mention that we love, love, love what we do. We love making cartoons. It's something we've always wanted to do. That helps.

What are some of the areas of research and development that are most likely to be successful over the long haul?

We've been really concentrating in two areas: developing animated properties (we just sold a show to Disney) and creating new forms of user interfaces, new forms of information visualization and navigation.

Can you explain what you mean by information visualization?

A typical example is how one would go about designing an interface for an on-screen channel guide for interactive television. Soon enough, there will be the proverbial five hundred TV channels. How does one go about navigating that in an informative, intuitive way? How can we design a customizable, updateable, dynamic, user-centered information display?

How do we make it not feel like you are not "navigating." Once someone feels like they are using an interface or dealing with a computer, they begin to have a different relationship to a given piece of technology.

Stuff like that. (Hope I threw in enough buzzwords there.)

In addition to online work, you've started a print publishing company. Well, company may be too heavy a word, but you have produced one book. What have you learned from this experience?

FG has always been a design company, working in whatever design medium is most appropriate—TV, digital, paper, whatever. It's something we've always talked about. Seeing something and saying, "This should really be a book." We decided to just finally do it. We have many book plans in the works. I guess we learned that we're our own toughest client. It took way longer to publish *Cola Madness* by Gary Panter than we first imagined. Setting up the distribution and sales was also an experience best left to professionals.

You've resisted letting Funny Garbage get eaten up by larger dot.coms. What is your plan for the future?

We will make the transition from a service company to a product company.

OWNERSHIP ABOVE ALL

with David SMALL, Principal
of Small Design Firm, Inc.

DAVID SMALL recently completed his Ph.D. at the MIT Media Laboratory, where his research focused on the display and manipulation of complex visual information. This was his third degree from MIT. Small began his studies of dynamic typography in three-dimensional landscapes as a student of Muriel Cooper, founder of the Visible Language Workshop, and later joined the Aesthetics and Computation Group under the direction of John Maeda. His thesis, "Rethinking the Book," examined how digital media—in particular the use of three-dimensional and dynamic typography—will change the way designers approach large bodies of information. In 1999, he founded the Small Design Firm, which has been designing information environments for a variety of clients.

You did not start out as a designer, yet you are enmeshed in design as part of your new media explorations. How did you come to be a "designer?"

I definitely came at design through the back door. I still sometimes think of myself as more of an engineer than a designer. Since I was young, I've done creative work—printmaking, photography, woodworking—but I never thought much about making a living that way. When I started working at the [MIT] Visible Language Workshop, it seemed very natural to ply my skills as a programmer in the pursuit of improving the visual aspects of computers. It took a long time for me to gain confidence as a designer, however, and I still feel that my contributions to design have more to do with improving the underlying technology than with "design" itself.

When creating your doctoral thesis project, the Talmud Project, did you have an inkling that you might be able to market this particular work or that it would lead to developing software that was marketable?

I never had the slightest intention of marketing the Talmud Project itself. In fact, I think it is wrong for students to try to create projects with the idea of marketing them—it goes contrary to the purpose of design research. I had to focus on the conceptual framework without limiting my ideas to the constraints of a market.

Nonetheless, I feel that the underlying conceptual work (with ideas of focus, dimensionality, animation, and juxtaposition) has great market value. Since that thesis work had corporate funding (for which I am very grateful—no student loans!), the intellectual property embodied in the work belongs to them, and these larger corporations are in a better position to bring these ideas to market. My goals are much smaller.

How did you get corporate funding for your thesis?

The Lab handles all of the corporate funding—all students have their tuition fully paid and get a small stipend. Students are not responsible for bringing in sponsorship. All lab IP is then shared out among all of the sponsors.

You have a design firm, and some of your works are consumer- or client-driven, others not. How do you make the distinction, and what projects are one or the other?

Almost every project I am currently engaged in is client-driven, even if the product is very personal. The vegetables I did for Martha Stewart (see top image, page 34) are a perfect example. I try to find clients who can support the work I want to do for myself, but can't afford. Because of the cost and time involved in developing new software, it is difficult to do personal work. One thing that I try to insist on is ownership of my work, which allows me to develop an increasingly sophisticated set of software tools that I can then use for other purposes.

You developed a process whereby you laser-cut letterforms into fruits, vegetables, virtually anything. Is this, shall we say, a meal ticket for you, or a blip in your continued explorations?

Ha! This is the least profitable project I've ever spent so much time on. It seems to have all of the ingredients of a blockbuster product, and yet it is totally impractical. What's value for me is in the doing of it and in all the intangible benefits of being able to bring it to such a wide audience.

Working within the digital realm, how do you reconcile being ahead of the curve? In other words, is there limited return in developing concepts where the world, or client, is not quite ready?

I think that the potential rewards of working out in front are enormous. These rewards are not primarily financial, but are instead about being able to influence the development of this new medium in a direction where I hope it will go.

Do you consider yourself to be entrepreneurial?

Absolutely—I turned down a lot of offers to work for other people and organizations; I could never reconcile myself to the thought of working for somebody else. My parents and my grandparents all had their own businesses, so I always took it for granted that I would found my own company after I finished school.

How would you define your approach to entrepreneurship?

I have a very simple business model—people pay me for my work, I take out all of the expenses, and everything left over I keep. It seems old fashioned, but it works well for me. As I get better established, I have more choices in the projects that I take on. I'm also learning how to take less work and have more time to relax. The advantage of being your own boss is the ability to take a day off and go to the beach. If you work yourself too hard, you might as well be working for somebody else.

Good point. At what point does an experiment bridge the divide between the speculative and functional? And in which of your projects do you think this is the case?

That is usually what the client brings to the table. I hope that the project for the Chicago Museum of Science and Industry will bridge the divide. Museum work gives you the freedom to innovate, but the audience will insist on a crystal-clear interaction and very direct and understandable information.

Please describe the Chicago Museum project.

The project is for the Museum's new exhibit on genetics. This interactive experience acts as the central hub of the exhibit and ties the lessons learned from animal models to the human genome. The idea is to give people a look at the human genome at a variety of scales and to use that structure to tell a series of stories about human genetics, such as mutation and cystic fibrosis, genetic engineering and the blood clotting agent factor 9, and the formation of identical twins.

As you see your company (and yourself) growing, do you envision more or less client-based work?

I think more. I find I need the discipline that a client brings to my work. Perhaps some-day I won't need that, but I doubt that purely self-directed work would ever fully satisfy.

What would you like to do that you have not already done?

A movie.

EXPERIENCING EXPERIENCE

with Edwin SCHLOSSBERG, Principal
of Edwin Schlossberg, Inc.

EDWIN SCHLOSSBERG is president and principal designer of Edwin Schlossberg Incorporated (ESI), a fifty-member multidisciplinary design company that specializes in museum master planning and exhibit design, public information systems, and entertainment sites. ESI creates dynamic interactive experiences in a variety of contexts, such as museums, retail stores, public attractions, television programs, corporate environments, and computer information systems. ESI's current projects include the design of two museums for the Los Angeles Children's Museum; the design of dynamic signage for the Reuters building in Times Square; an interpretive exhibit program and signage program for the John F. Kennedy Center for the Performing Arts; the design of an environment to be located in the Ellis Island Museum's main building, where visitors can examine general immigration patterns; and the design of a visitor program for the Pope John Paul II Cultural Center. Among other activities, Mr. Schlossberg lectures in the design field, has been a teaching fellow, and has published several articles and works, including *Interactive Excellence: Defining and Developing New Standards for the Twenty-First Century, The Library of Contemporary Thought; The Philosopher's Game;* and *Einstein and Beckett: A Record of an Imaginary Conversation with Albert Einstein and Samuel Beckett.* He has served on the Advisory Panel of the National Science Foundation and is currently a member of the Board of Directors of New York City Outward Bound. He has a Ph.D. in Science and Literature from Columbia.

You have said that you feel that you have been an entrepreneur all your professional life. In the sense that you own your own company, you are indeed an entrepreneur. So, how would you define design entrepreneurship?

I would define it as the wish to make something happen using all the available resources (time, money, taste, intelligence, etc.) and the willingness to take the consequences.

What was your impulse, indeed goal, in starting your company?

I was asked to design Macomber Farm, and I needed to build a team of people that I could work with to realize the ideas and dreams that I had. I was not sure that I was building a company as much as just trying to make a great project happen.

You carved out a unique niche in terms of inter-action or inter-relation design. Would you say that regardless of the specific project that this concept is your "product"?

Yes, except, of course, it is a process. I have been concerned that whatever I designed, whatever we designed, reflected a deep commitment to collective-collaborative composition and creation, as well as something that was fun, exciting, and worthwhile.

Would it be correct to say that your business is fundamentally rooted in an idea, and you fit that idea to the commissions that come your way?

I would not say an idea. I think it is a methodology or a series of assumptions about how people could experience things and why it is better if they experience things through the contributions of others to that experience. I also think that great experiences exist both between people and within them and that aiming to create such experiences is not the usual way that designers work, and so it is a good idea to experiment and work in this way.

I know that you redefine your problems, but in terms of clients needs, must they buy into the way you work? Or are you open to what they want to do?

I always work with our clients to create the experience and the designs with their input, review, and consideration. I think I am persuasive about the philosophical goals and methods I like to employ, and every project is a reflection of the conversation between the client's ideas and concerns and our ideas and designs that emerge.

Some designers market their styles. Do you have a style?

Not in the way I think you mean it. All our projects look different and use technology, materials, and media differently.

Given that your methods are so uniquely geared to making group experiences, have you literally invented hardware or software that facilitates this?

Yes.

In a recent project, you developed a PDA as a guide for users to identify natural surroundings. Is this a tool that you will be pursuing as a marketable property?

We have been working on the use of portable communication tools as part of exhibits for a while, and we are in the midst of setting up a new company that will use the designs and projects that we have developed as a basis for creating the business of developing these tools.

Have you given thought to how you might market this tool? Will you develop a separate company to handle it or find other means?

We will develop a company as a strategic alliance with a software and hardware company. The three members of the alliance will develop the marketing and development of the business.

How, in fact, do you promote yourself? Reputation is one means, but is there another way to reach clients?

Not really.

What does the future hold in store as far as entrepreneurial pursuit?

Mystery, success, failure, frustration . . . Many designers that I know tried very hard to start companies to produce their designs, and they proceeded to go bankrupt . . . It is a difficult process and one that requires enough success to make the struggle worthwhile. The challenge for a designer is that business requires disciplines based on costs, and design requires disciplines based on experience and a belief in the improvement of the world. These can work together, but sometimes they work at odds. I think the best situation is one where there is a design and business collaboration—each part contributing to the whole success. But, of course, I would believe that . . . Thanks for asking.

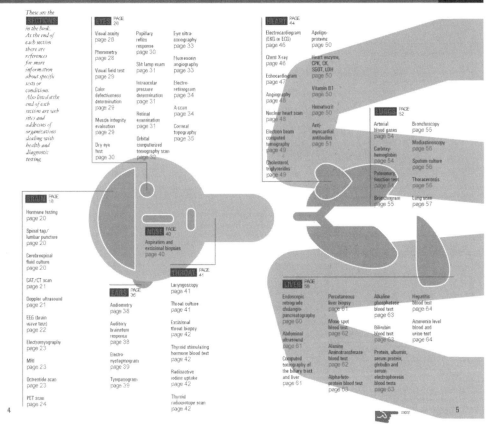

What are the tests, and where are they in this book

These are the
SECTIONS
*in the book.
As the end of
each section
there are
references
for more
information
about specific
tests or
conditions.
Also listed at the
end of each
section are web
sites and
addresses of
organizations
dealing with
health and
diagnostic
testing.*

EYES PAGE 26

Visual acuity
page 28

Photometry
page 28

Visual field test
page 29

Color
defectiveness
determination
page 29

Muscle integrity
evaluation
page 29

Dry eye
test
page 30

Pupillary
reflex
response
page 30

Slit lamp exam
page 31

Intraocular
pressure
determination
page 31

Retinal
examination
page 31

Orbital
computerized
tomography scan
page 32

Eye ultra-
sonography
page 33

Fluorescein
angiography
page 33

Electro-
retinogram
page 34

A-scan
page 34

Corneal
topography
page 35

HEART PAGE 44

Electrocardiogram
(EKG or ECG)
page 46

Chest X-ray
page 46

Echocardiogram
page 47

Angiography
page 48

Nuclear heart scan
page 48

Electron beam
computed
tomography
page 49

Cholesterol,
triglycerides
page 49

Apolipo-
proteins
page 50

Heart enzyme,
CPK, CK,
SGOT, LDH
page 50

Vitamin B1
page 50

Hematocrit
page 50

Anti-
myocardial
antibodies
page 51

LUNGS PAGE 52

Arterial
blood gases
page 54

Carboxy-
hemoglobin
page 54

Pulmonary
function test
page 54

Bronchogram
page 55

Bronchoscopy
page 55

Mediastinoscopy
page 56

Sputum culture
page 56

Thoracentesis
page 56

Lung scan
page 57

BRAIN PAGE 18

Hormone testing
page 20

Spinal tap/
lumbar puncture
page 20

Cerebrospinal
fluid culture
page 20

CAT/CT scan
page 21

Doppler ultrasound
page 21

EEG (brain
wave test)
page 22

Electromyography
page 23

MRI
page 23

Octreotide scan
page 23

PET scan
page 24

NOSE PAGE 40

Aspiration and
excisional biopsies
page 40

EARS PAGE 36

Audiometry
page 38

Auditory
brainstem
response
page 38

Electro-
nystagmogram
page 39

Tympanogram
page 39

THROAT PAGE 41

Laryngoscopy
page 41

Throat culture
page 41

Excisional
throat biopsy
page 42

Thyroid stimulating
hormone blood test
page 42

Radioactive
iodine uptake
page 42

Thyroid
radioisotope scan
page 42

LIVER PAGE 58

Endoscopic
retrograde
cholangio-
pancreatography
page 60

Abdominal
ultrasound
page 61

Computed
tomography of
the biliary tract
and liver
page 61

Percutaneous
liver biopsy
page 61

Mono spot
blood test
page 62

Alanine
Aminotransferase
blood test
page 62

Alpha-feto-
protein blood test
page 63

Alkaline
phosphatase
blood test
page 63

Bilirubin
blood test
page 63

Protein, albumin,
serum protein,
globulin and
serum
electrophoresis
blood tests
page 63

Hepatitis
blood test
page 64

Ammonia level
blood and
urine test
page 64

INFORMATION IS MY GAME

with Richard Saul WURMAN,
Information Architect

RICHARD SAUL WURMAN coined the term Information Architect. He says that the singular passion of his life is making information understandable, and he has built a business around this simple idea. In his best-selling book, *Information Anxiety,* in 1990, he developed an overview of the motivating principles that he continued in the *Yellow Brick Road,* the second of this series. Each of his books stems from his desire to know rather than from already knowing, from his ignorance rather than his intelligence, from his inability rather than his ability. Given this concern, he created an annual design competition for the AIGA in 1995—The Design of Understanding—and chaired the first jury. He is the founder of the TED conferences, which married the most significant developments of the three disciplines of technology, entertainment, and design. In addition to these entrepreneurial pursuits, Wurman continues to be a regular consultant to major corporations in matters relating to the design and understanding of information.

When, during your career as an architect and designer, did you realize that you were best suited for entrepreneurial pursuit?

I first learned at the age of twenty-six in an uncomfortable moment of self-realization that, inevitably, I could only work for myself. In 1962, I began as an assistant professor of Architecture at North Carolina State University, Raleigh. This academic situation allowed me the unjustified freedom of doing what I wanted in the classroom.

You started publishing in your garage, but what factors caused you to inaugurate your Access Guide series?

I did not start Access Press until 1980, when I was forty-five years old. Up until then, I had failed sideways at a number of occupations. I spent one year in city government as the Deputy Director of Housing and Community Development in Philadelphia. For another year, I worked as the Dean of Architecture, Urban Design and Landscape Architecture at California State Polytechnic Institute, Pomona—where I was fired. Finally, I started an architectural practice in Philadelphia (which seems like you are working for yourself, but what you are really doing is maintaining relationships with clients—trying to get them and keep them), which went belly up in 1976. So, my first moment, so to speak, as an entrepreneur was in 1980, when I started Access Press with the first *Access L.A. Guide.*

What were the pitfalls, pratfalls, and other difficulties in such a seat-of-the-pants start-up?

I began Access Press because I had just moved to Los Angeles, had been fired as Dean, had nothing to do, and my architectural practice back in Philadelphia was gone. I was living in L.A., and I did not know anyone and could not find my way around, and I could not find a guidebook that I felt comfortable with. So, I decided to create a guidebook out of my ignorance, and my lack of understanding of where I was both physically and mentally.

I made a rather concerted effort to find a publisher in New York and L.A. The few that would talk to me, and I mean few, chucked me out of their offices when I proposed the project on the basis that I was perfectly qualified by my inabilities and ignorance. My philosophy was that I had no expertise whatsoever, no deep knowledge of L.A., and since I couldn't find my way around and had never lived there before, I was the perfect person to do a guidebook. They did not buy that.

I eventually was able to get some money from Atlantic Richfield, now called Arco, and developed the first Access Guide. Only then did I discover that no one would distribute it, because I did not have a credible company with only one title. Distributors had no way of dealing with an independent publisher at that time.

How did you sell the books?

I ended up selling the books out of my car and stored them in my garage. I printed a shit-load, because I knew if I only printed the number of copies recommended by my most optimistic acquaintances, I would not sell any. I needed that bug up my ass. I needed that moment of terror. I needed that push over the edge to get these books out to see if people liked them. *The Access L.A. Guide* got good reviews and sold rather well.

My problem was that I was going bankrupt. I am sure that it is obvious that you cannot make a living from one guidebook to one city. Plus, since I was selling copies personally with no other guides in development, the profit just was not there. Frank Stanton, the former CEO of CBS Inc., saved my ass by investing some cash. He funded a new edition of *Access L.A.* and new guides (Hawaii and San Francisco), for 50 percent of the company. I owe him a great deal. Someone having faith in my book and my person, especially with that somebody being the ultimate suit and representing integrity and quality, turned the tide of my life.

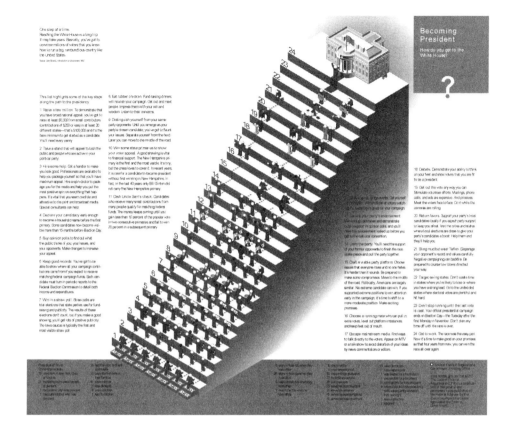

Regardless of the challenges, the Access Guides succeeded, set a standard for such publishing, and otherwise launched your own business. When and why did you decide it was time to sell the company and launch the TED conferences?

Because of the development of the guidebook for New York City as well as Access Guides on football, baseball, and the Olympics, I was traveling a great deal. The only interesting conversations that I was having with people sitting next to me in planes were with those who were in the technology business, the entertainment industry, or the design profession. These conversations were interesting when people told me about their projects that intertwined these three professions. Everybody else that I spoke with was unbelievably dull.

Why TED?

I thought that the merging and converging of technology, entertainment, and design would be the future of the American economy. Also, what I found interesting was the converging of these disciplines as they served learning and communication. In 1984, with Harry Marks and Frank Stanton as partners, I put on the first TED conference.

Conference management is a big business these days. I know of at least three companies that have bought magazines simply to have their conference assets. TED is a leader. How did you make it so? And what have you done to maintain the brand?

TED's success is due to the concerted effort I make each year. It is due to being a committee of one. It is a joyous indulgence. It is grand to have another chance each year to make the four days of the conference palpably better than anybody's expectations.

Is there a trick or formula to what you do, or is it continual reinvention?

Tricks and formulas are basically the same thing, so I do not relate to that question. Instead, I just try to do good work, and in order to do good work, be sure that you look at the things that do not work rather than the things that do work.

In addition to being the impresario of these shows, you must also have the vision to get ahead of the curve, especially in this competitive field. How do you accomplish this?

The key to creativity is not a better version of what you have already done, but rather an understanding of failure as the path to new ideas.

What's next?

I do not look at the TED conferences as my day job. This year [2000], I will have designed and published eight books. I own 50 percent of a publishing company, TOP, a joint venture with Ovations, a four-billion-dollar division of a twenty-billion-dollar company (UnitedHealthcare). We are developing a major series of books on health and wealth. These are the subjects that interest me the most.

I am always publishing books: three more in the understanding series (*Understanding Children, Understanding Children for Grandparents,* and *Understanding Healthcare*) similar to *Understanding USA,* which came out in 2000. Also, my own Who's Who of the thousand brightest and most creative individuals in America *(The TED Register)* is out, as well as a joint venture with *National Geographic Traveler* called *Healthy Travel.* Through a company called Sheer Bliss, my wife and I have published a book, *The Wizard Who Wanted To Be Santa,* which was illustrated by Seymour Chwast.

I will also be developing the third in my series of meetings on the communication of medical information, called TEDMED3, as well as the first EUROTED, which will probably be held in Dublin. There will be more TED Conferences. The best one in the series will be in 2002, which I initially have described as "Simply the Greatest Design Conference There Ever Was." TED12, known as 12@12, will address the ideas of design in relation to other fields, with twelve subconferences, including The Design of Your Life, The Design of Technology, The Design of Sensuality, The Design of Products, The Design of Design, The Design of Humor, The Design of Music, etc.

MAPMAKER, MAKE ME A MAP

with Stephan VAN DAM, Mapmaker

STEPHAN VAN DAM is the founder of VanDam's Digital Map Library in New York. He has created over five hundred maps covering eighty cities worldwide and the heavens above. Maps fall into four retail categories: StreetSmart (the United States and Europe), CitySmarts (the New York environs), NY@tlas (New York's most popular spots), and UNFOLDS (a unique folding map that covers parts of Europe, Asia, and even Mars). Van Dam's obsession with wayfinding began small; today, his aim is to chart the world.

Why and how did you get into the map business?

I fell into it by inventing the UNFOLDS® concept. At the time, I was intrigued by the folded metal sculptures of Merle Steir, a sculptor friend of mine. So, I started playing with folding sheets of paper and chanced upon a sheet-folding method that refolded automatically. It was aching for maps and other cartographic uses.

Through an attorney friend, I was able to secure a family of patent rights on the fold, the method of folding it, and the machine that folds it, which I built with a German engineering friend.

Now, I needed cartographic expertise, which in the early eighties still meant old-style cartographers scribing negatives on huge film overlays. A group of European mapmakers took me under their wings and showed me the ropes.

Did you realize that this would, in fact, become a profit-making business?

It had to be. I was out there raising venture capital to get the company off the ground. VCs were looking to get three times their money back in three years. The VCs finally agreed to fund the venture based on my ability to secure a major distributor for the line. So, I signed an agreement with American Express, my first customer, to offer UNFOLDS to its card members.

I presume that to provide maps to the public, you have to both be very confident in your ability to be accurate and convince your customers of this fact. How easy or difficult was it for you to build this confidence?

This goes to the heart of the nature of maps, which are at the intersection of art and science. We generally ascribe truth to maps, because they are assumed to represent fact.

Graphic design plays a key role in convincing users of this accuracy. The actual process of ensuring accuracy, however, is really more of an engineering and an editing process.

Where do you get your raw data?

For locational maps, we generally start with government vector data sets in various "shapefile" formats (Tiger, USGS, Census, etc.), which we visually process and reproject to suit our base mapping needs. We then export these files to a Mac graphics environment, adding up to seventy-five layers of illustrations, symbols, and text elements. Cartographic design clarifies these added realities. The editing process and on-location verification are annual rites.

On the other hand, maps are also miniatures. As abstractions, their very nature is to omit key aspects of reality. One pertinent example of this is the Epcot SkyCalendar we produced for Disney. While its planetary maps are accurate for every day of the year, these are really maps of ignorance, considering the fact that most dark matter in the universe (about 98 percent of the map) remains unknown.

Design plays an important part in the work you do. What training did you have?

I studied architecture and environmental design at Parsons here in New York City. But I am really a *bricoleur*, a professional jack-of-all-trades who acquires skills as they are needed. From origami to information design, cartography to Web-based GIS, from setting up large production runs to licensing intellectual properties, from doing 3-D magazine covers to visualizing history and representing ideas through maps, I make it up as I go. What all these activities have in common is that they are based on good ideas, which are the basis for good design.

What did you have to learn in order to become a viable business? Were there any models on which you base yourself?

Refine your product. Hone your skills. Make your clients happy. I know it sounds clichéd and sort of mundane, but making a business viable means buying cheap and selling dear. I learned this and a few other things from Richard Wurman.

What else did you learn?

From Nigel Holmes (former graphics director of *Time*), I learned about character. The central role typography plays in making cartography accessible. John Grimwade (of Condé Nast *Traveler*) taught me the art of ellipsis, what to leave out of a map.

How big is your operation? Do you design everything, or do you trust others with your properties?

We try to keep staff below ten people, so I can both manage and design. We are lean, mean and fast—usually working on three to four projects simultaneously.

I layout the direction, conceptualize content and format, then delegate. But I am also the final editor. While I try to remove myself from detail, it is a challenge to be detached and so closely involved at the same time.

What is the most creative part of what you do?

Coming up with the next thing. Conceptualizing new products and experiences. I like the playfulness and challenge of the process. It's like doing the mambo.

I presume that in the wireless Web world, maps are going to play a huge part in the data equation. How are you addressing this new future?

For the wireless Web, we are inventing the next generation of dynamic, location-based wayfinding. These are maps that play as interactive movies on the fly.

The big challenge is to create an open information architecture, bringing together interactive authoring, 3-D animation, wireless wayfinding, clear interface design, deep data that dance, and Web GIS, and to shape them into an immersive and memorable experience. The fun part is to bridge the gap between user and map by making the user part of the map. It's where the map and the model merge to create powerful new realities.

And how do you make further inroads into "old" media?

On the print side, it's been about representing ideas dealing with where and how history/politics and nature/culture intersect. In the RAINFOREST UNFOLDS, we mixed politics and nature by combining maps and poetry in engaging ways. NY@tlas is about looking at the metropolis in two ways:

- ❖ How to get from here to there: 320 pages of the best street-level data to New York City.
- ❖ How we got here from there: ten haiku histories showing how, at crucial moments in each of the ten decades of the twentieth century, New Yorkers changed the way we look at ourselves as Americans and how that process has shaped global contemporary culture.

How much time is devoted to new product?

At least 50 percent of my time. You are only as good as your next new thing. Reinventing previously published stuff isn't half the fun. But with a backlist of over eighty titles, it's half the reality.

As a designer, do you feel that your design ability has progressed or stayed the same in the process of making product?

Making product and building a brand heightens your awareness that good design makes all the difference. I think that I've become sharper in this area. I am also convinced that making the complete product (from concept to delivery of finished goods) allows us to quality-control every aspect of what we do. There are no excuses.

Your business has obviously found a niche market. Do you know who this market is?

Ultimately, we design for the end user. To reach as many users as possible, however, we are dealing with clients in three distinct markets.

- ❖ *Institutional*—We produce maps and atlases for federal, state, and city governments, not-for-profits, bids, chambers of commerce, etc. We just signed a five-year deal with AAA and have done map identities for the National Park Service,

NYCVB, LACVB, Heritage Trails, the Met, the United Nations, and the New York City Economic Development Corporation to name a few.

✤ *Custom Publishing*—We introduced the concept that guidebook publishers should have a companion map series to build their brand and increase their presence in stores. We convinced St. Martin's Press of this with the Let's Go map guides six years ago. The format, with over five million copies in print, has become the industry standard for people traveling on a budget, with most major publishers following our lead. Langenscheidt and Bertelsmann are licensees of our cartographic products in the United States and Europe, which greatly expands our reach and distribution.

✤ *VanDam Publishing*—Under our own imprint, we publish maps and books to cities around the world in three unique formats: UNFOLDS, StreetSmart, and @tlas.

Given your niche, do you plan to produce other products?

This is the time to invent new location-sensitive applications for the Web and e-commerce. They fill a real need, promise a viable economic model, and allow us to truly map the culture of congestion.

What haven't you done with your business that you'd like to do?

Create interactive museum exhibits that let users choose their level of interest.

Get our map movies to play on phones and in goggles around the globe and, in the process, change people's mental maps of their cities.

Is design still a determining factor in your work?

Yes, it's why I do what I do.

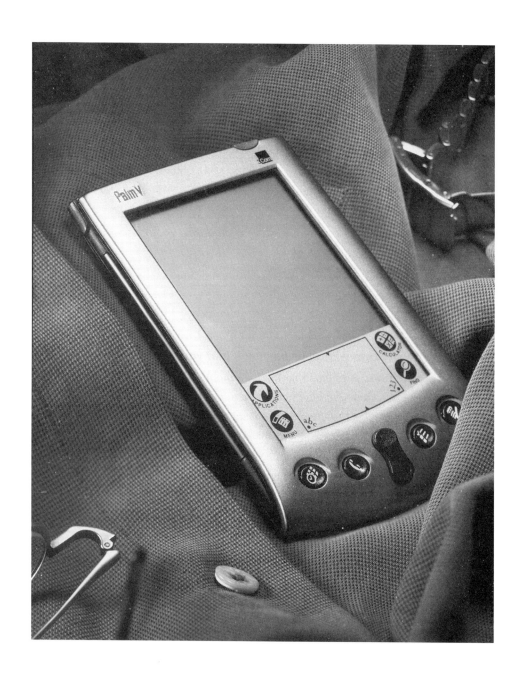

GROUP THINK

with David M. KELLEY, CEO of IDEO

DAVID M. KELLEY, founder and chairman of IDEO and a professor at Stanford University, is a successful California-based entrepreneur, educator, designer, and venture capitalist. In 2000, he was one of six architects and designers honored with the annual Chrysler Design Award, and the National Academy of Engineering elected him to its membership, one of the highest distinctions given to engineers in the United States, recognizing him for "affecting the practice of design." At Stanford University, Kelley is a tenured professor in the school's innovative Product Design program. When Stanford recently published a one-hundred-year retrospective on the one hundred individuals who had most epitomized its tradition of academic excellence, Kelley was recognized for encouraging "the melding of can-do spirit with limitless imagination."

Why did you become an entrepreneur?

My actual reason for starting the company was because I wanted to be in control of who I worked with all day. When I worked in big companies, someone else assigned which person sat in the desk next to me and who I would spend all my time with during the day. Since I wasn't letting anybody choose my girlfriends, I wanted to choose my work friends, especially since I was going to spend ten to twelve hours a day with them. So, I had very little choice but to start a company in order to enjoy my work life.

Do you see a conflict between being a client-oriented business and an entrepreneurship?

No. Clients have lots of latent needs that they're not really in touch with. So, there is lots of leeway to come up with big ideas and then convince them to go in new directions that they haven't considered. I never want to get into a situation where we have to take design direction from the client to the exclusion of what is right for the user. Seems to me you can always convince the client of the appropriate direction by representing the user's point of view and supplying user data to back up your claims.

What role does design play in IDEO? Do you begin with products in mind and find design solutions to frame them? Or is the design and function of products always totally integrated?

The initial conditions, so to speak, are almost always given to us by the client (except

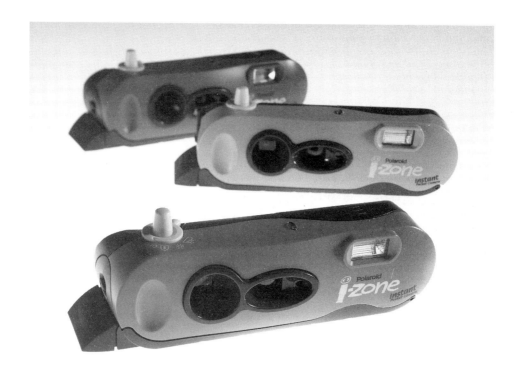

on IDEO's own products). So, let's say you're a toaster company. We can't come up with ideas for farm equipment—we have to do things in their market. So, we start by looking at the experience, in this case, of using toasters and other kitchen appliances. This leads to ideas about what would make a better toaster experience. Then, it is simply our job to innovate around appropriate technology and appropriate appearance for that environment and user group.

Do you look to the consumer as a benchmark for your designs? Or do your designs drive what you provide the consumer?

We definitely look to the consumer for inspiration; however, we don't expect the consumer to come up with the design ideas. We want to know what the users value as a group and what their intent is in a product area, then, it's our idea to visualize possible futures. Through user observation studies, we learn about the thing the users want, but can't articulate, and we use these findings to move forward.

What is your success-to-failure ratio? In other words, how much of IDEO is rooted in research and development versus sure things?

Some of our products do fail in the marketplace. Things rarely fail in the development process, because we're always changing the point of view through user research. We start out with a specification, and then, if we find out it's not possible technically or users do not resonate with the proposed direction, we change the specification. We don't just stop.

If one of our products does fail, it is because it cannot be delivered to market through a sales channel and with a manufacturing cost that people will accept. This is a messy process with no obvious right answers, and we also, of course, can fool ourselves about the size of the market.

Given that IDEO has become a fairly large company, how do you maintain a creative presence?

It's hard to have really creative hot groups that are very large, so we've broken our company down into quite autonomous groups we call studios. Although we share knowledge and resources across these groups, they are pretty much separate in the way they do business, how they get work, and how they govern themselves. The thing I am most proud of is that we've been able to maintain a unified culture, despite our separation, though it's a lot of work.

How much of the ideas of IDEO are generated by you?

Zero. Almost all IDEO ideas are group ideas.

Does being an entrepreneur change, in any way, your approach to design?

I don't really know. I do know that being outside of an individual corporation allows us to learn from many different companies. All companies are good at something, and, as consultants, if we are just mindful of learning from our clients, we can incorporate the best ideas into our methodology.

What haven't you done that you would like to do with your business?

I'd like to raise the perceived value of designers in corporate America—say, to half as much as they value lawyers and management consultants. Our thrust now is developing new business models that put us on the same side of the table as our clients, that allow us to work with them as partners, sharing the upside and the downside. This is happening more and more already.

bar tray

LOAD DRINKS CARRY LIKE THIS... ...OR LIKE THIS.

party tray

GET A DRINK GET A SNACK ENJOY.

shots tray

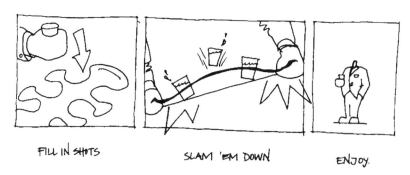

FILL IN SHOTS SLAM 'EM DOWN ENJOY.

IMPROVING EVERYDAY LIFE

with Yves BEHAR, Principal of fuseproject

YVES BEHAR is founding principal of fuseproject, a brand development and industrial design firm based in San Francisco. As design manager for Frogdesign and for Lunar Design, Yves Behar is widely noted for designing the Silicon Graphics O2 workstation, the JPS Global Positioning System line of products, and the inaugural Hewlett-Packard Pavilion product line, as well as its recent update, the Pavilion 2000. A designer working across a wide array of fields and media, he has also led design teams for Schick-Wilkinson, Omega, Mitsubishi, Kensington, and Apple Computer. Recent projects include a perfume bottle (spacescent) and cosmetics, and technology products (Hewlett-Packard Pavilion 2000), home goods (Lush Lily Trays). He has gone on to develop strategies and products for clients such as Birkenstock, Hewlett Packard, Microsoft, and Alcatel, as well as for prominent start-ups such as PeoplePC and Philou Cosmetics. Behar also contributes experimental design projects for the press and museums alike. Most recently, he was commissioned by the San Francisco Museum of Modern Art to design future shoe concepts for its exhibition, Design Afoot.

How would you define a "design entrepreneur"?

A design entrepreneur is one who sees an opportunity to improve or create a user experience and simply acts on it.

As a designer, do you prefer to solve the problems of others or make your own products?

Creating my own products is ideally something I can do while solving the problems of others . . . I think good designers find a way to make mainstream products personal, for others and for themselves.

Tell me more about fuseproject. After working for Frogdesign, what prompted you to start your own business?

Reaching people through my design work is always the motivation to do a project or get onto a business adventure. I felt I would be closer to my clients if I could create an environment that is truly focused on design and the stories that design can create. The fuseproject motto became, "fuse the clutter of detail into a rich narrative." [The quote is from A. Schlessinger.]

My first client was Javad Ashjaee, a genius scientist of the GPS world. After creating two other successful global GPS companies, he launched JPS (Javad Positioning Systems). I designed five products for the professional surveyor (GPS antennas, receivers, remotes, tripods, etc.), with an utter disrespect for the existing products in that category, which are typically heavy and uncomfortable articles of nondesign. The result was a line of bright green antennas that became an instantly recognizable icon by expressing a link to satellites, topography, and sci-fi. The JPS line made magazine covers, was exhibited (Cooper-Hewitt Design Triennial), and became a statement of what equipment-type products can be. The company was sold in October 2000, two years after launch, for $40 million; the president of the purchasing company lamented that the brand recognition JPS had acquired over the two years of its existence cost him a few million!

Where do you fit into the loop in a project like PeoplePC? Do you see yourself as entrepreneurial or serving the entrepreneurs?

When I am brought into a company that is in the process of defining itself, I tend to immerse myself in the challenge. The blank page is a powerful equalizer, which brings CEOs and advisers to an equal level. The design and its message are blended with the business: Ideas and vision dictate the character and personality of the design. I was also called upon to create a structure in which manufacturing could happen, a complex element that often escapes start-ups.

In order to be entrepreneurial, one has to feel deeply personal about the problem and exhibit a great deal of empathy at the same time.

With PeoplePC, specifically, what did you create that was entrepreneurial in fact and spirit?

The unique element of this collaboration was that PeoplePC was entirely focused on the user experience—not just the computer, but all the elements that affect the surrounding of the product. The traditional computer companies too often ignore the "total user experience."

So, we created numerous friendly "experience enhancers" that reside in the periphery of the computer. Several solutions for cable management and cable routing were developed (dealing with cables is the first element that disturbs the home environment); a "monitor saddle" that attaches to any size monitor and elegantly holds a piece of paper for typing, headphones, business cards, and a flower; a mouse pad with wrist rest and cable management integrated; a keyboard with a soft wrist rest, physical hot keys

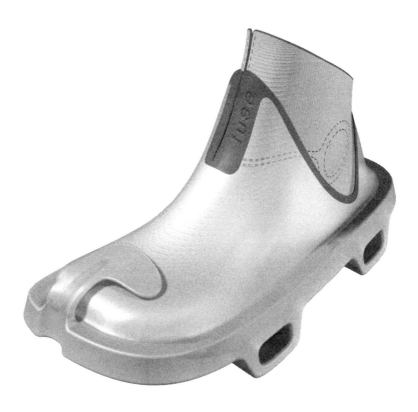

for bookmarking, and a pencil tray integrated. All the products are made out of soft fabric and foam: Tactile, practical, simple, and friendly, they epitomize a company focused on the user experience!

You do "experimental" work, like the shoe project for the SFMoMA. Are these just exercises, or do you see them as prototypes for real and future entrepreneurial projects?

I believe that, as designers, we have a responsibility to look for solutions and improvements to people's everyday life. As creatives, we can take the initiative and show a future direction for products and ideas, and hopefully, a manufacturer might move forward with this future vision

Experimental projects are first and foremost ways to envision possibilities, create future dreams, and express one's ideas. When done with sincerity and integrity, they often lead to possible design ventures. The shoe project for the SFMoMA led to a project with Birkenstock, the famed earthy sandals company . . .

Another example is our design of a future city-commuting solution: The Scoot is a response to the need for urbanites to get around town without breaking a sweat or the environment. Scoot's hydrogen fuel cell motor, a form of energy emergent in northern

Europe, propels the user along city streets without harming the environment. The hydrogen fuel cell ensures that the Scoot does not add to city smog.

"The Scoot folds into a compact and portable object in seconds for easy carrying or packing on buses and subways," says Johan Liden. Its folding mechanism, collapsible handle bar that turns into the product's carrying handle, and fenders that cover the wheels when the Scoot is folded propose a total solution that makes the Scoot a real commuter product.

The Scoot is designed as an elegant product. In contrast to the youth market's small scooters, the aesthetics of the Scoot fits a professional user. The design is an expression of both efficiency and modernist simplicity, bringing product design qualities to a new product category that resides at the intersection of the car, train, or subway and one's destination.

Tell me about other projects, successes or not, where you have taken the lead.

I recently created twelve product ideas in a week for a CEO who simply felt that push scooters could be much improved. Based on the rough designs, he quickly obtained an investment and a $4 million valuation for Znapz—not bad for a week of design exploration.

I partnered with Space, a lifestyle company who launched its first product, a high-end limited edition perfume called "spacescent." In a saturated market, the unique bottle and guerilla launch captured a lot of media attention, creating enough recognition to allow for the development of the next line of products. Rather than spending large amounts of marketing dollars, our strategy with Space (with its current and future line of personal products) is to let the product develop in the eyes of the public organically, through targeted launches in interesting spaces (Totem Gallery or Kbond in Los Angeles), press, and word of mouth.

I designed a line of shampoo bottles for Philou, a French-American start-up. Based on the novel perspective that the design has presented, the product was picked up by numerous retailers, including Sephora, and the CEO, Philippe Tordjman, was able to make a case for his new products on CNN.

A few words about the project and design: The world is full of clichés, and design is all too often a way of perpetuating them. For the Philou line of hair products, we looked beyond the typical designs created for teenagers for an expression of nascent purity and sensuality. The resulting Philou bottle is both fresh and refined, drawing attention far outside the teen audience. Adults react to the informed design, and Philou's vibrant colors and scents attract younger consumers. "The emotional response that the design of the bottle has created is incredible," says Philippe Tordjman, CEO of

Philou. "People are immediately drawn to touching the shape . . . Needless to say, the brand recognition the design has given us is very strong." Although a new company, Sephora immediately picked up the Philou launch items of shampoos and conditioners.

I also often find that through design consulting projects, I am able to cast a whole new perspective on an established company by approaching what might seem like an isolated problem in a holistic way . . . Once the door is cracked opened, a whole new perspective can be discussed.

Since you develop projects for producers, manufacturers, and retailers, why don't you produce, manufacture, and sell your own intellectual property?

As a creative, what I am good at is being the production machine of others. Recognizing that there is a limited amount of time available, I am focusing my energy on "creating and telling." Most designers that I know who have launched their own personal line of products really only spend 3 percent of their time on design, and design for me is the "fun stuff" I want to spend most of my energy on.

Of course, the temptation to launch my own product is always present . . . and when the right time comes, I certainly will not be able to resist the temptation.

PRODUCTS OF NEED

with Ellen SHAPIRO, Principal
of Ellen Shapiro Design

ELLEN SHAPIRO, a graphic designer and writer (her essay appears earlier in this volume), heads a design firm that specializes in identity and communications projects for corporate and nonprofit clients. She is also founder of Alphagram Learning Materials Inc. (*www.alphagram.com*), which publishes unique tools that help young children learn to read. She is the author of the book *Clients and Designers* and coauthor of *Ready, Set, Read!: Skills and Activities That Help Build Confident Readers*, a guide for elementary school teachers. She is also the Senior Seminar instructor at Purchase College, SUNY, and has taught at Parsons School of Design, Pratt Institute, and the School of Visual Arts.

How would you define entrepreneurship?

I would define entrepreneurship as risking your time, your money, and your soul to create a company that sells a product you believe in. You hope that at some time in the future, your company will make a profit.

And by extension, how would you describe the design entrepreneur?

The design entrepreneur doesn't have to hire another designer! The entrepreneur who is not a designer has a product or business idea. In order to visualize the idea, to demonstrate it to others, and to create what is needed to produce it, he or she must bring in a designer to make drawings, models, digital files. Something may get lost in translation. In most cases, the designer brings something to the table that contributes to the entrepreneur's vision and success. And often, the designer doesn't get paid enough to compensate for the value added to the project, or even for the time spent.

The design entrepreneur can be the visionary and add something new, useful, and beautiful to the world—whatever he or she can dream up, as long as there is a market for it. It could be a toy, a home accessory, clothing, a book, a Web site, a vehicle, a system, something that has never been imagined before. The design entrepreneur, ideally, is in control and can keep "all" the profits instead of getting a 5 percent royalty or whatever.

But instead of bringing in someone to design, the design entrepreneur must bring in people to teach us how to run a business that, in many ways, is very different from a design firm.

You began your practice as a graphic designer. At what point did you decide to develop your own products, and why?

I'm still a graphic designer.

I'd been fooling around with products off and on for years. I have a file drawer with several unsellable ideas.

All the best products emanate from a real need. When my son Alex was about six and a half and not learning to read, he was diagnosed as having dyslexia. I engaged the services of a tutor, who used (what I now know are) explicit, multisensory teaching techniques. In a relatively short time, she was able to teach Alex to look at a letter shape, listen to the sound and repeat it, and associate it with an icon or pictorial cue that represented that sound. Soon, he was able to put together two and three letters to read syllables and words.

As successful as her techniques were, the materials she used were homemade file cards with letters written with magic markers and pictures cut from magazines glued on. I knew I could do better, and I began developing a paradigm for a moveable flash card with a large letter, pictorial icon, and key word. Inspired by the flip books that let you make funny, mixed-up creatures with different heads, bodies, and feet, I created a flip book that lets you make more than a thousand three-letter words and syllables with consonant, vowel, and consonant.

Alex is now a very literate freshman at Oberlin College, studying Chinese and physics. I can't say my products were developed soon enough to help him, but they have been helping other kids for more than three years.

Your products are designed for educational purposes. What did you have to know about this area that you didn't already know?

I didn't know anything. I had to learn everything. The only thing I knew was that for some kids—about 15 percent of the population—learning to read is difficult. And that I couldn't find anything—anything that looked well designed and effective—in stores or catalogs. As just one example, typical phonics workbooks have pages crammed with letters, words, and pictures. Directions like, "Circle all the words that begin with . . ." are about other activities, like coloring, not reading. They confuse and frustrate a child with dyslexia, who needs to focus on one letter at a time, with no distracting elements.

I read books about teaching reading, both those written for professional and lay (parent) audiences. I consulted with reading experts, from whom I elicited valuable advice on everything from the right colors to the perils of "r-controlled" vowels. I visited elementary schools, tested prototypes with kids, gave out free sample prototypes with survey questionnaires designed to help me learn as much as possible from the teachers who would ultimately be using these materials.

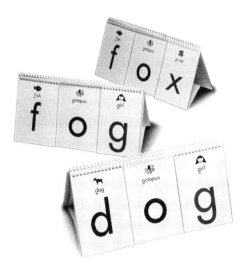

I went to reading conferences, for two reasons. I needed to see what the exhibitors were selling. Did they have anything like my idea? If I would soon be an exhibitor, would there be customers for my products? I also attended some conference workshop sessions to learn everything I could about teaching reading, especially to children with learning disabilities. What did teachers and tutors need to help them do what they do better? Alphagram's first booth was at a conference sponsored by the International Dyslexia Association. When teachers came out of their sessions, enough of them came by and said, "Wow, I could really use this," to show me that a market was there. They saw an attractive, inexpensive item that could save them days of work, that kids would like, and that would make their lives easier.

I've never stopped doing all of these things.

How easy or difficult has it been for you to conduct a design business and a product business?

Not easy! I have a schizoid life. I get e-mails to both companies routed to the same mailbox. I switch from minute to minute from designing a corporate identity or brochure to doing something for Alphagram, whether it's talking on the phone to a customer, marketing the Web site, or negotiating with a potential distributor. As you know, I also teach and write magazine articles, so I sometimes do feel stretched thin. But I wouldn't have it any other way.

Is there much or little crossover in the way you operate your businesses?

In certain ways, there is a lot of crossover. Quality is one of them. For example, I've designed every Alphagram icon (and there are hundreds) with all the care and attention that I give to a corporate logo. It shows. Teachers and parents appreciate the difference. Our icons were based stylistically on the AIGA/Department of Transportation Symbol Signs: the clearest, most graphic way to pictorially represent an object. Although there are a few notable exceptions, most educational publishers don't seem to spend much money on art or production. I find some of the materials on the market almost insulting to children and teachers. Alphagram manipulative products are manufactured by one of the top printing companies in the country. In the beginning, I tried to use a low-cost printer and had some problems with cards that didn't flip properly, stands that collapsed, pages that came out of bindings. There is nothing worse than dealing with unhappy customers and returns.

So, what do you do to avoid this?

The structure of each business is quite different though. The success of most graphic design firms is based on long-term, personal, consulting relationships. The success of most entrepreneurial companies is based on volume.

Entrepreneurial businesses often, ultimately, don't need their founders and have value in themselves: intellectual property assets, inventory, and customers. But they take much more capital to open. You have to have enough start-up capital to manufacture your products—there's no such thing as a one-product company—store them, advertise them, be able to take orders and fill them. You don't need to be McDonalds and try to reach every person in the world. But you do have to be able to reach your target market. You've got to have a real clear idea of who those people are, how to find them, and how to show them what you have to offer and why they should buy it.

How, then, did Alphagram begin?

After getting positive reactions to my first prototypes, I started Alphagram by renting a list of all the reading teachers in New York City and mailing a black-and-white flyer. The response rate was high enough to plan the next mailing to all reading teachers in the country. That's how we grew. With baby steps.

One interesting example of crossover is the Sappi Paper "Ideas that Matter" competition. You may have seen the ads in design magazines with a red 3-D light bulb–heart inviting designers to submit a proposal on behalf of a nonprofit organization "close to their heart" for a grant for up to $50,000 to produce materials printed on paper (design to be donated pro bono). I wrote a proposal on behalf of the International Dyslexia Association to produce posters and booklets on how to recognize and treat learning disabilities in young children in the nation's most economically disadvantaged school districts. Shapiro Design was one of a dozen U.S. winners, and we are currently completing this project. I couldn't have done it without the knowledge gained from all the research for Alphagram.

What is the most fulfilling result of your entrepreneurial pursuit? And the least?

The most fulfilling result is knowing that kids around the country are learning to read, at least in part, because of my efforts. The least fulfilling is knowing I have a warehouse full of giant cards that might not sell!

There were some exhilarating moments, like getting the patent and passing the first $100,000 in sales. And there were some weeks when so few orders came in, I thought I'd made a terrible mistake. After all, over the last several years, I'd put in a lot of time on Alphagram that could have been spent going after corporate-identity programs or annual reports. I'd been doing design jobs that were more bread-and-butter than creative.

But I've kept going and, I think, did things with integrity. That is, identifying top reading experts around the country, really listening to what they had to say, using them as consultants. To me, it was obvious from all the headlines about falling reading scores and the literacy crises that elementary reading programs needed revamping. I looked at what the research was showing and saw the winds of change in the air. If multisensory techniques can help kids with learning and language difficulties, they should be able to help all children learn to read sooner and better. And with words like "phonics-based" now on the lips of many mainstream educators, I will be pursuing opportunities to partner with larger companies with nationwide marketing and distribution clout in the hopes of bringing our methodologies to millions more K–3 children.

How have you grown your company since launching your first product?

I've grown the company by trying to fulfill teacher needs. Four or five times a year, I sit behind a table at reading conferences, meet teachers, and sell products. They tell me what they need. People call with requests. "Do you have . . . ?" If there are enough requests, we'll design it and have it manufactured. Individual packs of cards with digraphs, blends, and diphthongs that let you spell any word. A teacher's guide, *Ready, Set, Read!*, filled with lesson ideas and activities. Posters in Spanish, Hebrew, and Chinese. Laminated desk-size student cards. Well designed tools for handwriting practice. (Many kids who can read can't write.) Alphagram Tracing Letters in lower case and caps, manuscript printing and cursive, for which we developed a new cursive font. Games, like "Write the Right Word," which teaches vocabulary and spelling.

Do you have plans for increasing your product line, or are you content with what you are doing so far?

I'm never content with anything. Right now, I'm working on a handheld electronic word game, based on "Write the Right Word" (change one letter to make a new word that fits the clue); a phonemic awareness storybook, which is a prereading, auditory experience that will help children hear, identify, and classify sounds before letters are introduced as the symbols that represent those sounds; and a pre-K curriculum to propose to Head Start, which George W. Bush says he wants to turn into a phonics-based reading program.

Do you see a point in the future where you will devote yourself entirely to Alphagram in a total eclipse of your design firm?

No. In my future crystal ball, I'm an independent consultant working out of a comfortable, book-lined home office. I consult on the design of new educational products. I do a few select corporate identity projects. I teach. I write. I write a book called *How to Teach Your Child to Read*. I get a big advance. It is a bestseller. A total fantasy? I don't know. Talk to me in ten years.

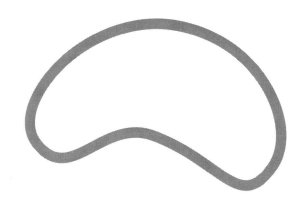

TOYS, GAMES, GIZMOS

3

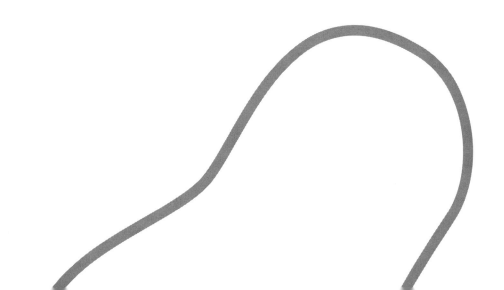

14

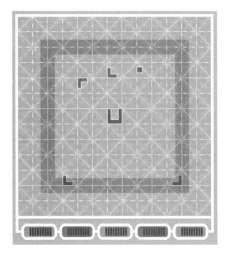

MAKING HAY FROM PLAY

with Eric ZIMMERMAN, C

ERIC ZIMMERMAN is a game designer, artist, and academic exploring the emerging field of game design. He is the cofounder and CEO of gameLab, a New York City–based game developer with a focus on experimental online games. Recent game projects include "BliX," "LOOP," and "SiSSYFiGHT 2000." Zimmerman has exhibited nondigital game projects at galleries and museums, including Artists Space (New York), Le Magasin (Grenoble), and the Bellevue Museum (Seattle). He has taught design at MIT, NYU, and Parsons School of Design and has published and lectured extensively on game design and digital culture.

How did you become a game designer?

It turns out that I have been making games my whole life. Growing up in the college town of Bloomington, Indiana, I was lucky enough to have a lot of spaces for play. I would draft neighborhood kids into test-driving elaborate haunted houses I would make in my basement, or play variations of "Kick the Can" or "Ghost in the Graveyard" with the kids on my block. Of course, I was an early computer game player (my fifth-grade class had a TRS-80, and my best friend had an Atari), and I was a "Dungeons and Dragons" supergeek in junior high and high school.

But I was always interested in making art, too—music, visual art, writing, and theater. I studied painting at the University of Pennsylvania for my undergrad degree. I was always making these diagrams about the relationships between the artist, the art-work, and the viewer—elaborate models for the creation and experience of art. After I left art-making to make pop culture in the form of games (during which time I received an M.F.A. in Art and Technology at the Advanced Computing Center for the Arts and Design at OSU), I realized that in designing a game, I am able to focus on those relationships to the exclusion of all else. A painter makes an object for passive contemplation. A game designer creates a system that only comes to life when it is inhabited and played by players. Structuring social relationships (even if it is between an individual and a responsive system) is a very unique kind of design activity, and I find it very satisfying.

In the digital environment, gaming is a key medium. What do you need to know that goes beyond the traditional realms of design?

First of all, creating a digital game is a highly interdisciplinary endeavor, like making a film. A gameLab team might include a programmer, a visual designer, a sound designer, a game designer, and a project manager. Instead of trying to address all of these roles, let me focus on game design. Game design is, after all, the one role that doesn't exist in any other medium. Programmers create all kinds of software (including games), but you won't find game designers doing anything but making games (unless they're unemployed).

One of the challenges of being a game designer is that there isn't really an established discipline of game design. So, it is difficult to acquire the fundamental skills of the field, or even to know what they are. In general, I would say that the skills a game designer needs are similar to those of an interactive designer or industrial designer. At the core is the ability to structure a participatory experience by understanding how dynamic systems function. The trick is understanding how these formal systems relate to the experiences of players in terms of desire, aesthetics, communication, emotion, representation, meaning, and other vectors of the multivalent play experience.

It's also important to have a sense of the twenty-year history of the medium, preferably as an avid digital game player. And of course, knowledge and interest in non-digital games is important, too. Finally, as with all of design, it is crucial to understand how one's own disciplinary knowledge intersects with other design fields and with culture at large.

Obviously, the term "video game" conjures "Dungeons and Dragons," "Myst," etc. How is what you do different from these extremely popular fantasies?

One of the things that drew me to create digital games is how formally innovative they are. More than any other medium, digital gaming really reinvents itself every few years. Some of the most interesting vectors of computer culture—real-time graphics rendering, complex interactive systems, massive online communities, procedural interactive narratives, nonstandard hardware interfaces, artificial life and artificial intelligence—find their most robust manifestations in gaming.

Yet, at the same time, the culture of games is somewhat stunted, mired in adolescent male power fantasies, like the pulp fantasy you mention. In my work, I have tried to incorporate narrative content and visual and audio styles that aren't normally found in games. Digital games are a pop-cultural medium, and it's time that they had the same sense of style, appropriation, and cultural subtlety that other pop media, like music and fashion, share.

Do you think "child" when you design games? Or do you think "everyone"?

The idea that "play" is for children is a deeply held belief in our culture. Along with this notion is the idea that the purpose of play is to make these children better citizens of the state by educating them cognitively, socially, or ethically.

There are many other ways of thinking about play as well. I like to think about play as a kind of subversiveness or mischievousness—the "play" of a steering wheel, for example, being the interstitial space that exists between utilitarian structures. I'd like to find those spaces and have players inhabit them.

So, no, I don't think of children when designing games. I'm not even sure about this whole category of "adulthood." I think of myself as a boy. . . .

You worked for game designers. What were the challenges of starting your own business?

Starting any kind of business is challenging. gameLab opened its doors in September 2000. At that time, it was just myself and cofounder Peter Lee. Since then, we've added three staff. Now that we have real personnel overhead every month, I would say that the biggest challenge is finding online publishers willing to pay what it takes to make great games.

We are unhappily sandwiched between cheap online games that you'd never want to play more than once and big, huge, expensive retail game titles. Although the game industry is well established, Web gaming is relatively new, and revenue models are still experimental. Publishers are very conservative about how they want to spend their money, and that's been our biggest challenge.

How much of your work can be categorized by the word "design," and what does that mean in terms of what you do?

I have a very broad understanding of the word "design," which I borrow from designer Katie Salen. Design is the creation of contexts from which meaning can emerge. In this very inclusive sense, everything I do, from teaching a class to designing a game to answering the questions of this interview, is a kind of design activity. That may seem like an indulgently vague understanding of "design," but for me, it is a useful definition. The challenge, of course, is, What kinds of meanings do you want to emerge from your designed experience? And how can you make it as meaningful as possible?

How much of your creative time is devoted to R&D, and how much to making money?

I don't make those kinds of distinctions. All time spent in the company is "creative time," and all time spent "making money" is also time spent in R&D.

Gratuitous (but earnest) rhetoric aside, gameLab staffers are expected to spend 20 percent of their time (about a day a week) in research activities, like playing games and developing side projects that aren't connected to a paying job. We've also integrated a number of research activities into our company, such as a research library (every gameLab staffer has a monthly budget for contributions) and periodic research sabbaticals. Too much West Coast game culture is about bleary-eyed developers putting in eighty-hour weeks and sleeping at work. Game development is a cultural practice, and it's incredibly important to us at gameLab that we have culturally robust lives outside of the office.

What, in your estimation, constitutes success? In other words, what are the goals of your business?

The goals of gameLab include finding new audiences for gaming, expanding the boundaries of the medium, and changing the culture of gaming.

How do you market your products?

We don't. The computer game industry is structured like other content-based industries, such as the music industry. In the game industry, there are two kinds of companies, publishers and developers. Developers play the role that musicians do, generating intellectual property in the form of computer games. Publishers are like record labels: They fund the development of games and also are responsible for manufacturing, marketing, and distributing them. Our company, gameLab, is a developer. So, we don't market our products to the public ourselves.

Yours is a fairly new venture. How do you see it evolving?

There are a number of economic, technological, and cultural factors affecting the development of the game industry. While the game industry has grown remarkably quickly (it now is comparable to the film industry in America in terms of revenue), it is like the Hollywood film industry without an alternative [independent] film industry.

Games are very expensive to make (a mainstream game typically costs $2–4 million). The equivalent of the "garage band" that can record an album over a weekend does not exist in the medium. Retail distribution is bottlenecked by a handful of store chains that lack sufficient shelf space and have a high turnover rate, which makes it difficult for games without a massive marketing campaign to survive on the shelf. The game industry is a hit-driven industry like Hollywood, and so publishers generally are looking for that one hit, rather than experimental or groundbreaking games, leading to hundreds of "genre-fied," "look-alike" game titles. Games tend to be made by and for "hardcore gamers," and therefore, games have been slow to find new audiences. Some hope that online distribution can alleviate some of these problems, but the challenge of making money from games online remains an unanswered question.

A question for me is, considering all of these factors, how will games develop as a medium? One possibility is that they will remain stuck in pulp adolescent genres, and like comic books, will never overcome their social stigma, regardless of how much experimentation goes on in the medium. On the other hand, games might become like music, a multifaceted pop medium in which there is room for both corporate, boy-band dreck as well as commercially successful experimentation.

Where will games end up?

Part of why I'm working in this field is to try and answer this question.

SERIOUS PLAY

with Byron GLASER and Sandra
HIGASHI, Founders of Zolo

BYRON GLASER and SANDRA HIGASHI, both natives of Southern California,
graduated from Art Center College of Design in 1978. In 1986 they founded a
graphic design firm, and the following year they created Zolo, the post-
Modern-looking toy that they assert "established a new free-form gender-neu-
tral construction niche" in the toy market. It was the first product in their own
line of many toys and the beginning of Zolo Inc., which includes toys, digital
products, and children's books. Combining their unique illustrative graphic
style with fun concepts, they've created such consumables as Mixostickers,
Curious Bonz, Sense-o-rama, and At Home products (including Splat Coasters
and Kooky Cutters).

Byron and Sandra, how did you begin as graphic designers and illustrators?

Sandra: My first public illustration showing was a crayon drawing of alien Martians I
did at age seven. It was shown on the *Chuck Jones the Magic Man* TV show. For a shy
kid living in South-Central L.A. it was the beginning of a dream. Later, I was fortunate
to attend a public high school that offered a course in advertising design, which introduced me to graphics and allowed me to build a practical portfolio. My art instructor,
Sam Uskovich, encouraged me to apply to the Art Center College of Design, and to my
disbelief, I was one of two students accepted straight from high school in the fall entering class.

    Byron: For me, it started in the fourth grade, when my teacher, Mrs. Bulara, would
let me get out of class to design the bulletin boards and display cases in and around the
school. She also told me that I would make my living in art. I was a believer. My seventh grade art teacher, Ditte Wolff, created a class for me, and one of my assignments
was to recreate Mexican whistles in clay. I sold them for a quarter, and by the second
week at lunch, Ditte and I walked out on the field, it was as if a flock of a thousand
nightingales had landed and were singing for me—even those who did not have the
two-toned whistles whistled on their own. At that moment, I realized the power of art
and commerce. Even the principal could not control it. I was found out and forced to
return all the money I had earned.

What was your impetus for creating the product Zolo?

Sandra: Back in 1986, we were involved in designing the interior graphics for the flagship FAO Schwarz store in New York. As we were researching, we gained a good overview of the toy market and realized that there was a big hole in the marketplace. It felt very corporate and uninspired. We wanted to create something with heart and soul, and a sense of amusement and humor.

Byron: I also remember wanting to create the best toy in the world! Something that would inspire creativity, something that would require imagination. We wanted a toy that we would like playing with.

Did you foresee that Zolo would evolve into a business?

Byron: "Evolve" describes exactly what Zolo has been for us, and no, we did not foresee anything. We had to do a lot of improvising along the way. Challenges we would never have imagined presented themselves to us daily. The toy industry especially was not open to Zolo as a concept. We were told the same thing by all the major toy companies. There wasn't a category for Zolo. Was it for boys or girls? What was the target age? Even the MoMA did not exactly know where to position us. Were we construction or art? Many people since then have told us that Zolo created a new category.

Tell me about the transition from Zolo as a cottage industry into a more widespread and well distributed concern.

Sandra: It wasn't really a choice, but something that was part of the natural progression. When you have a successful product, there's a good chance it will get knocked off by someone eventually. We wanted to be at the forefront, to at least be the first and the best. It's about survival. We also wanted Zolo to be a classic.

After Zolo, did you maintain a design business, or did you immediately launch your own product line?

Sandra: We did both. Once you have one successful product, it creates a huge appetite for "new" and "more" in the marketplace, every season, every year. You can either seize that opportunity or quit with your "winnings" and fold. We were enjoying the creative freedom and got such great feedback that we decided to build a business from it. Our graphic design business also helped to balance out our cash flow with the heavily season-driven product business.

How much freedom do you have to create the products you want?

Sandra: You can have total freedom, or you may decide to sacrifice some of it, depending on what's important to you. How many you want to sell, what the market will bear,

what your personal objectives are, and how much you care about the monetary success are factors that play into this decision. A lot of times, we'll opt for special materials or extra details over more profit, other times we'll make sacrifices if we price ourselves out of the market. At least you have the power to decide where you want to be. Licensing is another matter.

Given the constraints of the marketplace, have you had any difficulties in doing the kind of work that you want to do?

Sandra: In terms of licensing, this is where it often becomes a conflict. Licensing is great, because it can give you much greater volume, but your newfound partners might not always share your vision. Although we always include a "creative control" clause in all contracts for our protection, sometimes a licensee's decision is motivated by different factors than what a designer's would be. You eventually have to find a common place—sometimes it works, other times you just have to step back and look at the bigger picture, or you'll make yourself crazy and go nowhere.

Byron: At one point, we licensed Zolo to a toy company, and it became a struggle to keep the Zolo core values intact. Their marketing group could not handle using certain colors that would be perceived as too feminine. We don't adhere to color stereotyping. Especially with Zolo, where the concept is that all "colors, shapes, and sizes work together and the results are extraordinary." Usually, the constraints come from the budget. How much will it cost once it is manufactured, packaged, and shipped? Then the cost of getting it to market: How many hands are involved and how is it sold? The rule is, whatever it costs you is doubled, then the retailer doubles that. It's why the good stuff ends up being so expensive, and many of the best ideas are kept in a file. The idea is the easy part.

As your own clients, so to speak, what kind of strictures do you place on yourselves—aesthetically, philosophically, practically?

Byron: Usually, the strictures are defined by the market for whom the product is intended. Our approach always begins from the point of view that it appeals to us first. We have to like it or want it. Is it fun? Does it engage the end user? Will it last? How much does it cost? Will people buy it? Can the package be reusable? Will it win awards? Does it have purpose? Are we willing to put our names on it? Will we be cast into hell for adding to the landfill? Does it feel good? Will it make people laugh? Touch them? Make them think? We have not always been successful in reaching these ideals/objectives, but we try.

How do you decide into which products you will invest your time, energy, and money?

Sandra: Intuition mostly. This is really important. A lot of major corporations spend millions on market-testing products that ultimately fail, when a lot of times it seems obvious. We do also have a marketing partner now, who keeps us on track. She's also much more creative than most marketing people, so it works well for us.

Byron: We have recently joined forces with a former client who we did work for at Nickelodeon, Deb Hirschfield. She was the head of product development there, very talented and intelligent, with an intuitive sense of the marketplace. With a lot of creative ideas herself, she is also able to help us focus on a more strategic way of reaching goals. Having the ability to negotiate agreements and contracts is essential, and for Sandra and I, the least desirable part of the business, a huge energy drain. She [Deb] has a great business sense with a heart of gold, and the left part of the brain we lack. We now are able to make what we think would be great products, but have a better idea if they will be profitable or not.

As we grow our business, we are trying to stay focused on core product lines and develop them as brands, strategically. Before the development process, we take time to research the marketplace and to try and understand what's currently out there and what the consumer actually needs. As we begin to create the product, we start with functional attributes, incorporate the branding elements, and then the rest of the design grows organically from there. Most importantly, we make sure we can make a high-quality product that can be delivered to the customer for the right price.

Are your monetary investments your own, or are you in a position now where you can work with other people's cash?

Sandra: Equally our own, for our line of products, and also from others in terms of licensing. We don't have outside investors in our company as a whole—it would have to be a very unusual investment group.

How are your work and life integrated?

Byron: I can't really tell the difference. I remember a time, when we did not have our own design company, I was working at an ad agency in New York, and there were days that I would dread going in. Since Sandra and I have had our business, I have never dreaded "work." In fact, I never really think of it as work. That's not to say that there are not huge challenges, and at times we have felt, "That's it—man overboard! Ship's sinking!" What we do involves travel to exotic places, our own commitment to time, a true love of design, and a desire to spread the joy. We definitely adhere to the "live to work" principle. Mostly, we employ friends and even family, so the lines blur.

What are your plans for the future?

Byron: We created a set of fortune cards, called Q-cards. They never lie. I will draw from them now and see what they say. "Big Deal. Win/Win. Take a look at yourself. Share the wealth. Whoa, Nelly!" That sounds good. Who knows?

POWERED BY THE LIGHT

with Richard MCGUIRE,
Principal of Work Is Play

RICHARD MCGUIRE started his professional career by designing record sleeves, posters, and videos for his own band, Liquid Liquid (with which he played bass). Later, he formed his own toy company, McGuire Toys, and produced games, puzzles, and an Optical Solar Toy called EO. He has written and illustrated four children's books, and his illustrations have appeared in the *New York Times* and the *New Yorker*. Most recently, two animated spots that he created for PBS and his design of the Japanese Web site, "Willing-To-Try.com," have won numerous awards.

How did you become a toy maker?

As a kid, I'd make toys for myself. My grandfather was a carpenter, so it just came naturally for me to play with wood. I ended up studying sculpture. My sculptures eventually got smaller and smaller, and I made boxes for them.

The pivotal moment of becoming a "professional" toy maker happened when I had heard that Steven Guarnaccia was putting together a book called *Artists Who Make Toys*. I set up a meeting with him. There was one toy in particular that he liked, called Puzzelhead, and he wanted to buy it from me. We ended up working out a trade.

Then, I got a call from Byron Glaser, who saw the toy at Steven's. He said he could help me get it manufactured. Byron and his partner, Sandra Higashi, had created a toy called Zolo. They were having it manufactured in Indonesia by a small group of artisans they had put together. I met them at a time when they were looking for other products to keep this group working together. So, within a few weeks of meeting Byron, I was on my way to the island of Java to work, and then one toy led to the next.

It's one thing to be an artist who makes special things, like toys, but another to manufacture, distribute, and otherwise try to promote your "art/commerce." How did you make this work?

I was extremely lucky to have met Byron and Sandra, who had already been around the block a few times with the stuff. It was a great introduction to the world of manufacturing. After dealing with countless frustrations with trying to sell their ideas to toy manufacturers, they decided to forge ahead and do it themselves. They were just starting to work out the distribution part when I came along. I learned a lot from them. We rented a booth at the Gift Show, which is a huge show at the Javits Center here in New York. It happens twice a year, all the buyers from museum stores and small specialty gift stores from across the county come there.

I showed a prototype of Puzzlehead, and we started taking orders.

You succeeded in producing three toys. What was the easiest and the hardest?

I've created four toys, actually. They all had their unique set of problems to solve, but that can be fun or frustrating, depending on how you look at it. With Puzzlehead, I didn't know what I was getting myself into, which I think was a good thing. Before leaving for Indonesia, I had to get shots for typhoid and malaria and take three planes to get to this small village in the middle of nowhere. It took a while to get the group into the groove of the work. I had interpreters help me talk to the workers about technical problems.

For the box, we had to drive to Jakarta a few hours away to find a manufacturer. Finding good-quality cardboard was hard. To keep the cost down, I had to settle for something I wasn't completely satisfied with.

There were cultural differences as well, which got in the way. They would never say "no"; there are a million ways to avoid being that direct, which I think they find offensive. We had orders to fill for Christmas, and instead of saying straight up that they couldn't meet the orders, they would tell us what they thought we wanted to hear. When the orders did finally show up, they were late, and half of them were put in the boxes while the paint was still wet, so they were stuck to the boxes! Only a couple hundred made it out into the world.

That's terrible.

Ultimately, the story has a happy ending. I posted a photo of it on my site, and it was seen by a company in Chicago called Chiasso—they have a chain of stores and a catalog that reaches millions. They asked to carry my toys. Through my rep in Paris, Prima Linea, we were able to arrange a deal with a Swiss company called Naef. Naef is *the* best wooden toy manufacturer in the world. They do all the reproductions of the original Bauhaus toys. So, this is the deluxe edition that has a wooden box with a sliding lid, it's beautiful! They will manufacture it, and the distribution will be shared by Naef and Chiasso.

So, the next product was just as hard or easier?

I suppose the next product was the easiest. I decided to create a deck of cards based on the game "Go Fish," which I used to play as a kid. I thought, "How complicated could it be to just have something printed?"

I made a traditional mechanical with separations and chose three Pantone colors. Finding card manufacturers was easy. What I wasn't prepared for was the minimum orders, which were something like ten thousand units! Eventually, I found a printer in New Jersey who would do two thousand.

I remember, I wanted the corners to be curved, like a classic playing card, but I couldn't afford to pay for a die to be made. The printer said he had an old corner-cutting machine, and he set up his grandmother in the corner to cut them all! Two thousand decks!

It was by the next printing that I'd heard about international trade councils. I wrote to the Hong Kong Trade Council for names of card printers. I sent faxes to them asking about pricing, then narrowed it down to a factory that would do a relatively small print run of five thousand. The printing was incredible and at a quarter of the cost of doing it here. Getting them into the country was complicated. Getting them on a freighter, getting through customs procedures, then across the country by train, then by truck to a warehouse, it took a lot of calls.

It was a great product in the end; it sold steadily for years. It went though a few printings and allowed me to do another toy.

Does this mean it got easier with each successive project?

No. The next toy, EO, was possibly the hardest, but the biggest learning experience. It was a solar-powered toy. I made one for myself and put it in the window of my apartment, and everyone who saw it encouraged me to do it as a product.

It was a simple, flat figure with two different printed sides. The figure was attached to a motor and powered by a solar cell. There is something magical about seeing a toy start up all by itself when the sun shines on it. As the figure would spin, it would animate, with a very hypnotic effect.

One of the first lessons you learn making product is that there is a simple rule of thumb formula: The cost of your product per unit doubled is the wholesale price, and that figure usually gets doubled again when it goes retail. I needed it to sell for around $25, which means my cost-per-unit should be $6.25.

I couldn't afford to use plastic—that requires having molds made, and that is a huge start-up expense. I originally found the motor and solar cells in a hobby catalog. I made a bunch of calls trying to track down the source of the cells, which I found out were actually created by NASA and used for satellites. The only place that I could get them from was a surplus supplier.

The motor and the cells took up more than half the budget. I still needed the printed figure, packaging, and a wooden piece that could hold the motor and give it some weight, so it wouldn't go flying when it started up. What I didn't know was that wood "breathes"; it shrinks and grows, depending on humidity. The first part I had made absorbed moisture while it was sitting in the warehouse, so then the motors no longer fit. I had to have that part made again. This time, the wood was baked to get out all the excess moisture, and after the pieces were cut, they were sealed with paint.

When I went into production, the cell supplier ran out of cells. Desperate, I ended up calling up NASA directly, but went round in circles. The supplier eventually found some in a bigger size, but by then, I had already locked myself into the size of the base, so I had to work around that and make it fit.

Then, there were registration problems in printing. The figure was printed on paper, then glued to cardboard and die cut. The lining up of the two sides was crucial to make the animation effect work. The first time I had this printed, it was a disaster. I found a new printer, who was more expensive, but was confident he could do it. Then, there was a new problem: The figures started to warp. It could have been the gluing, or what one printer referred to as "the memory" of the cardboard.

You've always been somewhat entrepreneurial. Even as a musician with your own group, Liquid Liquid, you evinced the entrepreneurial spirit. So, how did you make the transition into being an editorial illustrator, working for a client rather than yourself?

There was a real roundabout way that happened. The band existed for about five years. I formed the band while I was still in school, and we put out a few records. I played bass and created the graphics for the sleeves and the posters. Eventually, I felt the band had run its course and it was time to move on, so I left to pursue a more visual work.

My artwork wasn't exactly making me a living, but because of my background in sculpture, I was able to get a job working in a place that made props. I designed and built sets for TV commercials. We would make incredibly realistic, magnified views of products, so they could be lit better when filming the "beauty shot." Or sometimes, we would create rigs for special effects. This was all predigital, so if a commercial called for a tree to burst into flames, we would figure out how to do it. It was fun working on a set rigging things up. The requests were fun to solve—making a rubber potato chip or building a Hawaiian landscape with hydraulic lifts to simulate an earthquake. It was fun, but a lot of the materials for this kind of work were very toxic, and I thought it was time to move on.

The transition came from a job that required that I design and construct three-dimensional sets for a cereal commercial. Animated characters would be added to the sets later. Somehow, after the sets were built, I convinced them to hire me to work on the animation, which I did. This led to more animation work, and at night, I worked on getting an illustration portfolio together. Around this time, I took a lecture class with Art Spiegelman, because I'd been a fan of *Raw* magazine. Art was working on the Garbage Pail Kids cards with Mark Newgarden at Topps Chewing Gum at the time. I became friends with Mark, and he got me some freelance work creating animated flip books on the backs of the cards. This was the first step to freelance work. A friend of mine was working at the *Village Voice* and introduced me to the art director. I started getting some work published, and after a short time, I was illustrating a regular column. Eventually, that led to other work, like the *New York Times Book Review,* and before long, a whole new career.

As a children's book illustrator, you are creating for your muse, but also addressing a very specific audience. What determines the themes of your books?

I'm thinking mostly about what I would like to do, rather than the audience. I like diagrams. I'm always attracted to interesting structure. *Night Becomes Day* was an exercise in trying to build a chain of connections. "River becomes tree, tree becomes paper,

paper becomes trash," then it becomes new from recycling. The book itself was printed on recycled paper. It's a collection of connections that loops back to the beginning. The idea came to me while I was working out another book, which was basically about karma and the chain reaction of events that became *What Goes Around Comes Around*.

The idea for *The Orange Book* came to me when I saw an orange on a subway track. I was thinking how this orange most likely had lived the good life up until this point, basking in the sun in Florida or California, and ended up here on the subway tracks of New York and will most likely be eaten by a rat. Which led me to think of the fate of all the other oranges.

Another book idea came from a *New Yorker* cover I did for April Fools' Day, with ninety-five things wrong with the cover. The cover had gotten a great response, so my editor suggested I try to do a book in this vein, which became *What's Wrong with This Book?* It was filled with optical illusions, die cuts, and everything else I could think of.

Have you tried to tie in your toys to your books?

I did do one toy with a book. A little doll. The story was called *What Goes Around Comes Around*, which I mentioned earlier. It was a story about a chain reaction of events that goes completely around the world. It starts with a boy throwing his sister's doll out the window, and it comes back and smacks him in the head at the end of the book. I wanted the doll to be packaged with the book, but it met resistance from my publisher. The marketing people weren't interested. They had a formula they were sticking to— "big dolls with small books"—there was no convincing them. I went ahead and had the doll made anyway and distributed it though my own channels. The doll had a tag to promote the book, but it could have been more coordinated.

Toys and kids' books. Do you prefer to work in the children's arena?

I love kids. I love getting fan letters and drawings in the mail, but there are many things I want to express outside of that realm. One book I'm working on now is based on the comic I did years before for *Raw* magazine. It was called "Here," and it's another story that plays with structure. It shows one location over time. If you can imagine, in the first panel, there is the image of a room. In the upper-left corner of the panel, you see it is marked with the year 2001. In the second panel, you may see a continuation of what is going on in this room in the year 2001, but it may also contain a smaller panel showing a glimpse of another time with another event that happened in that exact location. As it progresses, you are seeing a multidimensional view of time in this one location.

When I tried to sell the book, it met resistance from publishers, most of whom wished I would adapt the idea to a children's book. But I thought the idea was bigger than that. I want it to express a fuller experience, and I felt it would be compromised.

Eventually, I signed a deal with Pantheon, who had already contracted Chris Ware and Ben Katchor, and they understood what it was I wanted to do. But I don't think of it as comics really. It isn't a traditional narrative.

What haven't you done, entrepreneurially, that you still want to accomplish?

There are so many things that excite and attract me. I want to do more experiments with books, but I also want to work within multimedia platforms. I want to create more Web experiences.

I would love to incorporate music with some kind of kinetic experience. I'm not sure if that's through objects or some sort of virtual experience.

Last year, I was invited by the Swiss Institute to participate in a show. They had seen the "Here" strip and suggested I do it as an installation. That was a great opportunity, and one I want to explore more. I enjoy product design, and in the past year, I've been able to create a whole array of home furnishings for kids through a company called Land of Nod—rugs, sheets, quilts, pillows, chairs. That's been a great experience. Now, Chiasso, the company I mentioned earlier, asked me to design more products for them.

I recently designed a series of animated spots for PBS, and now, I have new doors opening there. There are so many possibilities.

Hole No. 15 at the Lookout Mountain Golf Club in Phoenix, Arizona. Photo courtesy of Pointe Resorts.

THE BIGGEST GAME

Forrest RICHARDSON, Principal of
Richardson or Richardson

FORREST RICHARDSON studied golf course architecture as part of an independent study program at the University of Dundee in Dundee, Scotland. He established his practice in 1988 and is the firm's current president. Richardson has worked in association with Arthur Jack Snyder since the mid-1980s. Together, they have completed new design and remodeling projects throughout the southwest United States, in California, Nevada, Arizona, New Mexico, Texas, and Hawaii. Internationally, they have worked in Mexico and Asiatic Russia, on the north shore of the Sea of Japan.

What in the world made you switch from graphic design to golf course design?

I had always wanted to be a golf course architect and even studied to do this. But I found myself working for a printer during school. Graphic design seemed fun, and I sort of gave up on the golf idea. Then, I got a terrific break to do a course after really being out of the golf picture for many years. I look back on that, I now realize what a once-in-a-lifetime break it was. Then, after doing several courses, I finally had to choose.

Are there any similarities whatsoever between playing with type and playing with greens and fairways?

Yes. It's all design. One is more permanent. Very often, the people you are working for don't have an eye for what you're doing no matter what the design problem. Concepts are hard to sell in either discipline, but I've found they are necessary in both, at least for the work to be nice.

How did you establish yourself in this world? I presume that landscape architects toil for ages before they can do something like this.

There are about four hundred people in the world who design golf courses full-time. It is really hard to describe the competition for the very few projects that are out there. The problem in this business is the celebrity golf-pro designers. It would be like having Martha Stewart put her name on a design project and then have a team of designers do the actual work. Wait a minute, that's happened, hasn't it? Oh, well, it's sort of like that. Maybe this is a better way to think of it: What if Martha Stewart all of a sudden got

2,500 commissions to design brochures and annual reports? How would it affect the graphic design industry? That's what this is like. So, naturally, we now work with a "name" pro, at least to help us get in the door and even have the chance to talk to a client.

How does this obsession manifest in terms of your design business? Would you call it a vocation or an avocation or a reason for tossing in the towel on graphic design?

I've always loved to love what I'm doing. Sometimes, I think, I made myself love what I was doing in graphic design just to satisfy this equation. Now, I believe I've found something I love without too many questions. And I admit, graphic design was becoming somewhat of a drag. I sensed that in other people, too. Clients and designers I worked with were feeling the time crunch and the effects of lots of things changing really fast. Probably too fast. Golf is much more steeped in tradition. It takes four hours to play and about two hundred acres. Those have really not changed much in four hundred years.

What must you know that you didn't know before?

Budgets and economic stuff. As a graphic designer, I never thought really beyond a campaign, and not often in quantitative terms. You know, the kind of facts and figures that we regard often as "gray" matter. Well, now, I'm expected to know about this stuff. How much money a course will yield is an absolute reflection of how much money I can spend on a building for my client. I also have to work with engineers, environmentalists, angry neighborhoods, MBAs, and virtually everything we do has to go before board and commissions, city councils, and other approval processes. Projects take years just to move from concept to schematic design. I need to know how to manage a thousand things and keep focused on the big picture. I also need to know a bit of everything—about civil engineering, turf, psychology, etc.

If working with graphic-design clients is sometimes difficult, how much more difficult is it to work with clients in this area?

Easier in that I'm working at such a small scale, most people cannot visualize what the end result will be. More difficult in that there are many more layers, and communication is sometimes very problematic and involved.

Would you describe this activity as entrepreneurial?

Not really. I'd call it superspecialized—if you have a reputation in golf design, you are almost automatically a guru, at least of sorts. None of us who do this are breaking new ground except in our own designs, certainly not in the profession.

Hole No. 8 of the Coldwater Golf Club in Arizona. Photo by Dogleg Studios.

What are the pleasures you derive from this work?

Seeing something come to life that truly is growing and a living ecosystem. Some of the courses I've done are wildlife corridors and trails, so wild animals can get from one side of a highway to another, or from a national forest to a greenbelt. It's a playing board, and I think designers get great pleasure seeing how people play with their designs. This is the ultimate. Also, my work will be there for generations. I think that part of most graphic design is really troublesome to designers—the end result is often trashed in a matter of months.

Okay, what are the main problems?

Getting new work. I've never worked so hard to get projects in my life. In graphic design, you can get work by being good, knowing somebody, or dropping your fee until no one can say "no." In this business, there is too much at stake. The people who get work are people who have a track record.

Have you played on your own courses?

Of course. We make fifty to sixty visits before they open and actually direct shaping work in the field. By the time they are done and the grand opening is scheduled, we are really a part of the team, too.

Do you see this evolving into some other kind of business?

Golf course architects design experiences. I have already influenced the design of communities and resorts. I'd like to be called upon more for that. To do whole concepts.

HOW ARE YOU PEELING?
Foods with Moods

SAXTON FREYMANN AND JOOST ELFFERS

FOOD THAT DOES NOT SPOIL

with Saxton FREYMANN,
Cofounder of eeBoo Corporation

SAXTON FREYMAN, an artist and illustrator, has carved a career from carving food. He received his first jackknife on his eighth birthday, which he used to carve his very first pumpkin. Years later, he used that same knife to create many of the characters in *Play With Your Food*, his first book comprised of anthropomorphic fruits and vegetables. Freymann and his wife, Mia, started eeBoo Corporation, which makes fun products, such as growth charts, cookie cutters, and stacking blocks. Later, he teamed up Joost Elffers, who had the idea of doing a book on carving veggies. Together, they immediately began working on *Play With Your Food* and *Play With Your Pumpkin*. Freymann has devoted almost a decade to finding the most expressive produce and bringing it to life. In the bargain, he has developed an incomparable business that is not only profitable, but healthy, too.

You were an artist/illustrator prior to launching a career in metamorphic food. What kind of work did you do?

I made mostly representational paintings, drawings, and collages, which were occasionally shown, mostly in group shows. I had a kind of "half-baked" commercial art career, doing whatever came along, in a variety of styles and media—mostly drawings. About five or six years ago, I helped my wife start eeBoo corporation, which makes beautiful things for children.

How did you stumble on to food as a métier? Had you seen the famous eggplant (circa 1968) shaped like Richard Nixon's head, published in New York Magazine?

I don't think I saw that one, although I have seen a lot of eggplants that look like Nixon. Tomatoes, too. In 1996, my wife met [the designer and book packager] Joost Elffers through a friend and learned that he was looking for someone to collaborate with to create a book about creative ways of carving food. I immediately wanted to do it, so I ran out to the corner, bought some fruits and vegetables, and made some characters. When Joost got the snapshots, he called me up and said, "Let's start right away." A few days later, we were shooting the first book with photographer John Fortunato.

Once you settled on food, how difficult was it to get a publisher to, well, bite?

Joost published the book himself, and it was distributed through Stewart, Tabori & Chang. Lena Tabori got it immediately. I think she came up with the title, *Play With Your Food.*

Play With Your Food *is chock full of inventive and witty transformations. Tell me something about your process. Am I correct in assuming that you see parallel universes in every fruit and vegetable these days? Do you start by seeing the hidden forms in the produce, or do you begin with a concept for which the food is made to conform?*

Play With Your Food was about finding resonance in the organic forms, opening your mind to what was already there, and seeing what can be brought out with the least intervention. The more narrative the books have become, the more the process is reversed, and the seeking is more directed. (Although you must always remain open to the possibilities suggested by the form. This is an advantage of writing the books as well as illustrating them.)

Why did your books become more narrative as opposed to, say, gag-oriented?

Since everything is made of food, and visual puns abound in the books, gags are already embedded in every page. *How Are You Peeling?* is about emotions, and the text is designed to let you pause and talk about what is happening in the pictures. That meant stopping short of a continuous, linear narrative. But the book form lends itself to narrative, and the continuity of narrative helps the created world feel like a real place unfolding in time, populated by living characters. So, the books that followed explore those possibilities. But there will be more nonlinear books as well. Each approach offers different opportunities.

This is clearly disposable art. How long does this stuff last? And does your studio look and smell like the back room of a greengrocer?

Most of the things barely last long enough to photograph. I buy most of the produce on the way to the photographer's studio. I arrive with bags of groceries, and Maggie Nimkin and Ed Parrinello wait for me to put something in front of the camera. It's more like a live performance than working on a painting or a sculpture. And since the final product is a photograph, the object becomes obsolete (and usually a little tired-looking) as soon as the exposure is made. The studio *is* usually pretty fragrant. When we are shooting mushrooms, particularly, it smells like a forest.

With someone new... a little shy?

How do you feel your work compares to those sushi chefs who make animals out of cucumbers or shrimp?

I think it was that tradition that originally inspired Joost to produce a book on the subject. I have only had a limited exposure to it, although I am always impressed by the skill and beauty of the presentation. *Playing With Your Food*, with its embrace of the irregular, misshapen, imperfect form, most clearly diverges from the Japanese aesthetic. I have not been to Japan, but I am told that all the produce in the stores is perfect and uniform. I'd probably be in trouble if I had to find expressive peppers there. But our books are very popular in Japan, so who knows, maybe I'll have a hand in corrupting them.

Do you have any rules or limits? By this, I mean, do you refrain from using nonorganic materials and nonfruit or vegetable substances in your work?

Only produce. Purity and elegance are the main criteria. But the rules really create themselves. The limits are not arbitrary: Sticking together a hodgepodge of elements just doesn't work. The original organic form must remain the central premise of the design, or the result would look forced. The wonder lies in seeing a face and a vegetable at the same time. There is a special pleasure in finding that an ant is not only made of cherries, but that its legs are nothing more than the cherry's stems. Nothing extraneous, just one very familiar form rearranged to become another familiar form.

This food play has become something of a cottage industry. What is the nature of this business?

This fall [2000], we published our third children's book with Scholastic, and there will be seven more books of various kinds. There are cards, calendars, magnets, and most recently, a line of kitchen and tableware. We have also licensed some images commercially. But the books are really at the center of everything.

The "play with your food" idea is not going to be fresh forever. There are, I presume, inherent limitations, such as repetition. And yet, you've produced a number of books for kids and adults (as well as an entire holiday issue of the New York Times Book Review) filled with new ideas. Do you think that there is a point of diminished return?

Organic form is such a rich starting point that there are a surprisingly endless number of directions to pursue. And the forms are so primal and familiar (not to mention those colors!) that it all still feels fresh, and . . . ripe with possibilities. The next Scholastic book, coming in fall 2001, is the most ambitious so far, depicting an entire world with architecture, vehicles, flora and fauna, and characters who will appear in future books. As in any art form, reducing your means often expands your vision, and the discoveries you make returning to the same forms again and again become increasingly interesting.

But do you run the risk of being too cute? Do you have a "cute meter" in your head, or is that not a big issue?

I think all artists have to decide where their own line is. Certainly, *Play With Your Food* was a bit colder, a bit more formal, and that is because Joost, who is Dutch, occasionally expressed concern when I would make something that seemed too cartoony. Growing up with American pop culture, I probably have a higher tolerance for those references. Now, with the children's books, I feel justified in sweetening up the characters a little. I don't hesitate to give them those big, black-eyed pea eyes.

As an artist, I know that you are consumed with this. But in what other directions are you going, or plan to go?

For now, I am very fortunate to be able to do something so playful and inventive and have such a broad audience. The response has been so gratifying, particularly from children (I have three). I am hoping that I will get the chance to explore animating this world of food. We have already done a few animated commercials, and the possibilities are intriguing. I am looking forward to seeing what direction I take when I return to painting, for which I've had almost no time for a few years. But the food project is like calisthenics for the eye and the imagination, so I don't feel out of shape.

Has playing with food altered your dietary habits?

It certainly keeps my kids eating a lot of fruit and vegetables. My wife has finally gotten used to slicing up the characters for dinner, and my children are eager cannibals.

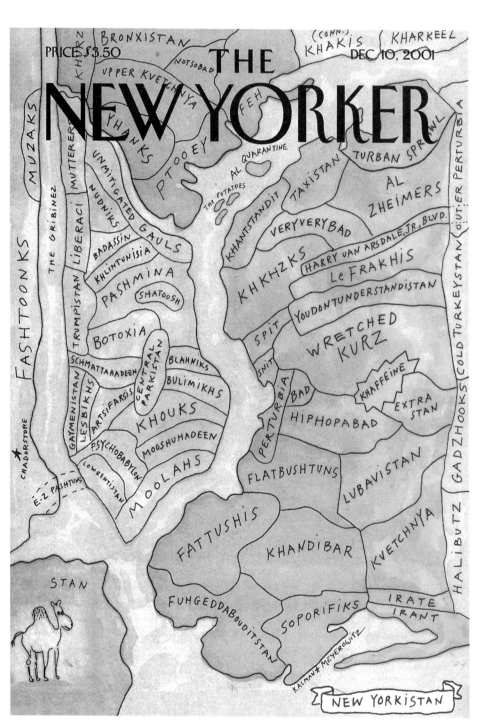

Courtesy Maira Kalman. © *The New Yorker* magazine.

COMMUNICATING WITH EVERY PERSON ON EARTH

with Maira KALMAN, Cofounder of M&Co.

MAIRA KALMAN was born in Tel Aviv, Israel, at a young age. She came to New York, where onions and hamburgers were frying on various coffee-shop griddles all over town. Her first entrepreneurial venture was babysitting at the Edmond Lee in Riverdale, New York. Not only was it a lucrative venture, but she was able to donate some of her time to philanthropic efforts. She was a candy striper at the local hospital. Some time passed. She did this and that. She is now the author/illustrator of ten children's books, including *Max Makes a Million* and *Next Stop Grand Central.* Her illustrations/articles have appeared in the *New York Times,* the *New Yorker, Interview Magazine, Atlantic Monthly,* and numerous other publications. As the head of M&Co. (the design studio she cofounded with her late husband, Tibor Kalman), she designs somewhat unnecessary but amusing products distributed by the Museum of Modern Art. She has designed fabrics for Isaac Mizrahi, mannequins for Ralph Pucci, accessories for the Whitney Museum, and lots of other things she can't possibly be expected to remember. Oh, yes, her most recent book is *un(FASHION),* a photographic compilation about what people wear around the world. She is dabbling in other things—record producing, filmmaking, radio reportage. She is not interested in cooking, thank you very much, but is willing to clean up.

Is it legit to say that you began your entrepreneurial pursuits with the development of the M&Co. products?

In 1970 (while we were working for Len Riggio at Barnes & Noble), Tibor and I conceived of and realized the now defunct but once liked bookstalls on Fifth Avenue and Sixtieth Street. That was, I believe, our first entrepreneurial collaboration. The products came later.

What was the impetus for these products, watches, clocks, paperweights? Did they develop from the Christmas gifts that M&Co. produced?

The holiday gifts led to the product development. I have no idea why we did it, other than curiosity and a desire to do everything.

How did your illustration career get started?

My sister was an artist. She went to Cooper Union in the early sixties, and I was exposed to the art world.

I went to Music and Art [High School] and studied music. I thought I would be a writer. I started to write in college. The writing stank. When I left college, I thought I might try something easy, like drawing. I started to make naive, narrative, surreal, cartoony things. Steinberg was an influence. Jim Nutt. Henri Matisse, Ludwig Bemelmans. Street signs, dreams, family stories, architecture, music. The drawings were journals of my life.

How did you become a children's book author?

I had been doing editorial illustration for about fifteen years. My style was childlike (maybe deceptively so), and it seemed a natural. Tibor orchestrated the notion of doing *Stay Up Late* by the Talking Heads. I was addressing a new audience of parents and readers, people who wanted their children to wear black clothes. It was sophisticated, but not negative. It was absurd, but optimistic stuff.

You helped carve out a child/adult book genre. I'm sure you get this question all the time, but do you think of your audience as you conceive, write, and draw?

I am obsessed with communicating with every person on earth. Adult and child. Having said that, I try, when I am working, to forget everybody and just get lost in my own cockamamie story. I do not *ever* think of what is appropriate for this one and that one. That would be the death of my work.

Authoring children's books makes you a bona fide author, but have you ever thought of merchandising your characters?

There have been a few attempts at merchandising. There was a Max doll. Very well made. T-shirts. Postcards—the usual stuff. I have not made any money from these things.

I guess that merchandising characters is like commodifying a piece of your life? How much of your personal existence is invested in your children's books?

My books are mirrors of my life, with gross exaggeration and outright lies. But that works for me.

Okay, it's one thing to make books and dabble in product development, but what about business? How much business acumen do you have? Indeed, how much do you want to have?

I have good instincts and terrible acumen. Or acute acumen. Or none. I limp along with luck and the kindness of lawyers and agents. It is a herky-jerky affair. I wish I were spit-spot at running a tidy little business. Oh, well.

You and Tibor nourished each other. With his passing, how do your unique ideas differ from your collaborative ideas?

Tibor passed? I hadn't noticed.

Okay. It is really too soon to tell who was who and what will be. He wanted me to continue running M&Co., whatever the hell that is now. I am beginning to see my momentum. Books primarily. Tibor was rather fearless and was a brilliant innovator. I am funny and not stupid, but I don't quite know how that will translate in the real world. Again, it's way to soon to tell.

You are a gadfly in the best sense of the term, in that you do not focus on one artistic or entrepreneurial endeavor. What are your goals in terms of production?

My goals are to make the most ridiculous communicative humanistic projects, ones that thrill me. Smart, unusual, nutty books, objects, films, shows, people clothes, dog clothes, stage sets, comedy writing, producing music CDs, graphic novels. I would like to travel a bit also and learn to play the accordion.

Is this anyway to make a living?

This might not be a great way to make a living, but it is an excellent way to live.

DESKTOP MONUMENTS

with Constantin BOYM,
Principal of Boym Studio

CONSTANTIN BOYM was born in Moscow, Russia, in 1955, where he graduated from Moscow Architectural Institute. In 1986, he founded BOYM Partners Inc. in New York City. His studio designs include tableware for Alessi and Authentics, watches for Swatch, and exhibition installations for many American museums, including the Cooper-Hewitt National Design Museum in New York and the National Building Museum in Washington. Objects designed by BOYM Partners are included in the permanent collection of the Museum of Modern Art in New York. From 1989 until 2000, he was a professor at Parsons School of Design in New York City. And in 1998, BOYM Partners started a three-year-long catalog project, "Souvenirs for the End of the Century," which are sold in museums and on his Web site.

How would you define design entrepreneur?

Being a designer is a tough job. It is hard enough just to design good, interesting, innovative things, but the hardest part is that one has to earn the *right* to design them. In other words, before you offer the world your great idea, you have to be asked to do it. And what if you have the idea, and nobody is asking? This is where design entrepreneurship comes about. In a majority of cases, it is not so much about business, but about one's desire to speak out, to make oneself visible, to offer your vision as promptly as possible and without any middlemen. Perhaps you can define it as the greatest professional shortcut. Some would rather call it professional gamble, with all the risks involved, and with characteristically remote chance of success. Design entrepreneurship is, by the way, a purely American phenomenon, which goes hand in hand with our independence and determination and our disregard of conventional professional and economic structures. When I first played with this concept in the mid-1980s, having started a small furniture production (on a shoestring, with $5,000 of borrowed money), my friends in Italy, where the furniture was to be manufactured, simply didn't understand what I was trying to do. We, designers, are supposed to make designs, not chairs, I was told too many times. Now, this situation is perhaps changing. Not surprisingly, the American way prevails. [The company, called Nota Bene, survived for merely two years and closed shortly after the market crash of 1987.]

You are something of a part-time entrepreneur with your growing Souvenirs project of the "Missing Monuments" product line. How and why did this idea begin?

In a strange and not very typical way. Originally, the first monuments (of the Missing Monuments line) were made for an exhibition, in 1995, as one-of-a-kind wooden pieces. *Metropolitan Home* ran a half-page article about them, with a photo. Suddenly, the phone began to ring. We were confronted with hundreds of phone calls, with people asking where and how they could buy these souvenirs. At this point, I said to my studio, Hey, we have to *make* this stuff. Which was not easy.

Originally, I wanted to have them made of cast bronze: the truly indestructible, "monumental" material. Since the building referent does not exist, the souvenir becomes the only tangible material manifestation of a memory, or of a concept. And the object has to be as permanent and long-lasting as possible. Bronze casting proved to be prohibitively expensive, even though we decided that the price point could be pretty high. Eventually, we had to settle on bonded bronze, a composite material that has the appearance and feel of metal, yet could be cold-cast in rubber molds. This material was formulated for restorations and is sometimes used for museum reproductions. Ours was one of its first uses for new products. All along, the telephone requests were compiled in computer, to form a mailing list. Once the first (postcard) catalog was ready, we sent it along and filled the first orders. That's how it all started.

This is a rather quirky foundation for a business, but totally engaging. It taps into the need of people to collect souvenirs that seem arcane and limited. Do you see this as becoming a successful business? And what determines what your content will be? Is the product line finite or infinite?

To answer, I have to step back, into Boym's general design philosophy. If there is such a thing as "critical design," for me, it is design that deals with the margins: aesthetical, social, cultural, even technological. Souvenirs belong to one of those margins of industrial design. Even though, by its connection to tourism, souvenir production is one of the world's largest industries, there are hardly any designers of note who would attach their name to a souvenir design. The subject is never offered in design schools, rarely discussed in design press or conferences. That's where we usually step in. It so happened that souvenirs ended up in the Miniature Building typology—perhaps because I have collected those for some time (some say it's because I am a frustrated architect—by education).

One of the main points I have tried to make is that these souvenirs *are* design, even though they seem not to have a clearly defined function. We call it "fuzzy function"— that is, one whose purpose is not immediately clear. Such is the case with collecting.

Why do people devote their lifetime and fortunes to this seemingly useless activity? Yet they do it, and it is our role as designers to respond. Another thing that was superimposed onto all this was the Millennium celebration.

This makes sense, products need a hook.

Back in 1998, the Millennium still loomed as something exciting and wonderful. We somehow wanted to contribute creatively, and to mark the event with specially produced souvenirs seemed like a natural idea. That's how the project, "Souvenirs for the End of the Century," took off. "End of the century" (fin de siècle) always had this connotation of retrospection, of closure, of reflection. Missing Monuments have been included as one of the lines. The other (and the most successful) one is Buildings of Disaster—replicas of famous structures where some tragic or terrible events happened to take place. This is not only a comment on our media-fed fascination with disaster, but also an alternative view on architecture: one based on populist emotional relationship, not on scholarly authority.

Originally, the plans for the catalog were very ambitious: I wanted to invite other designers and creative people to participate. This was way too difficult to coordinate. One collaboration, with jewelry designer Meredith Beau, did not prove commercially successful, even though I personally liked the results. There has been much debate whether to make the objects limited edition or not. The final decision is somewhat of a compromise. All objects are numbered, but not limited, yet we promised to finish production when the end of the [twentieth] century comes.

How are these manufactured? And how much of a personal investment are you making?

The objects are made at a small factory in Long Island City, which specializes in museum sculpture reproductions. I bring them an original monument, which is meticulously handmade of wood (mostly by myself), from which they produce rubber molds used for casting. The great thing about this project is that it required very little personal investment. The cost of rubber was only a couple hundred dollars per building. The objects are made in batches, fifteen to twenty at a time, so we can recoup costs before paying for a new batch. The larger investment is design, printing, and distribution of catalogs. At least we never invested in advertising, always relying on editorial coverage and on word of mouth.

What amount of time does this take from your industrial design practice?

Here lies the big problem. In spite of all help, sometimes, it feels that my whole day is devoted to dealing with the manufacturer, buyers, journalists, UPS, and so on. At this point, the creative component of the project is nil; it's mostly management. And we all want to design! And financially, the studio has to have other work to sustain itself. Somehow, I was able to foresee all this, when we decided at the outset to make the catalog a three-year-long project only. The production is supposed to stop on December 31, 2000, at the official end of the twentieth century. Now, everyone is saying, Come on, you can't just close it like that! I guess it will continue for a while, in a somewhat different guise.

It makes sense that industrial designers would invent their own products, but what are the problems in terms of producing and selling them yourselves?

It is possible to produce anything, but to sell it consistently and profitably is another, more difficult matter. We were lucky with the critical attention of the press, the museums, the media—which just *loved* this project. As I mentioned before, the *Metropolitan Home* article essentially had the project started. And then, one thing led to another. An article to a museum exhibition, to more articles, to a TV show, and eventually, some high-end stores (like Moss, or OK in L.A.) asked us to sell the souvenirs. This almost guarantees some sales every month. Could this be a new model for some high-end, conceptual, artistic production?

Do you foresee a time when this work could supercede your client-based work?

It would be possible (theoretically) to turn all this into a *real* business. But then, we will have to have new lines every few months, travel to and show at the gift fairs, produce substantial catalogs, have a warehouse, and so on and so on. More importantly, the production will have to be cheaper, and perhaps be dumbed down, to reach a larger audience. I, personally, am not ready to make this commitment. If I only could find somebody to deal with all this business. . . . but then, all design entrepreneurs say that.

MAGAZINES, BOOKS, PERFORMANCE

4

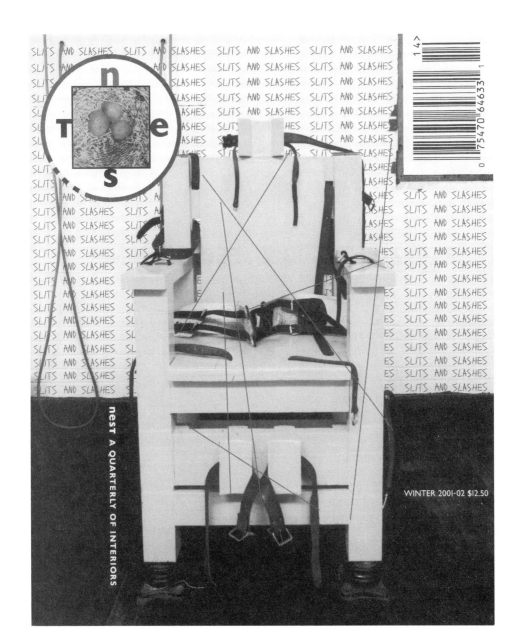

SLITS AND SLASHES SLITS AND SLASHES SLITS AND SLASHES SLITS AND SLASHES SLITS AND SLASHES SLITS AND SLASHES SLITS AND SLASHES SLITS AND SLASHES

nest A QUARTERLY OF INTERIORS

WINTER 2001-02 $12.50

NESTING MAGAZINES

with Joseph HOLZMAN, Publisher,
Editor, and Art Director of *Nest*

Nest, A Quarterly of Interiors is a cacophony of visual excess and unrefined typography and the brainchild of its publisher/editor/art director, JOE HOLZMAN, a self-taught interior designer and decorator who, in 1997, untrained and inexperienced in the magazine and graphic design fields, switched from "chintz-slinging" to publishing. Despite its amateur beginnings, Nest has become one of the most daringly innovative and audaciously progressive new publications to hit the newsstands in recent years and the two-time winner of the National Magazine Award. Holzman's cult publication has grown into a bibelot of the quirky shelter set.

You began as a designer of interior spaces. Why did you start a magazine?

I was always interested in interiors, and since childhood, I committed to memory the contents of my mother's issues of *Architectural Digest*, etc. By the time I began *Nest*, I had several decades of them well stored away. My principal work as a designer was, in fact, a very large apartment I acquired in Baltimore. My early thirties were spent on this project. The idea for the magazine, which came to me rather suddenly, was my first venture into the real world. I was encouraged by several people to get out of my shell, and I realized that I had it in me to try a magazine. Blessedly, I could not have known how many challenges and headaches come with starting a magazine.

You are not a graphic designer, and typography was not your métier. How did you learn graphic design?

In designing *Nest*, I did have the help of Alex Castro, a highly experienced graphic designer, for the first issue. But that issue was as much my work as his, and even then, I had ideas that I wanted to take further than he did. Perhaps some of my earlier experience helped. I had taught studio art at a junior college for about five years. However, my own college experience lasted one year. I am one of those people who learn better from myself than from others, I guess. Even now, I do not look at other magazines. I would rather avoid being influenced.

How did you have the temerity to start a magazine without magazine experience?

A good question. For one thing, I did not know what was involved. My learning curve was pretty steep, starting from ground zero. Except I must say, I did work out a very clear idea of what kind of magazine I wanted to do, from the very beginning. If you look back at the first issue of *Nest*, you will discover the matrix for all the following issues. I had a basic idea about how to treat advertising, what sort of production values I would require (high ones), and a certain view on content (broad from feature to feature, yet specific in each feature). Instead of trying to find out what some marketing-defined group ("them") might want, I already knew what I wanted to give "you," meaning whomever might be interested. Also, I was convinced of my creative abilities. In that area, at least, I'd been preparing—without knowing it—to take this kind of perhaps foolish step for much of my life. And I was lucky enough to have some very supportive friends to give me the push I needed.

The uniqueness of Nest: Were you certain doing it your way would work?

I was not at all certain doing it my way would work. But I did have a way, and I have always done things my way. I am not capable of doing things any other way. When I was a child, I made up my own language, etc., etc. I could not even manage to stay in college. I have never been interested in going the conventional route. And of course, as you would expect, the consultants I consulted assured me that my ideas would never fly.

What in Nest underscores your artistic personality?

Let's simply say that I design every page. There are, as well, a few ideas behind each issue. These tend to flower as the issue is being made. It is a creative experience in the sense that I do not really know where the work is taking me until I have arrived. Some of our best features are last-minute inspirations. I should explain, too, that the literary side of the magazine is the work of novelist Matthew Stadler. I trust him completely and have given him the last word on our writers and texts. We plan each issue together, but our domains are separate after that. I read a great deal of contemporary writing, but do not consider myself especially suited to be a literary arbiter.

Has not catering to advertisers been a problem?

No. I am trying to convince advertisers that the *Nest* approach enhances their impact. Ads look very good on fine paper and with art-book-quality printing. Restricting ads to full pages also makes them look good. The ads form a bloc in our issues and acquire an interest they would not have otherwise. It is a little like wholesalers all concentrating in

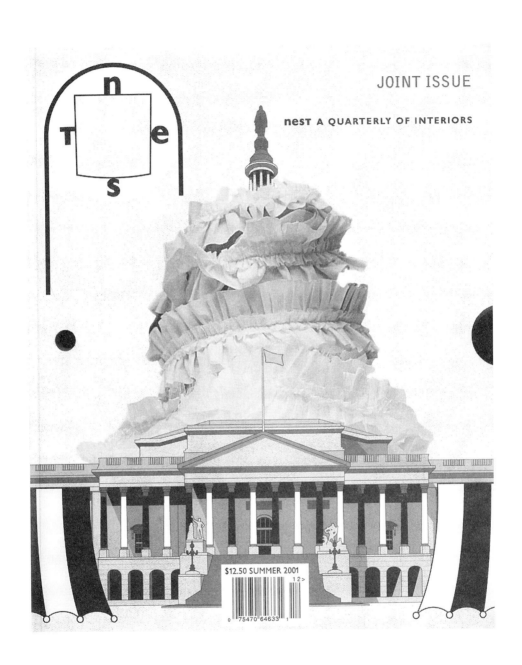

JOINT ISSUE

nest A QUARTERLY OF INTERIORS

$12.50 SUMMER 2001

one area of a large city. All the formative creative powers of the ad pages benefit from a new synergy. And on the other hand, there is an upper limit on ad pages, in that I will not have more than one ad page for every two of editorial (so far we have not bumped up on this limit). So, in the bigger picture, there will always be an ample editorial environment in which our ad pages float.

Some advertisers get into the spirit of *Nest* and respond in their designs to our special die-cuts, etc. And we play with them, too, with witty juxtapositions. Our up-front story is a special area of the magazine, the one place where we do place ads against our own pages. We get a huge kick out of dreaming up provocative content for the up-front story, bringing out the subtexts of an ad, for example, or creating visual rhymes between our images and theirs.

As of now, our advertising is skewed toward fashion, which I take as a tribute to *Nest*'s commitment to design. I would like to broaden our advertising base, but that will take time. We are not a large-circulation magazine.

How do you decide what new thing to do, what new object (Nest being in its way an object) to come up with, with each new issue?

I get inspirations, fortunately, in time for each issue. A lot of my time is spent thinking about design, or maybe just dreaming. And the last thing anyone should worry about when dreaming is whether something is plausible or not. That part comes much later—from our production manager, usually, whose job involves worrying about things like cost. Then, the challenge is to figure out how to do what I'd hoped to do anyway—in spite of all the obstacles that might lead others to say it *can't be done*.

As for what we won't do—I really couldn't say, at least not in advance. I try not to close off avenues.

What have you learned about magazine publishing in the last three years?

I believe more than ever in following one's own drummer, in putting the money we have into content and keeping our operation cost-efficient. We at *Nest* are driven by creativity and deal with the practical issues as they arise. Then, we learn about them and deal with them as best we can. It is not easy addressing practical problems with our tiny staff. We do not have specialists in-house, and we do not have depth in our staffing, only frontline talent—both in our creative and our business people. More generally, I have come to admire the energy and talent that is devoted to many magazines, not just ours.

What do you do to maintain the interest of readers?

Be ourselves, only better with each issue.

How do you plan to grow the magazine?

We are not satisfied to merely do what we are doing. We need to grow to ensure our financial health. I believe that despite the publicity *Nest* has received, we remain to be discovered by many potentially loyal readers. We have ideas for how to develop further, but I would prefer to discuss them some other time. There are several possibilities we are exploring. All take effort and patience to work out, and describing our thinking would be premature.

#16

$6

also
in this
issue

GORILLA-SUTERY | NARCOTICOS! | DUNKING BOOTH AT BURNING MAN
PATTY COMICS | OPERATION HOOTERS | WHAT IS NEOTOTALITARIANISM?

HERMENAUT

THE
STOCKHOLM
SYNDROME
ISSUE

T. W. ADORNO
cannot accept the usual mode of thought

DAVID MAMET
considers the sources

DAN ZUKOVIC
sustains some degree of media exposure

TI-GRACE ATKINSON
fights metaphysical cannibalism

NOT JUST A MAGAZINE ANYMORE

with Josh GLENN, Editor and Publisher,
and Anthony LEONE, Art Director, of
Hermenaut

JOSH GLENN is editor and publisher and ANTHONY LEONE is art director of
Hermenaut, an irregularly published journal of philosophy and pop culture that
has been described as "a zine that gives voice to indie intellectual thought," "a
scholarly journal minus the university," and "a sounding board for thinking folk
who operate outside the ivory tower." Founded in 1992 by an amateur group of
what they refer to as "outsider intellectuals," *Hermenaut*, which actually sus-
pended publication in a print format in 2001 and can now be found at www.her-
menaut.com, uses the tools of philosophy, sociology, and critical theory to
explode the received notions of academia and the hipster demimonde alike.

When did you start Hermenaut, and why?

Josh: I started *Hermenaut* as a twenty-six-page, photocopied zine in 1992. In 1989,
while I was still in college, I'd stumbled upon the world of zines and loved the idea that
if there were no newsstand magazines out there that you enjoyed reading, you could just
make your own. I started publishing a monthly zine—called *Luvboat Earth*—that was
just a hodgepodge of things I'd written, found items from old textbooks and magazines,
that sort of thing. I'd hand them out at parties, swap with other zine publishers via
mail, leave them in public places. In the fifth or sixth issue of *Luvboat*, I started publishing articles that were more intellectual—about ideas and thinkers I was studying at
the time. By 1992, I was in graduate school briefly, and not enjoying myself very much.
I didn't like the way ideas were discussed in the academy and the way scholarly books
were written—all the jargon, the opaque prose, the dense thickets of footnotes. So, I
decided to start a second zine that would just be about my more intellectual interests,
leaving *Luvboat* to be more about my personal life.

And the name Hermenaut, where did that come from?

Josh: The name *Hermenaut* was an original coinage: It comes from "hermeneutics," a
ten-dollar word meaning "interpretation"—an example of the kind of jargon that bothered me in the academy—and "astronaut," because I've always been attracted to 1960s
space-race imagery, this exciting sense of exploring new worlds. A "hermenaut," then,
was my term for an outsider intellectual, a traveler in search of new meanings. I decided

that in each issue of *Hermenaut*, I'd profile such a figure, and I've done fifteen of them by now, from Nietzsche to Bruce Lee, and from Oscar Wilde to Philip K. Dick.

I was also fascinated by pop culture, particularly the TV show *Beverly Hills, 90210*—so we laid out the cover to look like *Sassy*, or some other teen magazine—with big, kissable photos of Luke Perry and Shannen Doherty, and so forth. The idea was that this would be a magazine of philosophy and pop culture—but unlike trendy academic journals, which *commented* on pop culture, we'd *be* pop culture. The magazine itself wouldn't be a book to put on your shelf, but a disposable piece of pop culture that you could roll up and stick in your pocket to read on the subway.

What was your background?

Josh: As far as my background goes, I've never studied journalism or business, or even English. I've just always loved magazines—particularly digest-sized ones, from Alfred Hitchcock's *Murder Mystery* to *Cricket* (for kids), and from *Popular Mechanics* to the *Partisan Review*. I worked for a couple of years as an editor at *Utne Reader* magazine—a digest-sized national magazine out of Minneapolis—and I was editorial director of a Web site called Tripod, which was acquired by Lycos just before I quit to do *Hermenaut* full-time. (Well, I'm a writer—that's how I pay the bills at home.)

How has the magazine developed in this time?

Josh: The magazine has evolved tremendously over the past nine years, and it's not just my magazine anymore—we have a staff and a network of regular contributors, and advertisers and distributors and ten thousand readers. But it's still more like a zine than a journal or magazine, in the sense that it's the product of a personal vision, and our editorial decisions are impulsive and deeply felt ones. I'll turn this over to Anthony now, since it's really become a whole new enterprise thanks to his redesign in early 1999.

Anthony, how'd you get involved in this project?

Anthony: I met Josh and the others in early 1999. I was working in a design studio at the time, but I'd also coedited and designed my own zine, *Commodity*, a hardcore/punk zine, from 1994 to 1998. *Commodity* came out of a thesis project my friend Josh Hooten and I'd done in design school, at Mass Art [Massachusetts College of Art]. Green Day had just signed to a major label, so we interviewed them and other punk bands who'd crossed over. We decided to self-publish the interviews, so *Commodity* started as a photocopied zine about exploitation. The front cover was a photocopy of the cover of *Men's Health*, and the back cover was some women's magazine. We published two hundred copies.

After getting written up in *Maximum Rocknroll*, we got a lot of letters and decided to keep doing it. We started having the covers offset-printed, but it was still about the exploitation of punk rock. As we progressed in design school, the design kept improving. We didn't have a set format—each spread was designed differently. Josh Hooten and I didn't collaborate too much on the design; we each did it our own way. By the time we graduated, we'd both used the magazine in our final review portfolio, and it really split the faculty: Some of our teachers loved it; others wanted us to prove that we could do corporate design work and not just independent work. I thought it was unfortunate that the others didn't see how great it was that we had a vision of our own; they claimed our portfolios "didn't look like Mass Art portfolios." It was very frustrating!

And Hermenaut?

Josh: We published *Commodity* sporadically for a couple of years after graduating and called it quits after the fifth issue, which had a circulation of 1,500. By that point, I was getting tired of spending 75 percent of my time on the logistics of publishing it. Josh was more interested in the content side of things and went to the magazine *Punk Planet*, eventually. I was more interested in the design side of things and started working full-time as a graphic designer—but I was looking for a magazine project, where I could do the art direction without working on the logistics of publishing and editing. When Josh and the others approached me, I immediately knew that this was the opportunity I'd been looking for—because they already had an entire editorial and publishing team in place.

Josh, where did you get your start-up capital?

Josh: Capital? I published *Hermenaut* as a photocopied zine, and then as a offset-printed journal, out of wages from these other jobs I've mentioned. Besides being a professional magazine editor, while publishing *Hermenaut*, I've worked as a bartender, a handyman, a courier, and all sorts of other things. After I quit Tripod/Lycos, I cashed in all my stock options and used about $80,000 to relaunch the magazine with a new design (by Tony), with an office that wasn't in my house, etc. That money is all gone now, but we've recently incorporated as a business, and we're selling stock—we've sold about $50,000 worth so far. We make pretty good money selling ads, subscriptions, back issues, but some months, we make more money selling the *Hermenaut* T-shirts Tony designed than copies of the magazine. We're always on the edge of bankruptcy, but it keeps us on our toes.

Anthony, your capital [for Commodity] was a bit makeshift, wasn't it?

Anthony: Commodity was funded by our credit cards. We were college students, so when we got those student credit card offers, we signed up for as many as we could. After a while, we started selling advertising, and that covered the printing costs. We found a great cheap printer in Madison, Wisconsin.

Did your magazine take shape at the time of execution or over time? What role does design play in your plan?

Josh: Designwise, although it's evolved over time quite a lot, in some ways it's just like it was the first time I ever published it, by myself, with scissors and glue and a photocopy machine. The magazine was originally laid out on legal-sized paper (8½" × 14") and folded to 8½" × 7". Although we no longer do paper-and-glue layouts, and although we're offset-printed now, with a perfect spine, over two hundred pages, and a six-color cover—it's still 8½" × 7". That format has survived even though our distributors always complain about what an awkward, unusual size it is.

Also, right from the beginning I wanted *Hermenaut* to be a piece of pop culture, a cultural artifact in its own right. So, we started off with these covers that were intended to look like the cover of a teen magazine—I did those myself, with scissors and glue. By the time I was working on the third issue, I'd met Scott Hamrah and Jennifer Engel, who came on board as coeditor and art director, respectively. Jennifer knew something about design and had Quark on her Mac, though she'd never really studied the program carefully—but thanks to her, we started really laying out the pages properly.

For our ninth issue, we switched from ersatz teen magazine to ersatz pulp sci-fi magazine. Jennifer would build little models of astronauts or whatever, and we'd have them photographed—by that point, we were printing the covers on glossy, heavy stock, so they looked really great. But the whole thing needed an overhaul—we'd just kept adding on to previous formats, and I was impatient to start from scratch. So, when Jennifer quit to pursue a career in film design, I was looking for someone who could realize my inchoate vision.

Anthony: When I came on board as art director, I listened to Josh and Scott a lot, trying to get them to explain what their vision of the magazine was, in a graphic design sense. I asked them about the word "hermenaut" and took my cue from their answers to my questions. "Hermenaut" is a word that combines the scholarly and the space-adventurous, and the magazine itself was supposed to be something like a synthesis of a literary journal and a fifties sci-fi journal. They handed me a stack of old digest magazines—*Amazing Science*, *Les Temps Modernes* (Sartre's magazine), *Partisan Review* from the 1940s, etc.

They also told me they wanted to run a lot of original illustrations, and not just keep cutting images out of old books. I looked through all the journals and developed a format—one that combined the pulp sci-fi journal and the more straightforward literary journal—that wasn't going to be overly retro, but still had elements from the pulp sci-fi

genre. From literary journals, I wanted to preserve the easy-to-read format. I based my grid on that idea—keeping the type clean, easy to read, not too design-y, plenty of white space, ample margins. The type choices were based on typefaces commonly used in the 1950s: Century Schoolbook is the body copy, the headings are Clarendon, and I used Trade Gothic for support copy and the masthead.

To set *Hermenaut* apart from every other literary journal I'd seen, I left plenty of room for original illustrations and photography. I came up with a formula for the articles: Most of them would start off with a spread that juxtaposed a full page of original art against a page of clean, simple type. It made it easy for me to assign artwork to illustrators, because they had an entire page to work with—like I said, I wanted to keep my process very easy. Most of my friends are working artists or illustrators, and I had always dreamed of having a project where I could involve them. I set this formula up so I could bring them all into the project easily.

How do you integrate print and Web into your formula?

Josh: I've worked at a Web site before, and I was very frustrated by the experience. The fact that you can do all this great work—editorial, writing, design, programming—and then have it vanish overnight if your boss gets tired of it was a bummer. Also, I'm old school: I like print. I like holding a magazine in my hands—not so much because you can take it into the bathtub, as people always say, but because I like to handle magazines and admire them as objects. I have a huge library of magazines.

However, I think a Web site can be a tremendous asset to an existing "offline" product, like *Hermenaut*. So, going into the process of creating the site, we wanted it to do a number of things. Simply by existing, it would give our readers—and people who'd never heard of us—a way to access us twenty-four hours a day, from anywhere in the world. We wanted to put up articles from back issues that were no longer available, to keep them in circulation. And we wanted to be able to publish articles weekly, or daily—because the magazine only comes out once or twice a year. Finally, we wanted to create a conferencing system, so that our readers could create a community of interest with one another and with us.

Anthony: The challenge for designing the site was how to minimize the disconnect between the site and the magazine. It became a mini-branding problem. I revisited my criteria for the magazine—creating a shell for images and information to flow in and out of. I've designed a branding bar that runs across the top of the site, that includes the logo, navigation, and a space for internal advertising: animated gifs or Flash art. The rest of the site is dynamically driven—there are no static pages—so we just used a similar type as in the magazine, some similar colors, and so forth. *Hermenaut* is an ongoing branding project—we're always improving upon past efforts.

How are the roles set up? Who does what?

Josh: I'm the publisher and editor, very hands-on in both roles. I write for the magazine and play a large role in setting themes, assigning articles, and copyediting everything. I have a small editorial staff. We also have half a dozen contributing editors who lend a hand as needed, but who mostly don't come into the office. We normally have one paid intern who helps with publishing tasks: filling subscription orders, etc.

Anthony: I'm the art director and designer. I do concepts for article layouts, I do all the design for the entire issue, I work with the illustrators and photographers, and I handle all the production. I have half a dozen regular illustrators. Michael Lewy, a photographer and painter who introduced us all, is our art editor. He does photo research, works with me on concepts for article layouts, and offers his opinions on assigning illustrations—he's from an art background and not a design one, which is sometimes a blessing and sometimes a curse—and he's done the past two covers and some illustrations.

Are you all partners in the venture?

Josh: In the business sense, no, we're not partners. I own 51 percent of the stock and have complete control of all business decisions. In an artistic sense, however, it's pretty collaborative.

Do you have a long-term goal that involves other entrepreneurial ventures?

Josh: Frankly, it depends on how much money we can raise. We're already selling 15 percent of the issues for ads and could easily go up to 20 or 25 percent, as long as it doesn't start to feel like a whorish newsstand magazine. We'd like to all quit our day jobs and do this for a living. We'd like to do four to six issues a year. We'd like to publish books, produce films and records. We even have a plan on the back burner for an intellectual publishing/design residency program. We have the location picked out and everything. We just need capital!

Do you consider yourself a business, or is this a passion that consumes?

Josh: It started as the latter and has become both in the past few years—for me, anyway. Michael, Tony, and Carrie draw small salaries, and we pay all the writers and illustrators, but Scott and I don't get paid. I spend a lot of time running the business end, which I enjoy—but I wouldn't keep doing it if it weren't also a passion for me.

 Anthony: For me, it's really important to be involved in something that isn't trying to sell a product. At *Hermenaut*, no one in a suit ever calls me up and tells me to make his logo bigger. I've always struggled with being a designer, because you're always communicating other people's ideas. It's nice to be able to have this outlet, where I can put forth my own ideas and help people whose ideas I believe in communicate through design. I'm all for the underdog.

baseline

international typographics magazine   No 35 2001

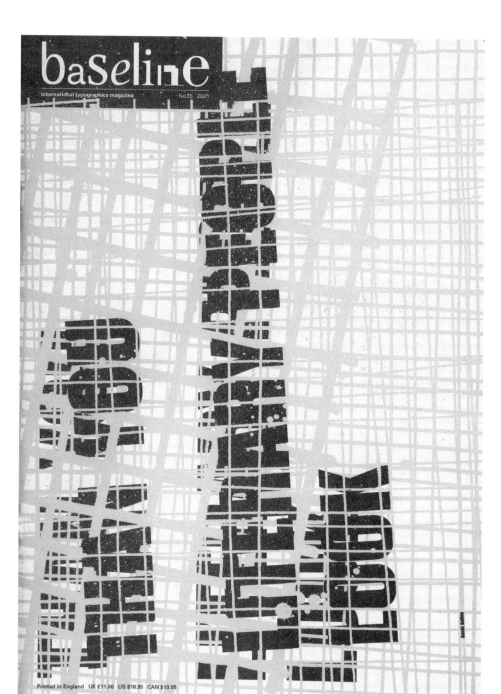

Printed in England   UK £11.00   US $16.95   CAN $19.95

AN EXPRESSIVE JOURNAL

with Hans Dieter RICHERT, Editor,
Publisher, and Designer of *Baseline*

HANS DIETER REICHERT started his design career in 1987 working in Holland
for Total Design and BRS Premsela Vonk. He moved back to England and
founded in 1993 the design studio hdr design and in 1995, as codirector, the
publishing firm Bradbourne Publishing Ltd. Reichert is publishing, art directing,
and coediting the International Typographics Magazine *Baseline*. In 2001 he
produced the book *Metaphors* in the new series "Baseline Editions," together
with Ken Garland. Reichert also lectures at the University of Reading. He has
received many awards for his work, from the Art Director's Club and Type
Director's Club New York, Type Director's Club Tokyo, Brno Biennale of Graphic
Design/Czech Republic, and Leipzig Bookfair, among others.

Why did you purchase Baseline *from its original owners?*

As a design company, we were involved with *Baseline* number 17 and 18 (still under
Letraset ownership). Letraset was a dominant international graphic supply company
that treated *Baseline* as its flagship publication. During 1993–94, Esselte, the parent
company, decided to close Letraset. All public relations activities stopped, and the magazine was consequently axed. Letraset wanted to sell the publication, and we (myself
and Mike Bains) put a business proposal forward, which Letraset accepted. We saw
potential in the magazine and took it on as a challenge. Another reason was to have the
autonomy to run the magazine as publishers, editors, designers, and distributors (subscription database) and have the total responsibility.

Was the idea to publish the magazine while attending to your professional design work, or did you see a phasing out of one in favor of the other?

The idea was to publish the magazine while attending my other professional design
work and gain additional experience in the publishing industry.

What are the different responsibilities you have as publisher as opposed to solely a designer?

My responsibilities as publisher are to produce a product that is initiated (concept of
projects and commissioning), published (edited, designed, and produced), and distrib-

uted and sold. As a designer, I am mainly engaged in visual aspects of a job, from initial concepts to the realization.

It's one thing to run a design firm, which has its own set of problems, but as publisher and editor of a magazine, are there issues that you never anticipated?

Yes, you can say that. Dealing with authors (ha, ha, ha—don't take it personally). Making sure that the quality standard is there and the production cycle is kept (frequency of publication). Footing the production bill.

How does this business impact your design business?

The magazine helps to promote our [hdr design] business. Each edition is a kind of visual design manifest that the design works together with the copy—not against. It shows visual variety in the application of type and images, depending on the contents of the article. It shows the eye for detail, the care taken to design, and the production (printing and finishing) of each issue.

How does this impact your design?

There is a fair amount of verbal exchange among the designers. They learn a lot while designing/working on the magazine. You can see the magazine as a kind of visual playground. The size is quite a graphic design challenge. We try to push the conventional boundaries (all depending on our basic design principles: color and readability of text, budget, and production). We do not like to be too trendy or avant-garde; we like to keep a certain "reference feel" to the magazine. Our objective is to draw you into the article via the visual impact of the displays.

How is the magazine staffed?

Publisher (four directors), two editors, one editorial assistant, one art director, one senior designer, three designers, two student designers, one distribution manager.

Do you have plans for future growth, or is everything the way you want it?

We have established the magazine as a serious publication with its current three issues a year (spring, summer, and autumn/winter). Besides the magazine, we published *Baseline* diaries during the years and a limited edition of "McKnight Kauffer cotton labels" in an attractive, handmade box. As for the future, we are starting an in-depth series of *Baseline*-related publications called "Baseline Editions," where we want to elaborate on previously published articles. The pilot issue is called *Metaphors*, by Ken Garland.

Would you say this is a viable business venture or an act of love?

It is primarily an act of love. But it is also a viable business venture. It pays the costs, and additional money goes straight back into the publishing venture.

Critique

THE
MAGAZINE
OF
GRAPHIC
DESIGN
THINKING

$18

WIT
SUMMER 1997

A MAGAZINE OF HIS OWN

with Martin NEUMEIER,
Publisher and Editor of *Critique*

MARTIN NEUMEIER, designer, editor, and writer, opened his design studio in
1973 in Santa Barbara, California. Working solo for the first three years, he
designed, wrote, and illustrated advertising campaigns and design programs
for agencies and small businesses. By 1980, he was working with a team of
five, working on corporate identities, annual reports, advertising, brochures,
and book design. But in 1984 he moved to Palo Alto, California, to focus on
communications for the burgeoning technology industry, specifically, Atari,
Sun, Adobe, and Apple. Eventually, he narrowed the studio's focus further, spe-
cializing exclusively in the design of software packaging. In 1996, he intrepidly
launched *Critique* magazine to fill a gap that he saw developing between professional magazines like *Communication Arts* and design-culture periodicals
like *EYE*. The idea was to offer professional criticism free of theoretical jargon
and yet more incisive than typical trade "crits." He self-funded the venture and
the quarterly *Critique* ran for eighteen issues, until 2001, when profits from the
design firm and income from the magazine could no longer keep pace with the
growing demands of the combined business.

After closing the magazine in early 2001, Neumeier has reinvented his firm
to take advantage of emerging trends in business and design. The new firm will
specialize in brand development for technology clients, including positioning,
naming, icon development, retail packaging, Web branding, brand advertising,
and client workshops. Here, he talks about his attempt at design entrepreneurialism and the successes and failures he encountered along the way.

After running your own design firm for so many years, what gave you the temerity to start a graphic magazine?

Temerity is a good word, because in retrospect, I was more foolhardy than brave. It
took me twenty-five years of hard work to turn the design studio into a real business. I
don't know why I thought I could master an unfamiliar skill set on the fly.

I'd gained a little experience with magazine design in the mid-1980s, when I
worked part-time at *Communication Arts* as an editorial consultant. I enjoyed the work
tremendously, and I admired the way the Coyne family had built the magazine on subscriptions rather than advertising. I took a guess that there might be room for a premi-

um magazine that could take that model to an even higher level, both in content and design.

A magazine is a unique animal. I mean, you have to come out on time, pay the bills, fulfill subscriptions, get advertising. How did you imagine that this scenario would play out?

Before we launched, I developed what I thought was a conservative business plan (for internal use only, since the project was self-funded), which accounted for all the things that make a magazine go. But it's possible to develop a perfectly logical business plan that bears no relation to the real world.

For example, I calculated that, for a subscription-based magazine, the toughest challenge would be to create a product that people would pay a premium price for—one with high production values, timeless design, and content that would be perceived as essential to a practitioner's work. It was a challenge, but far from the toughest. The toughest was building circulation.

I laid the groundwork for failure when I estimated the size of our potential audience: I figured we could sign up 20,000 subscribers within five years. We never passed the 4,000 mark. We did sell an additional 6,000 copies in bookstores each quarter, but newsstand sales don't add up to much; they only help if they lead to subscriptions.

On average, about 30 percent of our revenues came from subscriptions and newsstand sales, 10 percent from advertising, and 60 percent from client work in the design studio, which we kept going for that purpose. In the end, we couldn't keep up the pace. We were exhausted.

Of course, much of what we're talking about is in hindsight. The magazine had a nice run of eighteen issues over the course of nearly five years. It earned a following and might have garnered more readers over time. So, what did you learn from your "failure" that you would do differently given a second chance?

What I've noticed about designers is that we often try to transform business problems into design problems. For example, instead of cold-calling clients to get more work (the direct method), we design an award-winning mailer (the comfortable method). Instead of laying off employees in a downturn (the business approach), we generate busywork for them (the creative approach).

With *Critique*, instead of focusing on circulation, advertising, and production, I focused on product quality. In other words, I turned it into a design problem. I'm exaggerating a little, because I did care deeply about the business side. But by setting the design and editorial standards so high, I was forced to spend less time and fewer resources on business initiatives. Result: creative success, business failure. Let this be a lesson to all would-be design entrepreneurs.

The main insight I received about successful magazines is that they're not really about content. They're about selling. The word "magazine" means storehouse—in this case, a storehouse of advertisers. The editorial is there to attract a certain class of readers to the ads. A clever sleight-of-hand is accomplished by distracting people from the business purpose of a magazine by playing up the editorial information. Most people don't realize that the quality of the editorial is necessarily compromised in the process. The truth is that editorial isn't crucial to a magazine's success, except as a PR vehicle for advertisers. In publishing, the mixing of editorial and advertising intentions is known as "blurring church and state." The best magazines create an illusion of separation, but church and state have to work together to bring the price of the magazine down to what readers will pay.

So, would you mix church and state more if you had to start over?

No, because our idea was to mentor designers in the purest possible way. But near the end, we hatched a plan to slim down the magazine, increase paid advertising, and decrease editorial pages, which would have allowed us to lower the newsstand price from $22 to $12. It's a good thing we didn't follow through, however, because magazine advertising dropped off precipitously in 2001. And I just read in the *Wall Street Journal* that total newsstand sales have decreased for the first time in magazine history.

If I had to start over, I'd seriously question the delivery method we chose. It may well be that the market for design magazines was already saturated, and we needed to explore other ways of delivering our content. For example, we could have started a series of traveling workshops, backed by an educational Web site and a cheaply produced newsletter. Or we could have simply produced a series of books, which would have had higher price tags and a longer shelf life. But we didn't feel like doing that. We used the Frank Sinatra method—we did it our way. And we lost a few million bucks in the process.

We always talk about business success and failure in dollars and cents. But this was your baby, so to speak. What kind of emotional toll did it take?

I went from having a permanent smile in the early days to having a permanent grimace at the end of five years. In between, we experienced a roller coaster of highs and lows as we built the magazine and battled with finances. Every comment from every reader seemed like life or death, especially since we were committed to publishing any and all critiques of the magazine. It helped that my wife, Eileen, supported me at every step, especially the more difficult or dangerous ones.

But, hey, I got to share deep thoughts with some of the brightest people in the industry: Paul Rand, Saul Bass, Milton Glaser, Paula Scher, David Stuart, Kit Hinrichs, Richard Saul Wurman, Alan Fletcher, and even some guy named Steve Heller. That privilege by itself might have been worth a few million bucks. And I was able to work with a brilliant, brave, and loyal group of teammates, including Nancy Bernard, Chris Chu, Dustin McGahan, and Chris Willis, all of whom are sticking around for the next adventure.

I also deepened my knowledge of design by delving into craft and business as I researched and wrote articles for the magazine. I earned a hard-knocks Ph.D. that I can bring to future entrepreneurial efforts. All that makes me feel very happy.

How much of your primary business did you sacrifice to make your magazine work?

In the beginning, our client work took about half our time. At the end, we had few clients left, because we stopped investing in client relationships. We took only work that came in on its own, then used the revenues to pay magazine bills.

And now that Critique is kaput, what must you do to regain stability?

Well, unfortunately, we've been hit by a triple whammy. First, we've let all our client relationships lapse; second, the magazine has left us in debt; and third, we're starting over in a bad economy. The economic climate may be called a downturn in some quarters, but in the technology sector, where we work, it's a disaster. All we can do is cut costs, make arrangements to pay our creditors, and start rebuilding our client base.

Much of your graphic design business is built around the flagships of the digital revolution. Many of these are sinking fast. What adjustments must you make?

The real flagships in our sector, like Apple, Adobe, Sun, and Hewlett-Packard, are not sinking at all. To some extent, their funding has been sucked dry by the dot.com investment craze, so now, they're being cautious with their budgets. We missed out on all the dot.com feeding frenzy while we worked on the magazine. Now, luckily, we don't have to downsize our expectations like other firms who counted on easy Web money to build their firms.

When we halted *Critique*, my first order of business was to lay off a third of the staff, mainly magazine people. Very sad. Then, I set about "repurposing" the remaining folks. Nancy Bernard and I threw ourselves into a brown study, reading and absorbing the last few years' worth of thinking about branding and design. We developed a business model that we hope will capitalize on the trends we found.

In your new business plan you intend to create a product, rather than solely provide a service. How will you go about making this work for yourself?

The general trends we want to align with are specialization, collaboration, and audience focus. The result will be a new-generation design firm, poised to take advantage of the next business cycle. I wouldn't call our new business a product, although you could say that some of our services will be packaged and priced like products. An important part of our plan is to surround our services with information and to open up our design process to the full view of our clients and collaborators. We're doing away with the notion of design as mystic priesthood.

As a designer with a decidedly entrepreneurial bent, do you see yourself as going further into the realm of making products, rather than packaging clients' products?

I see a few educational products in our future, such as books, seminars, workshops, and maybe videos about design and branding. After we stabilize our client business, we may be looking for some interesting projects to give our designers some variety and a break from client work.

Whenever you're thinking of designing your own product, it's important to search your soul for your real motivations. Do you sincerely want the world to benefit from your product, or do you simply want to practice design without the interference of clients? Because most products, even design-centric products, are only 10 percent design and 90 percent sales, distribution, management, and finance. You learn very quickly that design is the least important part of the mix.

I've asked you what you would do if you could have a second chance with Critique. But what would you do if you could start your entire business over from scratch?

I'm doing it right now. It may seem as if I'm running back to the safety of my old studio business, but the new firm will operate on a much higher plane. The experience of running *Critique* has stretched my mind; I've become acclimated to a more complex business model. The old model was like a one-celled organism—do a project, do it well, then move on. The new model will be an interdependent mixture of education, relationship building, experimentation, and growth. I'm looking forward to it with barely concealed glee.

50 CHAIRS

Innovations in Design and Materials
Mel Byars

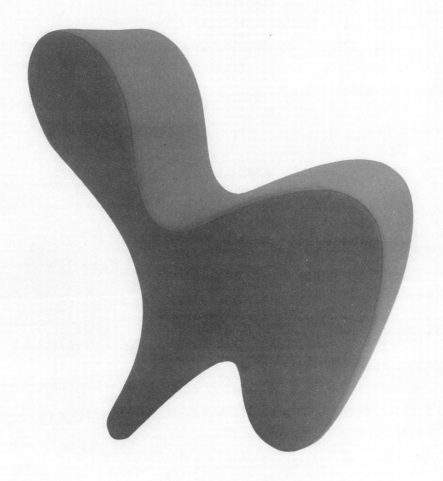

WEBZINE ON DELINE

with Mel BYARS, Author
and Webzine Publisher

MEL BYARS is a design historian and the author of several books, such as *The Design Encyclopedia, 50 Lights, 50 Objects, 50 Sports Wares,* **and** *50 Chairs.* **He is also a frequent contributor to several design magazines, including** *Metropolitan Home* **(USA) and** *Form* **(Germany).**

What prompted you to start Designzine.com?

Originally, we founded designlog.com (a products database for designers and architects). The site needed editorial content, a calendar, and more. After more than a year of work on designlog.com, we discussed the idea, and it was pointed out that collecting international design magazines every month was difficult and costly.

The nine featured magazines we choose have great content but very limited distribution outside of their respective nations and a high per-issue price.

In addition, we wanted a comprehensive calendar, audio interviews, book reviews, and more features to keep our viewers coming.

What were your backgrounds in design?

I have been in the design business for about sixteen years, first in Italy as a vice president of overseas sales and marketing at B&B Italia, a prime high-design furniture manufacturer. In 1990, I moved from Milano to New York and started my firm (I.L. Euro Inc.), an agent and distributor for manufacturers such as Cappellini, Flexform, Fontana Arte, Ingo Maurer, and Kartell. In 1994, I founded the North American distributor of Luceplan, a prime Milanese lighting manufacturer.

Starting a Web site is fairly easy, but starting a site that is this content-heavy is not. What were the problems you faced, overcame, and, for that matter, have yet to overcome?

Logistics with the nine magazines, overcoming diffidence and indifference, collecting data, organizing it, and designing a functional interface.

New Electronic Products By Mel Byars

UNIVERSE

Do you see yourselves as entrepreneurial? By this I mean, is this a big risk for you?

We are financing this with our money, and we are putting our time in it, so I think this purely entrepreneurial. Also, we work by "old economy" standards, in the sense that our dreams are realistic, and we will be making money!

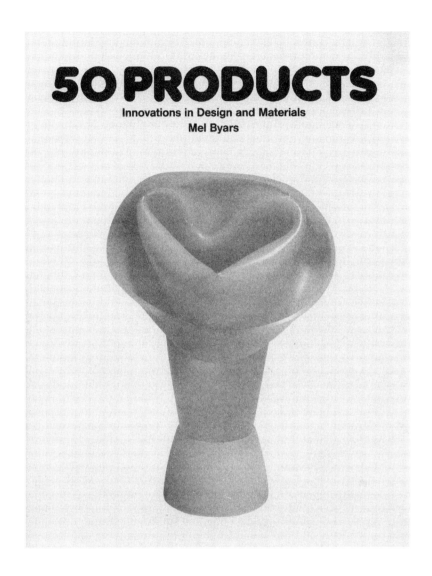

50 PRODUCTS
Innovations in Design and Materials
Mel Byars

What responsibilities has this venture placed on you that weren't there before?

Continuing to "make" a product that is always ahead of the pack, rich of content, and not too intellectual.

What's in store for the future?

More interactive features, alliances with other sites, continue with the promotion of the e-commerce site (designstand.com), expanding the B2B database (designlog.com), integrating the three sites.

FRENCH
FRIES

BOOK AS PERFORMANCE

with Warren LEHRER, Writer and Designer

WARREN LEHRER is a writer and designer whose books and theatrical works explore the music of speech, the complexity of personality, and the impact of social structures on the individual. His books, acclaimed for capturing the shape of thought and reuniting the traditions of storytelling with the printed page, include *The Portrait Series: A Quartet of Men*; *GRRRHHHH: A Study of Social Patterns*; *French Fries*; *I Mean You Know*; *Versations*; and *Type Dreams*. With his wife, Judith Sloan, he cowrote the plays *Denial of the Fittest* and *A Tattle Tale*, which have been produced at venues including La Mama ETC, The Public Theater, Independent Art at HERE, Theater Workshop at the Edinburgh Festival, The New York Theater Workshop, The Knitting Factory, and The Jewish Museum. Other plays include *Social Security: The Basic Training of Eugene Solomon*, written with Dennis Bernstein, and *The Search for IT and Other Pronouns*, a CD/opera cocomposed with Harvey Goldman. Lehrer is also an Associate Professor of Art at SUNY Purchase and a member of the graduate faculty at the School of Visual Arts' "Designer as Author" program. You can reach him at *www.warrenlehrer.com*.

How did you start as a graphic designer?

I was trained as a "fine" artist—and always wrote as well. When I started combining words as part of the mark-making in my paintings and drawings, most of my teachers didn't know how to address what I was doing. They warned me against this direction, which stimulated my interest even more. I continued to work from inside my own vacuum. From early on, I was interested in time-based forms. I was doing some animation, but mostly scrolls—on anything from adding-machine tape, to rolls of paper used to line the shelves at grocery stores, to canvas.

One day, in a semi-intoxicated stupor, I took a knife to one of my painting scrolls and chopped it into segments, then stacked the segments on top of each other. I brought the stack in to the one great teacher of my life, Louie Finklestein. He looked at it and said, "Uh . . . Warren. It's called a book." I thought, *book? Book—good!* It could have been a wheel I came up with, and I'd probably still be making wheels now. Louie turned me on to the work of Norman Ives and Dieter Roth and Kurt Schwitters. He mentioned a graduate program in graphic design at Yale that was doing this kind of work, concrete poetry and the like. I thought, *graphic design—good!* I was under the false impression that graphic design was a kind of esoteric, experimental field of visual literature.

When I went to the interview at Yale, Norman Ives was pretty sick. He had a patch over one eye, and his hands were shaking as he inspected the wrong side of my scrolls. I said, "Excuse me, Mr. Ives, the painting is on the *other* side. The backs are just incidental." (Newspaper had stuck to the gessoed back side of each canvas). He insisted that I should be proud of what I had done. I got into the program, but Ives died, and I never got to study with him.

On one hand, graphic design had little to do with my interests. On the other hand, I was very curious to find out about how things got printed, to learn about typography and photomechanical reproduction and semiotics and a lot of the history of design before it became an industry.

When did you shift into what we'd call an "authorial" mode, and why?

I never shifted. I was always just doing my work. Why should I want to solve other people's problems when I had rows of my own cued up in my head? When I first started coming out with my books, graphic designers and design students would ask me how I got away with some of the things I was doing. It struck me as an odd question.

Your books are a marriage of theater and graphic design. What prompted this unique confabulation of forms?

My writing was always very oral, which led naturally to writing for performance, both out of the tradition of lyric and spoken poetry and into theater. The invention of moveable type was a great thing, of course, but it also helped lead to the decline of direct people-to-people storytelling, and to the rise of writing for the page as a be-all and end-all. I think my work has always been an attempt to rebridge the printed word with the roots of storytelling, both oral and pictorial. The model of the crystal goblet, of the neutral typographic column, was always unsatisfactory to me.

In my bonehead years, I used to say I was after a "psycho-acoustic translation" of thought, speech, and ambiance. Would you want to go to a theater where casting and lighting and set design wasn't carefully considered? Where the actors or the musicians performed without expression, inflection, movement, dynamics, pacing, color, nuance? Why make a book that succumbed to such restraints? As a writer, who was also a visual artist, I couldn't cut off that part of the brain that had visual impulses to the composition of a text. What is the shape of these thoughts that I'm writing? How do they connect? In the end, my books are vehicles for the performance of a text, not only as a script (for plays/performance works, opera, radio), but for a reader, reading quietly alone.

As I get older, I try to separate these things more, to make a book or theater or radio piece that just functions in that one medium, but I can't control other people making these connections. For instance, the book *GRRRHHHH: A Study of Social Patterns* was never intended to be performed, but a choreographer named Janet Bogardus loved the book and based a dance piece around it. And nowadays, even a piece of bubble gum has a Web site and a T-shirt and everything else connected to it.

Your book French Fries *is a key element in the development of a "new expressive typography." I know that it is not simply a stylistic conceit. What is the rationale behind this remarkably complex design and narrative?*

Yeah. It's not about style. Even going further back than *French Fries*, I was working on coming up with a framework for a kind of real-time notation. Traditional punctuation seemed efficient but lacked an experiential dimension. Instead of notating a pause, for instance, why not create an actual pause on the page, as poets do in verse. If all thoughts are not linear, why should they be always stuck in lines, let alone columns? What about fields of thought? What about the shape of dialogue versus a quintet of voices?

These early books of mine, *versations* and *i mean, you know*, and *the song combines*, were very much about creating structures for multiple voices. It always bothered me, when you read a script of a play, you have to keep reading the name of the character over and over again. How about just naming the character once at the top, and whatever dialogue falls below is theirs, combined with setting characters in a distinct typographic configuration, not to mention color when available. What does it look like when one person dominates a conversation? When two people rise above a field of sixteen voices? When twelve people are talking in the same room? Is it just noise? How can I distinguish a subtext, a description of physical activity, or commentary from the main body of the text? Speech versus thought? Can a book be experienced like a movie? These were some of the things I was trying to find answers for.

And your answer?

My answer was all these books and scores I was making. They may have seemed complicated to some people, even to me right now, but at the time, it was a pretty accurate reflection of how I perceived the world.

With *French Fries*, which came out in 1984, I was also working on creating a setting that played off of American fast-food culture. I didn't think of the word "vernacular." If any one was talking about that, I was unaware of it. The book looked like a box of McDonald's french fries. The colors were bright and suspiciously cheerful, and the typography rapturously inelegant. Beneath the happy families and the reassuring cuisine was disease and violence and inequality and dream. The book is jammed with a lot of youthful energy, detail, and ideas. The reader has to make choices at every turn, as to where to go next and what constellation of activity to enter.

The dense pages in the political argument section probably garnered the most attention at the time. For me it diagrammed the voices of seven people in a heated argument set against a cold-war backdrop and a fast-food joint replete with a throbbing video arcade. For some, these pages might have been a *cool* overlay of layers and colors. I remember seeing a student of mine use a page spread from *French Fries* that was reprinted in a design annual as a textured background for one of his designs. He had no idea that this "borrowed" image originated with me or what it was about. Since then, computer programs have facilitated "layers" at the stroke of a button. Design curricula teach *typography as metaphor* and *deconstruction*, and Mike Mills gives a lecture called "the layered thing," reacting to his design education and a proliferating look that, like a style of clothing, one ought no longer wear.

I appreciate you and others who have made note of my contribution. I suppose I was at the front end of a wave, but I'm not so much interested in the style question as much as the ideas and the subjects that continue to fuel the work and the resulting emotional or revelatory impact it may or may not have.

What determines what projects you will do?

My "Portrait Series" project is based on my experience of always meeting or being sought out by people who are on the edge of madness and brilliance. Where do project ideas come from? I was actually on the toilet one day, when I had a vision of doing an ongoing series of books based on these uncelebrated "eccentrics." Each book would be proportional in size to a standing human figure, with a standing photographic portrait of them on the front cover; on the back, a portrait of them from the back; and inside "the body of the book," the guts, life stories, and perspectives told through me in first-person monologues. All books (and typography) are metaphorical vessels for human experience, and this idea seemed like a very clear expression of that. All I had to do was finish two other projects I was working on, then seek out the people. When I finally was able to start the project, I realized most of the "subjects" were already around me.

French Fries grew out being at the West 4th Street McDonald's with my friend Dennis Bernstein, realizing it was living theater in there—a perfect setting to capture an essential American experience.

Right now, my wife, actress and oral historian Judith Sloan, and I are working on "Crossing the Boulevard," a large project that attempts to penetrate the mundane, if not hideous, urban landscape of our home borough of Queens (New York) in search of story, culture, and home. Like so many of our neighbors, we live isolated, disconnected lives longing to be elsewhere. While waiting for the subway day after day, year after year, dreaming of exotic, far away places, Queens has become the most ethnically diverse locality in the United States. By becoming travelers in our own home turf, Judith and I get to see the world through the eyes of our largely immigrant, refugee neighbors. It is a book and a series of public radio segments. And, oh yeah, a performance. And, oh yeah, a Web site.

How involved are you in the actual marketing of your products? Your work is so rooted in the art of the book, how much of you is devoted to the business of bookmaking?

I started out producing my books, and even theater pieces, in the way any artist does whatever it takes to make their work happen. Bookwise, that began for me as one-of-a-kind books and then small, letterpress editions. Set the type, mix the inks, cut the paper, bind the thing, and move on to the next one. Then, I graduated to offset lithography. Three hundred copies. A thousand copies. A part of me just wanted to get my one copy to see what it looked like, and then be characteristically disappointed and move on to the next project.

But a funny thing happened on the way to the next project. People were reading and reacting to these things. There was feedback with an audience, critical and admiring, understanding and misunderstanding, which was very helpful. When you're writing for the theater, you can try something out and hear what works and what doesn't and what changes need to be made to be clearer or funnier, or whatever it is you're after. In books, it's printed, and then it's out there, and if you don't see how people are reacting, especially when you're inventing something relatively new or different, you could just be talking to yourself. In addition to wanting recognition, I think it was that shift from being an artist in his studio communing with higher forces to being a storyteller engaged in some kind of dialogue with others that motivated me to do some peddling.

This notion of connecting with your audience is fascinating. So, it's not simply doing the performance, it's about making sure it reaches its audience. How is this done?

When I published my own work or copublished, I was fairly aggressive in my own tiny way about marketing. I kept up a mailing list and sent out prospectuses that were designed to make you want the thing. I hated writing and designing this stuff, but I knew it was necessary. Wherever I went, I'd meet with booksellers and museum-store buyers and curators. One antiquarian book dealer leafed through my first offset book, an oversized volume printed on translucent all-rag paper. Then, he slammed the book shut, smiled, and said, "Magnificent. Come back when you're dead." The owner of the

Drama Book Shop made me an offer, "If you can find one shelf that that thing will fit on, I'll buy your whole edition." When I found copies of *French Fries* shelved in the cookbook section at Books & Company next to the Whitney Museum, I told the buyer, "It's a play. It can go in the theater section, or you can put it in art or design or American studies, but it's not a cookbook." He told me it was doing really well there and ordered twenty more copies on the spot. I couldn't argue with that.

With the help of grants and a small but growing following, I'd churn out another seemingly unmarketable book, which in turn became collectors' items that sell for ridiculous amounts of money. I tried to price things so that the kind of people these books were about could afford them. Instead of doing a markup of five times (or more) the cost of production, I'd sell the thing for slightly above cost, thinking, well, it was subsidized by public funds and foundations, so I can get it to the proletariat, guilt-free. Thirty or forty dollars, hardbound, Smyth-sewn, archival paper, two colors, three colors, sixteen colors, 150 to 500 pages—cheap! We sent *French Fries* to people in a custom box, wrapped with paper napkins, a blue plastic fork, and two packets of ketchup. *GRRRHHHH* is wrapped in press sheets that people frame and put on their walls.

Now, others publish your books. How has this changed the process?
Now that I'm not publishing my own books, it's hard to control the quality and love and attention to these kinds of things. But I'm a pathetic businessperson, really, so I'm better off focusing on the work as much as possible. I don't want to talk to people on the phone and in a zillion e-mails about an order that was never sent, and I don't want anyone running around my studio packing boxes while I'm in my underwear trying to think.

How does performance play a role in what you do? Is the performance piece envisioned after the book, before, or during?
The performances used to be envisioned at the same time as the composition of the books. It finally dawned on me that folks don't want to read stage directions when they're cuddled up in bed. Now, a project can have different components, but each manifestation is usually very different. The stage needs a different script than the text of a book page. There are four plays that I've written that were never published as books, although some have been published as scripts. Also, I've discovered, in my own backward way, that the text in a book is best served if it's more interior and contemplative, while the text for performance is more active.

You have also produced CDs. How does this fit into the holistic approach of your work?

I cowrote and cocomposed an opera with Harvey Goldman entitled, *The Search For IT and Other Pronouns*, which was released as an audio CD. I designed the packaging and the booklet as well. *Crossing the Boulevard* will also include an audio CD. I'm reluctant to make a CD-ROM, because everyone tells me I must and that it makes total sense for me to combine the music composition and the theater and the typography in this medium. I would love to start making films, but I don't want to do anything that will oblige anyone to sit in front of a computer for more time than they already do.

You've published yourself and you've sold "packages" to other publishers. What is the preferred way to do this?

I think I've mostly answered this, except to say, while I may not be interested in publishing my own work at the moment, I do continue to work out of an entrepreneurial model of producing self-initiated projects. It's very encouraging to see how more and more books in nonspecialty bookstores have odd, visual things happening between the covers. Two examples besides my own work: In Irvine Welsh's (author of *Trainspotting*) novel *Filth*, a subtext, which turns out to be the voice of a parasite, visually breaks out of the narrative of the piggish detective and eventually takes over the storytelling. Mark Danielewski's novel *House of Leaves* employs typography to juxtapose different perspectives.

While literacy and literary endeavors are imperiled by a plague of short attention spans and gross commercialism, we're also experiencing the nibbling around the edges of a possible renaissance in visual literature. We talk about the "designer as author," but I'm particularly excited about the potential of the writer, writing away on his little desktop or laptop computer, taking control of the shape and dimension of his work. I continue to feel privileged to be able to give form to my own work, without having to rely on a strict tradition or any intermediary technician, and it makes a lot of sense to me that others are discovering that the means of design need not be limited to serving the commercial or editorial ideas of others.

Can you make a good living through your art?

Between teaching, performing, lecturing, getting intermittent fellowships and grants, advances and some royalties, I manage to stay alive, buy some equipment, drive used cars, and subsidize whatever the next project may be.

Courtesy Gary Baseman. © 2001 Disney Corporation.

STORYTELLING IS EVERYTHING

with Gary BASEMAN,
Creator of *Teacher's Pet*

During **GARY BASEMAN**'s fifteen-plus years career as an editorial and advertising illustrator, he has produced a lot of comic, raw, and ribald characters. Yet most have been in the service of clients, including *Time*, the *New York Times*, *Rolling Stone, G.Q., Forbes, Blab, Reader's Digest*, and the *Atlantic Monthly*. His international corporate clients include Nike, Gatorade, Celebrity Cruises, Mercedes-Benz, Labatt, Thomas Cook, IPIX, and Capitol Records. His art has also been animated for television commercials. But last year, he made a quantum leap from mere illustrator and accomplished what most of his peers only dream about. He created an animated children's show, *Teacher's Pet*, about a dog who wishes he were a boy. It was bought by ABC/Disney and is currently the most sophisticated show in their Saturday children's lineup. As the show's executive producer, Baseman shepherds the look and feel of his characters. In this interview he talks about how he developed the show, what he had to sacrifice in the bargain, and the rewards (both present and future) of making a weekly show work.

You have been an illustrator for many years. Was the animation impulse in you from the beginning?

I loved animation since I was very young. In fact, I believed when I was a child that "perfection" was the old Warner Brothers cartoons from the thirties and forties. I took one animation class as an undergrad at UCLA and realized that it was too hard for one person alone to produce animation. The animation bug laid dormant until Nickelodeon called to see if I had any ideas for TV shows. I lied and said yes, then started cranking on ideas.

What is more important for you, animating your drawings or telling stories?

In creating a TV series, storytelling is everything. I love funny drawings. With interesting visuals alone, you can capture someone's attention but for a moment. It is important for me to keep the images looking like my artwork and to keep challenging myself aesthetically. I work very hard to make sure the stories are complete and consistent. We try to bring in as much emotion and humor into each episode. I have the greatest partners in Bill and Cheri Steinkellner as writers. Their scripts are a work of art. Reading their scripts are like dessert.

A few years back, you started doing some fairly visible animated commercials. How did this come about?

R. O. Blechman has always been an inspiration to me. He gave me encouragement from my first trip to New York and was the first to animate my work. He also was the first, along with J.J. Sedelmaier, to allow me to write and design animated shorts for a short-lived series, *The USA Today Show*. J.J.'s studio also did a wonderful job animating my work for a "Celebrity Cruise" campaign.

Teacher's Pet *is your first network cartoon series. I know many artists who sweat and toil for years even to get a pilot. How long did it take to get to the point of having a weekly program in the Saturday morning slot?*

Seven years from my first pilot to getting a series on the air. I did two pilots for the same show, *Louie Louie,* for Nickelodeon that unfortunately did not get picked up. The second *Louie* pilot is brilliant, and I was dumbfounded that it did not become a series. Maybe someday. I was determined to get a series on the air and moved back to Hollywood. I pitched all over town, and Disney offered me a development deal.

Tell me something about the genesis of the plot. The story centers around a dog who decides to pass for a boy. Where did this idea come from?

I have always been an animal person, and I spent many a day watching my and my wife's dog, Hubcaps. I like to use animals to tell very human stories. I started to wonder what Hubcaps did when I was not around, assuming he would be bored just napping and rolling on the grass, as he did in my presence. Did he watch TV, read books, call pizza delivery, etc.? Then, I imagined a dog who was bored staying at home while his boy master went to school every day.

Teacher's Pet *is a beautifully crafted and sharply written "kids" cartoon. Certainly, compared to most of the other fare on Saturday mornings, this is high art. What, in the development of this project, enabled you to have such a large degree of quality control?*

Dumb luck. And hard work. I was not willing to settle for a show I could not enjoy. I admired *The Simpsons* for being the best-written TV show. I needed to work with writers whose work I respected. I admired how complete and consistent and funny Bill and Cheri's spec script was. Also, my director, Tim Bjorklund, whose inspirations are a combination of the '20s Felix meets R. Crumb, is a talented director. And I really made an

Courtesy Gary Baseman. © 2001 Disney Corporation.

effort to make the show look like my art (all the way down to painting all the backgrounds on canvas). But even with this wonderful team in place, we have a special chemistry that I can only account to "luck." I have seen many other shows that are produced by talented people that just fall flat.

Do you maintain control over the animation? Or is this a collaborative sharing of power?

A television series is a collaborative effort. There are many people involved, and you have to let people do what they do best. We maintain as much control as we can with a crazy television deadline. We try to inspire and challenge our storyboard artists to better the scripts that come in. Make the jokes funnier, and stronger visuals. I want everyone on my crew to feel like they are learning and growing on this show. We work with two overseas animation studios, and we also have tried to inspire them to do their best work. Tim and I are both big fans of old Bob Clampett cartoons and have tried to do the best emulate the timing with a TV budget.

Courtesy Gary Baseman. © 2001 Disney Corporation.

Did you have to learn new skills to draw for animation that builds upon the quirks and characteristics of unique characters?

I have to oversee everything, so I don't draw as much as I would like. Tim was able to take my characters and make them animate-able. I wanted artists who can draw my characters better than me. Who can draw them in any angle or any expression. I try to learn a little every day.

On what models did you base your characters?

I designed the characters to optimize their personalities. I tried to make Spot an ordinary mutt. An ordinary blue mutt. But when he is a boy, I wanted him to be extra smart. My wife and I loved to watch the old *Superman* TV show from the fifties. And it is so silly that no one could tell the difference of Clark Kent and Superman cause he wears glasses. Well, I wanted to take that one step further. That no one could tell Scott is a dog cause he is wearing a beanie cap and glasses. I made Leonard to be an ordinary kid, but I wanted him to stand out from the rest, so he is the only one who is off-white in color. A little sickly. Mrs. Helperman: I wanted her sweet and to be attractive enough for her students to have crushes on. Tim really made her sexy, but "standards and practices" toned us down.

Thank heavens for the keepers of the moral flame. In a series like this, acting is extremely important. So, did you have a say in who was cast for the voices?

We had a say. We gave Disney our wish list, and they gave us their choices. We are overjoyed by our talented cast for our show. Nathan Lane has added so much life into Spot/Scott. He is great. David Ogden Stiers does an amazing job with Mr. Jolly. Jerry Stiller is hilarious as Pretty Boy. Debra Jo Rupp is a wonderful Mrs. Helperman. Shawn Fleming captures Leonard so well. And Wallace Shawn adds so much character to Principal Strickler.

Okay, a sensitive point. Many artist believe that getting a TV show is an instant ticket on the gravy train. Is it?

Depends on where your gravy train is heading. I make a fine living, but I made a fine living as an illustrator. Children's TV does not pay the same as prime time. With the success of this show, I would hope that someday, I will be rolling in gravy.

Disney produces Teacher's Pet. *Does this mean that you hold any of your own intellectual property rights? Or for the opportunity of doing such a feat as this, did you relinquish these rights and opportunities?*

I hold my own intellectual property rights to my other projects. But I did have to give up the show to have the "privilege" to work with Disney and get it on the air. It was something I was not very comfortable about, especially coming from the illustration community, where one usually sells only first-time rights to your art.

As executive producer of the show, what are you duties?

Executive producers have different duties, depending on who they are and what type of project they are working on. On my show, I am a full-time, working executive producer. I oversee the whole show with my partners Bill and Cheri, and Tim. I come up with stories, gags, designs; oversee and approve scripts, storyboards, character designs, backgrounds, layouts, returning animation, voice recordings, music; and take and implement notes from the network. I also work hard to keep the corporation inspired by coming up with new ideas to support the show, working with their different departments. I hand-paint the title cards for each episode.

And what is your relationship to Disney?

Disney retains my services as Creator/Executive Producer on the show. I am not an "employee."

How do you foresee Teacher's Pet developing? Do you look at this as a finite, self-contained world or as an expandable universe ripe for continued innovation?

I see unlimited potential with *Teacher's Pet*. The characters are very rich and dimensional. I am not sure what you are asking, but I do not see the characters aging like *Teacher's Pet: The High School Years*.

That's what I'm asking. So, as a follow-up to the above, with this experience under your belt, do you have other properties in the works?

Yes. But it is hard to concentrate on anything else right now, since I am so in love with this show.

ART, WRITING, OBSESSION

5

SPIRITUAL, OBSESSIVE, AND SACRED

with Marshall ARISMAN,
Painter and Illustrator

The paintings and drawings of MARSHALL ARISMAN have been widely exhibited both internationally and nationally, and his work may be seen in the permanent collections of the Brooklyn Museum, the National Museum of American Art, and Smithsonian Institution, as well as in many private and corporate collections. His original graphic essay, *Heaven Departed,* in which paintings and drawings describe the emotional and spiritual impact of nuclear war on society, was published in book form by Vision Publishers (Tokyo, 1988). The Chairman of the M.F.A. degree program at the School of Visual Arts in New York, Arisman was the first American invited to exhibit in mainland China. His series, Sacred Monkeys, appeared at the Guang Dong Museum of Art in April 1999.

You are a painter, sculptor, illustrator, writer, and god knows what else. In your role as artist, I see you as very entrepreneurial. Would you agree?

Necessity is the mother of invention . . . or so they say. My problem is that I can't figure out who *they* are. I know *they're* out there. Occasionally, I meet *them* in the form of gallery owner, collector, or art director, and they seem like perfectly nice people, but I don't trust them. Consequently, I try and present what's on my mind in a variety of written and visual forms. To put it bluntly, I am "covering my ass," so *they* can't gang up on me.

So, what is it that makes you an entrepreneur?

Fear of rape and fear of too much masturbation—artistically speaking, of course. I look for themes that become obsessions. Obsessions require a variety of forms of expression. I guess that makes me an entrepreneur.

It is one thing to create paintings for a patron (or client, as the case may be), but you've built worlds out of your artistic themes. Would you say that these are products?

They are all products, including film, writing, painting, or illustrating. It's tricky. My hope is that the expression serves my obsession and not my sense of greed.

How do you market your wares?

I do all these things to clarify issues in myself. Not knowing the answer before I begin, I have to complete the project before I am comfortable showing it to anyone. This is generally a bad marketing idea. I have found, however, that it is better marketing for me to find an interested person, who then suggests how I might market the finished product. They always know more about this than I do. I try and stay open and listen carefully. Then, I decide what marketing scheme I can live with.

Do you feel any compromise in being an artistic jack-of-all-trades? Is there any sense of sellout?

There is a natural compatibility between destruction and transformation. The only time I feel I am "selling out" is when I am trying to solve someone else's problem and not my own. I have done this, and it's always a painful and unpleasant experience.

What is your ultimate goal in creating things that reach the public?

The Belgian surrealist René Magritte said, "Painting can't teach anything. When your work reminds the viewer of what they already know, you have communication with the public." That is my ultimate goal with the work I create. What Magritte didn't say was that your public could be very small. In my case this is true. It's good to know this when trying to go into the mass market.

When I think of artist/entrepreneurs for whom design is a major component, the names Keith Haring and Kenny Scharf come to mind. Do you see yourself as ever developing an Arisman store? Or do you do anything like that now?

I think Keith Haring and Kenny Scharf reached a much larger public than my work does. I would love to have an Arisman store, as long as I didn't manage it. It would be painful to be reminded of how small my public really was. Listening to comments like, "I can't imagine what he was thinking of when he made this," would not promote good mental health in my brain.

How much do you involve yourself in the realities of business?

The realities of business only produce more visual junk. It pollutes the eyes. We are drowning in a sea of visual garbage already. I would like to not add to it.

What is it that you would like to do, entrepreneurially, that you have not yet done?

At the moment, I am making a ten-minute digital film that was an outgrowth of an illustrated novel I did. At age sixty-two, this is my first film venture. I love the process but find it frustrating that everything I have to say at the moment can be contained in ten minutes! (It's too long.) My belief is that the work will suggest other forms when it's appropriate. It is a leap of faith. I look forward to new avenues.

CHEESE
MONKEYS.

A NOVEL *in* TWO SEMESTERS

BY

CHIP KIDD.

DESIGN À CLEF

with Chip KIDD, Author and Designer

CHIP KIDD is a graphic designer and writer in New York City. His book-jacket designs for Alfred A. Knopf have helped spawn a revolution in the art of American book packaging. In 1997 he received the International Center of Photography's award for Use of Photography in Graphic Design, and he is a regular contributor of visual commentary to the Op-Ed page of the *New York Times.* He has been the design consultant for the *Paris Review* since 1995. Kidd has also written about graphic design and popular culture for *Vogue,* the *New York Times,* the *New York Observer, Entertainment Weekly, Details,* the *New York Post, ID,* and *Print.* His first book as author and designer, *Batman Collected* (Bulfinch, 1996), was given the Design Distinction award from ID magazine, and his second, *Batman Animated* (HarperCollins, 1998), garnered two of the Comics Industry's Eisner Awards. *The Cheese Monkeys,* his first novel, was published by Scribner in 2001.

The "designer as author" has been something of a buzz-term for designers who produce their own content, regardless of media. You, however, have taken this quite literally and have authored a novel. What prompted this muse?

A lot of things, but first and foremost, it was a need to tell a story I've been wanting to tell since I graduated from college (in 1986), and a novel seemed like the best way to do it. As far as I was concerned, design was always supposed to be a stepping-stone to writing. It just took me fourteen years to get my act together. The goal is not to be, finally, a "designer as author," but to simply be an author who writes about, among other things, design. When I first approached my agent with the idea for the book (many years ago), she said, "Oh, you should do it like a *Griffin and Sabine* kind of thing." But I was firm about wanting it to be strictly prose.

I know a few artists and designers who have written novels, but yours is actually about being a design student. Is this a roman à clef?

Technically, yes—that is, there are characters in it that are certainly based on real people. But it is very much a fiction. It follows two semesters in the freshman year of an unnamed art student (who bears an uncanny resemblance to me) at a rather plain mid-Atlantic state university. When my friend and former colleague Barbara deWilde (who I also went to school with) read it, she said, "It's weird, because it's half true, and it half isn't." And I said, "Yes, that's why it's called a 'novel.'" I find that the events, as they happened, were far too long and drawn-out to make an enticing memoir. Fiction frees you up to get rid of the dull parts of life and goose up the juicy ones. And no messy lawsuits!

I presume that a subject of this kind allows you to, well, purge yourself of certain demons (or peeves). What are some of these?

Strangely enough, I didn't really have the peeves 'til I started teaching senior portfolio at SVA in the mid-nineties. A major figure in the novel is this uber-tyrannical but brilliant teacher, not unlike a few that I had (and no, I'm not naming any names), who rules with an iron hand and tosses any kid out of the room who doesn't have their assignment for crit. Which is pretty much as it was. I personally thrived in such a highly disciplined atmosphere and found it an excellent environment for learning. Yes, it took its toll at the time, but anything worth doing does. I have no resentments about it at all.

So when I got to SVA, it was a shock. Kids may or may not show up for class, they may or may not have their assignments if they do. And if they don't like what you're teaching, they switch midterm to go study with the guy from MTV. So, I felt like *I* was being "tested," not them. The plus side was that the average talent level of the kids was much higher than what I was used to, and they "got it" much quicker. And those who stuck it out were terrific, and I ended up hiring a lot of them.

So, I guess if there's any payback aspect to the book, it's against a sort of laconic attitude about design, about work.

Much of your design work is rooted in ironic and sardonic juxtapositions of imagery. Was any of this transferred to your fiction writing?

I leave that up to whomever reads it. I know I couldn't keep myself from infusing it with a lot of wisecracks. The narrator is something of a smart aleck, because so am I. For better or worse.

You have written articles and reviews and a book about Batman artifacts, but these are not novels. How difficult or easy was it to build a contiguous narrative and keep it flowing?

The hardest thing was figuring out what the book was actually going to be. Which took years, I'm embarrassed to admit. It was the classic situation—I sat down to write one book and ended up writing another. There was this event I learned about my freshman year in Psych 101 that completely changed my way of thinking, and that was what I originally intended to write about. But before I could get to it, I had to do the back story of the main character before the event, and that grew like a virus and eventually became the novel. I still haven't gotten to the subject I really want to explore (though it has a lot to do with design—everything, really), and I'm hoping that if the book does well, I could do a sequel (jumping the gun, I know). My original proposal was for a massive, three-part epic, and my agent said, "This isn't one book, it's three. Lose the first and last parts and make the middle part the novel." And she was right.

Anyway, to answer your question, once the structure was set in place (two semesters—two assignments in the first semester, five in the second), it was just filling in the blanks. Or, at least, it felt like it.

You are a prodigious book-jacket designer. You've done jackets and covers for some of the finest contemporary literature. Knowing as much as you do about literature, was this scary, daunting, or not an issue?

Yes, I know. It's a good question, and of course the whole prospect is horrifying. In fact, at first I didn't call it a "novel" at all, because I didn't think it was good enough to earn the title. So, I called it an "entertainment," which is what Graham Greene used to call his fictions [that] he didn't think had the proper weight or emotional heft. But my editor said that was too confusing, and now, we've settled for "a novel in two semesters," so everyone will know what they're getting into before they pick it up. Or just ignore it altogether.

I have no illusions that I'm a great writer, or even a good one. But I think what I've got going for me is that I'm well connected in the publishing world and know how to grease a few palms. Also, perhaps more importantly, while it's true I've done jackets for some of our best living writers, to date, none of them have seen fit to write a novel about graphic design, so I'll have to do in the meantime.

By the way, did you design your own jacket? How were you as a client?

I was fabulous. Very loving. Gave myself *miles* of leeway.

Actually, this is the first question that everyone asks me (except you—congrats!), which I find strangely irritating—sort of like asking the Monkees if they really played their own instruments.

Contractually, I have approval and can design it myself, if I wish. But I'm acting more as art director on it and collaborating with my friend, the cartoonist and designer Chris Ware (more about him below). Also, I should add that I've talked with Scribner's new art director, John Fulbrook, about it, which is a relief, because he's an excellent thinker and designer. And because of that I don't mind another cook in the kitchen.

But all that said, the jacket is weeks and maybe months from completion as I answer this, and I've learned that anything can happen. The publisher could reject whatever we come up with, and then, who knows?

My only concrete thoughts about it are that I don't want anything like a traditional jacket, whatever that means. It should also be simple and direct (like me!). And beautiful (not!).

Does becoming an "author" in the traditional sense change your attitude towards your main profession of designer? Or is this just another part of the creative puzzle that is your life?

It's usually more puzzling than creative. Sometimes, I'm certainly past "burnt out" on designing book jackets, but then, a project will land on my desk that I just can't not do, and on it goes. Whatever happens happens, but if I could write for a living for a while and give the book design gene a rest, that would be swell.

And as corny as it sounds, writing *is* design. It's designing with words—choreographing people's emotions and putting specific ideas into their heads using a bunch (twenty-six) of abstract symbols that in and of themselves don't mean anything. There's everything to figure out when you write. First, its content: the story you want to tell. After that, it's form: how you're going to tell it—how long sentences should be, where a page should break (I wrote the book in Quark, by the way), who the characters are, and what they should and shouldn't let on about—the power of saying things by not saying them. All of that, to me, is purposeful planning as I've always done it: i.e., design.

In addition to being a novelist, you also edit graphic novels. This is an entrepreneurial feat in its own right. How did you initiate this, and where is it taking you?

Editing Chris Ware and Dan Clowes at Pantheon grew out of wanting to see their books get published properly while expanding my role here at Knopf/Pantheon (without becoming the art director—which Carol Carson does brilliantly and I wouldn't have the patience or stamina for). They were the right projects at the right place and time. And incidentally, Ware and Clowes both *hate* the term "graphic novels," but for better or worse, it seems to be the nickname the culture's chosen.

I'd been a fan of them for many years, and I brought their books into the house, just as Louise Fili did in the mid-eighties with Art Spiegelman's *Maus*. My champion in this cause is an editor at Pantheon named Dan Frank, and he helped me convince Sonny Mehta, Knopf's CEO, that we should publish them. It wasn't as hard as it could have been, really. And at the risk of sounding like a guest on the *Tonight* show, I can't say adequately how much I love those books. That I was able to make them happen here is a great privilege. (I know, violins are swelling, and we have to go to commercial. Sorry.)

Anyway, at this point they are doing quite well, and we have several others in the pipeline.

What are the newest books?

It's absurd, but I have four coming out this fall (though compared to you, I realize that's nothing): the novel (Scribner); a collaboration with Art Spiegelman on the life of the cartoonist Jack Cole and his creation, PlasticMan (Chronicle); the *Batman Collected* book (finally) coming out in paperback with new material (Watson-Guptill); and a massive book on *Peanuts* and the work of Charles Schulz that I'm editing, designing, and writing for Pantheon.

It's silly for them all to come out in one season, but I don't really have any control over that. At least they're all very different projects and publishers.

Blonde Like Me

The Roots of the Blonde Myth in Our Culture

Natalia Ilyin

"Natalia Ilyin takes a premise as wispy as a strand of baby blonde hair and weaves it into a surprisingly rich and entertaining tapestry." —M. G. LORD, author of *Forever Barbie*

BLONDES SELL MORE BOOKS

with Natalia ILYIN, Author and Designer

NATALIA ILYIN is a writer and designer. She was Director of Programs at the American Institute of Graphic Arts in New York, and she has taught semiotics and cultural theory at The Cooper Union and at Yale University. She currently owns a design consultancy, which specializes in communications for nonprofit cultural organizations. Her articles on design and media have been published internationally. Her first book, *Blonde Like Me: The Roots of the Blonde Myth in Our Culture*, was published by Simon and Schuster.

Why did you become a designer in the first place?

I became a designer because I thought graphic design and fine printing were the same thing. This is inexcusable but true. When I was twenty or so, I worked in Berkeley, running a small press for David Lance Goines, and his was the life I wanted to lead: Peet's coffee in the morning, esoteric remarks all day while sitting and inking things, a good dinner at Chez Panisse in the evening. I knew nothing of design or of the Arts and Crafts Movement, or of Modernism or of anything. I just wanted to live the way he lived. I went to New York and applied this fine press routine to being an art director at a music company. The result was hybrid, to say the least.

Let's cut to the chase. Why did you shift to writing?

I was hanging on by the skin of my teeth in grad school, not knowing a thing about design, having been an English major in undergrad, and I just remember reading everything I could about design and editing things for professors so they wouldn't throw me out. I was so blocked by the magnificence and talent of my peers that I didn't design another thing for ten years; I think my first shaky effort was a postcard for the AIGA. This year, I made a hydrangea wreath for the holidays, so I think I might be getting some feeling back in my design ego.

Did you imagine that from writing the occasional article or lecture that you had a book in you (and one, in particular, that was not about graphic design)?

I live a double life. Sadly, neither side is terribly seamy. I run a design firm that focuses on the design problems of nonprofit organizations, and I write because everyone in my family is a writer. It is sort of the family avocation, like dousing. I always avoided writing because everyone told me I should, and ran off to be a designer and wear black and all that. But the design business got me into an interesting area: the effect of design and advertising on everyday people. And so, the *Blonde* book is not about the nuts and bolts of design, but it is very much about my primary design concern: what happens when you show people pictures of the way they should be, the way they should act, and the things they should aspire to.

Tell me about the genesis of Blonde Like Me.

After grad school I taught a lot at Cooper Union, New York, in Continuing Ed. I was supposed to be teaching semiotics, but over the years, my courses became about the stories we learn in American advertising—how advertising affects us like a sort of consumerist mythology. I wrote a tremendous tome about a number of the starring icons of these myths—the Marlboro Man, the Blonde, and that sort of thing—because I was afraid to get a design job, and I figured I could hold my head up at parties if I said I was writing a book. My agent gave it one pass-around to a few editors and said it wasn't going to fly and that I should use the manuscript to prop up infants at table. But just then, an editor at Simon and Schuster said that she wanted me to write the Blonde chapter into a book and that she wanted me to put in some of my own experiences. And so, that is how I have become the person you call if you are writing some article about blondes and you want a quote. Who knew. It is an odd expertise.

As a designer, how much of your energy was concentrated on the design of your book?

Contractually, I was not allowed to touch the design of my book and had no hand in it at all.

Obviously, you did not object to these terms, but did you feel odd ceding this responsibility—your expertise—to another?

I did object to these terms. They let me rail, but changed nothing: I had zero pull as a first-time author. My editor did a good thing, though, and gave me by far the best designer they had on staff. They shot a good front cover, I thought, though the type left me lying on the rug despondent.

Do you see yourself as an author, or was this book something of an anomaly for you? Will you continue to practice graphic design?

I do see myself as a writer. And luckily, so does my editor, and soon, I shall plop another manuscript on her desk. But I run a design business, and design has gotten far more interesting for me since I got involved with Web work. My business's nonprofit angle is a good one: I bypass a number of the ethical conflicts that designers in business usually have to deal with. It is the part of my life that gets me out of my wonderful self and lets me use what I have learned about design and about business to bolster the communications of those that spend their lives doing good in the world.

What is the most important difference in your creative life at this time?

Since the book came out, people pay me to stand up and say things, and this is a great happiness.

FURNITURE, CLOTHES, ACCESSORIES

MATERIALS AND THE BODY

with John MAEDA, Associate
Director of MIT Media Lab

JOHN MAEDA is Associate Director of the MIT Media Laboratory, where he is
also Sony Career Development Professor of Media Arts and Sciences, Associate Professor of Design and Computation, and Director of the Aesthetics &
Computation Group (ACG). His mission is to foster the growth of what he calls
"humanist technologists"—people that are capable of articulating future culture
through informed understanding of the technologies they use. The ACG is an
experimental research studio that was founded in 1996 as the successor to the
famed Visible Language Workshop. A major component of the ACG's efforts
involves outreach to the design and art community in the form of workshops
and events that introduce the underlying concepts of computing technology, as
exemplified in the ongoing Design by Numbers project. Maeda is also an
auteur, who has produced a variety of digital typographic narratives and a 480-
page retrospective of personal work, entitled *MAEDA@MEDIA*. Currently, he is
developing two new strands of endeavor, painting and furniture design, that
may or may not merge into one discipline.

*You are doing some serious re-vectoring of your creative life. You became
very well known as a graphic designer working in the computer realm, but
now, you are shifting gears into furniture and art. Will you tell me why?*

Because the computer as we know it is continually degrading as a medium for reliable
human communication. Demands for greater functionality have spawned great complexity, to the point that when the computer does not work, it is impossible to fix. I
have lost confidence in the computer as a material.

*What elements of your previous professional life can you carry over into
your new entrepreneurial life?*

I believe that my goals as a conceptual entrepreneur, peddling thoughts through action,
remain consistent.

Can the problem-solving graphic designer coexist on any footing with the artist in you?

Designers solve problems for clients. Artists solve problems for humanity. The latter is the greatest problem.

How do you reconcile some of the tenets of graphic design that you have made part of your life and work—particularly the lessons you've learned from Paul Rand—with your new endeavors?

I continue to explore, clarify, and deconstruct my system of beliefs. Nothing has changed.

Having devoted so much of yourself to stretching the boundaries of the computer in design, is this something you will do in terms of furniture and art, or are these separate activities?

They are separate but related activities. Furniture is a staging ground for my study of materials in relationship to the body. Graphics was a study of the relationship of materials to the mind.

I presume your furniture is aimed at some kind of market. How would you describe your work and to whom is it targeted?

I am creating objects that will not be manufactured in quantity. These are being made with the Italian furniture maker Sawaya & Moroni. I have been fortunate to work with a company that does not acknowledge a specific market and consistently aspires to create the best.

How, then, would you describe your furniture? Is it solely about materials? Or does human interaction concern you? Are these pieces about comfort or something other? And your art, can you describe the motivations here and your ultimate goal?

I aspire to create art that is worthy.

You've said that you are "un-becoming" a graphic designer. Do you see an eventual shift away from the applied arts entirely?

I never was a "good" designer, as I was never sensitive to the client's needs. Never. This mythical way of the likes of Paul Rand is no longer valued, nor needed. I figured, rather than continue to cause friction as a matter of economic need, I chose to head towards a purer lifestyle.

MAVERICKS IN THE RAG TRADE

Michael Patrick CRONAN and Karin
HIBMA, Founders of Walking Man

The husband-and-wife team of MICHAEL PATRICK CRONAN and KARIN HIBMA founded Walking Man, a line of men's clothing, as an extension of Cronan Design in San Francisco. It quickly became an integral business. Walking Man's philosophy is, "You spend your days leading the pack, chasing your dreams, changing the world—you need clothes that are practical, easygoing, great to travel in." Cronan, who continues to direct his graphic design firm, provides the designs and inspiration, Hibma designs and runs the company. The products are made in the U.S.A. of the finest-quality fabrics. "The clothing is innovative and durable in both design and manufacture and lasts for years," they say.

How did Walking Man get started?

Through the eighties, we worked for a number of large, brand-name companies. During those years, we created and developed a lot of the design around consumer products, from the logos to the packaging, from ads to environments, but never the products themselves. It was something that was the logical next step. We wanted to be responsible for the process from start to finish.

Walking Man began as a set of definitions about what we would like a brand to be. We decided to create clothing, because there is an inherent usefulness to it. When some bit of clothing is well-designed, you really experience it in a tactile way.

Was this a whim? Unfulfilled dream? Or a real attempt to found a business that was totally apart from graphic design?

I'd say that although there are whimsical aspects of the Walking Man attitude, and there have been dreamlike experiences over the last ten years, it was an attempt to create something that would take us outside the bounds of service to a client (i.e., creating solutions for problems and implementation defined within their parameters) into direct contact with the consumer, offering solutions within parameters we'd defined. Walking Man is still aimed at someone who understands design, recognizes quality, looks for distinctive things, and cares to afford to own and enjoy a few good things rather than scores of cheap ones.

Did you always want to be, or know, you were a clothes designer?

Not any more or less than being any other kind of designer. We were fortunate to learn about and experience "design" as a continuum, like a single point of view brought to many materials and processes. We were reinforced in that perspective by our friends and colleagues, many of whom do buildings, furniture, and Web sites in the same practice.

Was there ever a chance that Walking Man would overtake your fundamental graphic design business?

Not really. The nature of the product and economics meant that the idea would, by definition, stay small. Over the years, we have avoided handing it over to others, and, as it turns out, the growth of the Internet has allowed us to remain in contact with our customers, worldwide.

Where is the nexus between Walking Man and your graphic design business?

Karin Hibma has run Walking Man from the very beginning, so my role has diminished over time to sharing letters from customers. Still, I use what I've learned from Walking Man every day. It has given me a useful perspective that I had been denied in my professional experience to that point, that of being the client. It is tough to be a client. I have great respect for those who embark on the task. To paraphrase Ralph Caplan, being a client is a part-time job that requires mastery from day one.

How did you establish this business? Is it a business within a business, or a separate operation?

We incorporated a separate business, Cronan Artefact, for Walking Man because inventory accounting is different than a service business and because it has separate management and business relationships.

The fashion industry is not the easiest to be afloat in. What have been your heartaches and successes?

We have pretty much stayed away from the industry because it would have predetermined what we would have to do to market ourselves, and we neither had the desire nor resources to go that way. One early example of this is our first experience with a manufacturer in South Carolina whom we contacted to make some knit yardage to a particular specification that we had worked hard to develop. To do business with this company, we had to first make a huge deposit with their "factor," a financial organization that acts like an escrow company to whom manufacturers "sell" their invoices for a huge percentage. Factors are common in the garment industry because there is no standard of trust, unlike 98 percent of all other industries. After they missed the delivery date, they straightforwardly admitted that they had shown our sample to Esprit, who had bought the first run of what had been ours. They offered to remake our order at an increased price, because they were now busy supplying Esprit. We declined and received our deposit refund a year later. From then on, we decided to manufacture no farther than a day's drive away.

Our successes are not from the fashion industry, but from the individuals who have made Walking Man part of their lives: from the repeat customers who order favorite items over and over, to those who have one or two of everything we've made, to the customers who reorder something they've worn for ten years and finally worn out, to the customer who finds us for the first time and gets that thrill of discovery.

I guess this really is a cutthroat business. Are you taken seriously as a fashion concern? Or has being from the outside been a problem?

I don't think it has been an issue for us. A dear friend of ours is Nick Graham, the creator of Joe Boxer, who has done very well by not being taken seriously. Being from the outside is not a problem if you choose to stay small. If you look at the scores of exquisite chocolatiers in Paris, staying small is what they do very happily and successfully.

Finally, why the name Walking Man?

The logo came first, from an antique Japanese drawing book. This naive-looking chap is out for a walk. The name simply came from this little sketch. We see him everywhere in the city, especially at street crossings, where he is the symbol for "go."

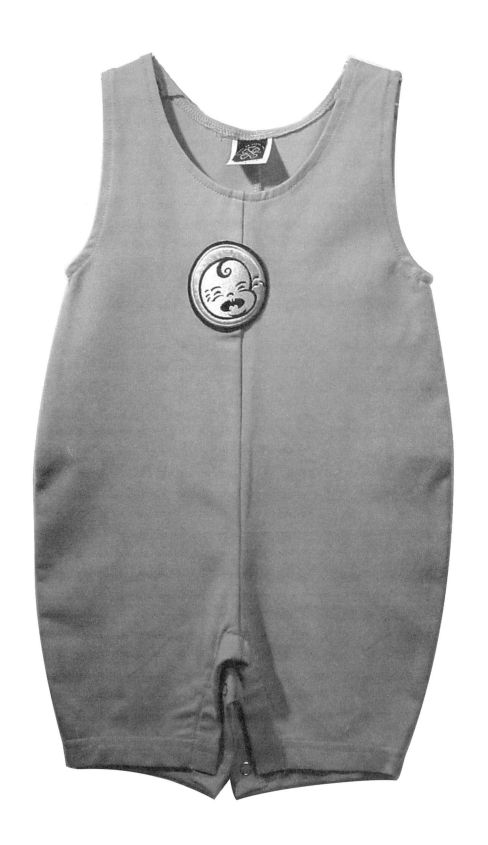

NAME ON THE MARQUEE

with Jay VIGON, Graphic
and Fashion Designer

JAY VIGON was born in Chicago and is a graduate of the Art Center College of Design in southern California. He has earned a reputation for designing classic logos for some of America's best-known music companies, movie campaigns, and fashion companies. His clients include George Lucas, Prince, Cole of California, Leon Max, Esprit, Gotcha, and Swatch. In 1996 Vigon opened his own boutique, Made On Earth. The store carries gifts, clothing, and art, all of which are designed and created by him. Made On Earth now sells nationwide. Vigon is also the author of two books, *Marks I* and *Marks II*.

How, when, and why did you start a retail store?

In the early 1990s, I stopped doing graphic design at a point when my broadcast graphics became a full-time endeavor. I was burned out on logo work and more than happy to leave that part of my career behind. But old habits die hard, and I never really stopped drawing. As a matter of fact, drawing for myself became immensely enjoyable. The end result was a rather vast library of images that had not been commissioned.

These drawings sat and gathered dust. This is when the idea of the store was conceived. I had created many successful logos for other people, why not myself? I needed an outlet for these images.

You produce products based on your own designs. What was the impetus for engaging in this entrepreneurial pursuit?

At first, I think it was something I needed for my artistic ego. Now, the store is likely to become a full-time, moneymaking endeavor. So, five years ago, my wife and I just jumped in with both feet, not really knowing just how hard it would be to make a going concern of a small business. We rehabbed a tiny space in Studio City, California, and opened the doors. This was financed by the money I was making directing TV commercials.

How is being a store owner different from being a creator? Or, how much of your business is devoted to business versus creation?

As a store owner, I am really sort of the marquee name, and I am the creative corner store. My wife, Margo Nahas, is an extremely talented artist in her own right and has much more of a head for the day-to-day running of the business.

I purposely limit my involvement in matters other than creative. I contribute the art to the store; it's what I do best. If I'm not creating art, I believe it's a waste of time and talent.

In deciding what products to produce, what standard or method do you follow? Do you test? Or is this purely intuition?

Introducing new products to the store usually begins with a new character. We give it the "T-shirt" test. If it sells on a T-shirt, we feel we can move to the next level and start applying an image to other products. The funny thing is, you never really know what is going to catch on. So, we never rush production.

Since so much of your energy is devoted to this, do you still act as a designer/illustrator?

As far as my energy goes, it is almost entirely devoted to being an artist. It's all I really know how to do. It's how I maintain the income of our corporation. There is no other thing I can do to help out more. If I can generate moneymaking images, my wife will manage it. It's a good partnership. If I'm not working on art for the store, I'm working on a logo job or a television commercial.

The fashion business is not the easiest in which to stay afloat, certainly as a principal owner. How do you navigate the vicissitudes of fashion and create the work that satisfies you?

Fashion is a tough business. That's why we do many things besides clothing. We are manufacturing some garments, but we also do furniture, housewares, silk-screen edition prints, etc. We don't put all of our eggs in the fashion basket. We do make clothing that tends to be somewhat basic. We are not ruled by trends or fads. We do what we do. That approach has always worked for us throughout our careers. It's what makes us happy.

How often do you change your stock of products?

We are constantly adding new products to the store. We have adopted a sort of constant trickle of new items, as opposed to big seasonal collections.

Do you feel that you've developed a clientele that returns for more of what you have to offer?

We have cultivated a very loyal client base. Not only retail shoppers but an ever-expanding wholesale market that is showing great promise.

How have you set up your business? Are you on the premises of your store all the time, or do you delegate?

You have to delegate as much as possible, but you have to check all the work that you delegate. I am almost never at the store. I drop in from time to time. I do, however, hang out a lot more during the holiday season. It's a great way to see customers who have been showing up for years and getting to know new clients who really enjoy meeting the artist.

Do you ever see a point at which you would grow and expand your retail business? If so, how?

Expanding the retail business is not the top of the list now. Expanding our wholesale is the main thrust of our long-term plan. Made On Earth International has a very nice ring to it.

If you had to do this all over again, what would you do differently?

Doing it over again? Our naiveté got us into this. Finding out how hard it is to make this a truly successful business almost got us out of it. This answer may take a bit more thought.

There are two standouts in this question. One is just lessons learned about display and merchandising in the store.

Two is harder. It has to do with financial backing. Do we or don't we seek a money partner? If you asked me two years ago, I would have said "yes" immediately. Now that the store is paying for itself, I'm not so sure. We would grow faster with more money, but we would give up a percentage of control. Artists who start business endeavors are the target of people looking to take advantage. We have had a number of these types approach us over the past five years. We've become a bit gun-shy. I guess if the right situation arose, we would be interested in a partner, but part of the joy of ownership is the autonomy. In another year or two, I may feel different.

GL084 / TEMPLATE / MENS SIZING
☐ WHT

GL085 / TAPE / ZIP HOOD - M/W SIZING
■ BLK ■ NAVY ■ RED ■ HEA

GL087 / BIRD / WOMENS SIZING
■ MAG ■ NAVY ■ TEAL ■ LT BLUE

GL088 / TEMPLATE POSTER /
18x24"
OFFSET LITHOGRAPH

GL086 / TAPE / MENS SIZING
■ BLK ■ NAVY ■ CHAR ■ OLV ■ BRN ■ RED

GL090 / SNAKE / 16" COTTON PILLOW
■ BLK ■ OLV ■ LT BLUE

CLOTHES FOR THE STREET

with Gary BENZEL and Todd ST. JOHN,
Principals of Green Lady

Part streetwear company, part ongoing obsession, Green Lady has grown steadily since designers GARY BENZEL and TODD ST. JOHN produced their first line in 1995. What began as a side project of making clothing for friends now sells in Japan, the United States, and Europe. Green Lady's graphics explore relationships between humans and technology, consumers and corporations, individuals and the group, often with sardonic treatments and deceptively simple designs. Both St. John and Benzel operate their own design practices as well. St. John runs a studio in Brooklyn, New York, and Benzel operates his office in San Diego, California, and also oversees production of the Green Lady line. They are launching a second product line and opening a store in California that will carry theirs as well as a small range of other brands.

Green Lady exists primarily as a graphics-driven series of printed shirts, posters, and accessories. How and why did you enter the clothes business?

We grew up involved with skateboard/punk music culture and having some interest in streetwear brands and graphics, which came out of those scenes. After studying design and working in the design field, we wanted to create a project independent from clients and also fill a gap of streetwear companies by producing a line not directly tied to a particular sports category (e.g., skate clothing, surf clothing, etc.). This posed an opportunity to create a line with the emphasis on the graphics as the product, as opposed to the graphics promoting or selling another product.

As a graphic designer, how much of your skill, expertise, and talent is applied to your streetwear business?

The yearly exercise of creating the graphics for the line offers the opportunity to do more experimental work than client-related work sometimes allows initially. Many times, the design work in the line turns out to be our strongest work for that year.

Do you design the actual clothing?

Yes, we have designed and developed all of the graphics in the brand and the limited amount of cut-and-sew produced to date.

Had you designed clothing before this?

We really started working on developing small lines and runs of shirts for friends in high school and continued through college.

Who is your audience, and are you successful within that customer base?

It is mainly a sophisticated streetwear youth-market buyer, looking for alternatives to name brands, ranging in age from eighteen to thirty-five. Eighty percent of our product sells in Japan, so it operates on a different level there than domestically. In the United States, the line is sold only in select boutique-style stores which promote graphic-forward labels. In the United States, the line is successful in its placement, while the Japanese market does grant more success in terms of quantities. The Japanese have a greater awareness and demand for lines like Green Lady.

What did you have to learn about fashion that you never needed in the graphic design business?

Financing in general is much different for the garment industry than the business of graphic design. One of the most difficult aspects is in logistics for production of large quantities of merchandise while fulfilling orders. There is a lot of planning ahead to ensure on-time delivery prior to an order's cancel date.

You have a design studio. Are you able to efficiently juggle the two businesses, both in terms of business and creativity?

The two ventures seem to feed off one another. Green Lady graphics generate interest from clients and agencies and thereby sort of operate as an underground PR tool. But working on both projects definitely impacts free time and having a life outside of both ventures.

Do you see giving up graphic design for this entrepreneurial endeavor?

Design is very integrated in the Green Lady process, so it is unlikely that anyone would have to completely forfeit design to continue doing it. However, managing all the aspects of the line and its production definitely impacts the amount of time one spends doing design versus other things related the project.

Has this taught you any lessons for making your graphic design practice more entrepreneurial?

Perhaps in understanding the impact of relationships with customers the most. And knowing how to negotiate your role and positioning within a specific market.

Into what areas will Green Lady grow in the future?

We are working on a second line, which will be launching this year. Also, hopefully, Green Lady will grow to incorporate and be a vehicle for the work of younger up-and-coming designers who can help Green Lady and be helped by Green Lady.

GL075 / INTERFACE / MENS SIZING
NAVY BRN KEL GRN RED

GL076 / SNAKE / MENS SIZING
BLK CARD RED OLV TEAL

GL077 / SNAKE / WOMENS SIZING
RED CARD BLK TEAL LT BLUE

GL078 / GRID / MENS SIZING
WHT

GL079 / XACTO / MENS SIZING
OLV RED GOLD TEAL LT BLUE WHT

GL080 / PLANE / MENS SIZING
CHAR TEAL LT BLUE RED

GL081 / LOVERS / WOMENS SIZING
MAG RL BLUE KL GRN WHT

GL082 / LOVERS / MENS SIZING
RED HEA WHT

GL083 / PUNCHCARD / MENS SIZING
BLK NAVY OLV WHT

FROM A LONG LINE OF MERCHANTS

with Sandy CHILEWICH,
Founder of Chilewich

SANDY CHILEWICH founded HUE Legwear with Kathy Moskal, and the partners revolutionized a tired hosiery industry with innovations in technology and merchandising. By the time they sold the company in 1992, it was earning $40 million in annual sales. Later, she founded Chilewich, a Manhattan-based design studio which produced RayBowls, her first product for home and industry, leading to RayBoxes and RayTrays. Recently, she started the HarryCarrys line of handbags and continues to experiment with materials for tabletop, handbags, rugs, and placements.

You began as an artist. What was your métier, and how did it lead into your entrepreneurial venture?

My life as an artist was very short lived. I moved very quickly from making sculptural pieces and collages, involving a wide variety of materials, to the more commercial enterprise of designing jewelry. It was an intuitive process . . . I come from a long line of merchants . . . maybe it was in my blood. There is something about making products that are functional . . . that people choose to buy and live with, that pulled me away from art. I never felt I had something that important to say as an artist. It was really very much about the aesthetic for me, and I thought my work was too decorative and not intellectual enough to be called "art."

How did HUE legwear develop? Was it a sideline that became a business?

While I was designing and selling jewelry, I met my neighbor Kathy Moskal, an art teacher. This is in the late seventies. A little tipsy on wine, we began looking in her closet and wondered why the cotton Chinese shoes, that "all of us artists" were wearing, only came in black. That night, we bleached out the black and dyed them in fuchsia. That weekend, we bought lots of shoes in Chinatown, dyed them in lots of colors. Friends and family loved them. I brought them up to *Vogue*, and they featured them in a two-page spread . . . "shoes by Kathy and Sandy." HUE Shoes was born . . . We imported 20,000 of them from China . . . and in my loft we set up a bleaching-and-dyeing operation. Retailers and editors wanted to know what else we did, and so we introduced other kinds of accessories that we brought to market in a wide range of colors. We offered cotton stockings in fifteen colors, and they were a big hit. After going down south . . . falling in love with the knitting machinery and seeing such a dearth in the marketplace for innovative legwear . . . we slowly eliminated everything else, and we became a legwear company. Our sales volume was just under $40 million when we sold the business in 1992.

You base your designs on a fluency of different materials. How did this knowledge accrue?

I really have no academic knowledge of textiles . . . I think I just process what I see in a personal and unique way. When I look at objects, textures, and patterns, whether they be from nature or handmade, old or new, I am always imagining it in a different way, a new application or interpretation. I am always very interested in joining different materials together.

Tell me about RayBowls. Was this a sculptural expression turned functional product, or were you focused on creating intriguing design for mass consumption?

After I sold HUE . . . I stayed on as president for a couple of years. In 1994, I left and began thinking of what I wanted to do. I had a number of ideas that I decided to take to a prototypical state and then stand back and see what had the most potential, both from a personal fulfillment point of view and what had the most commercial potential.

One of the ideas was inspired by the shape of the butterfly chair. I imagined it as a container . . . with removable covers . . . so you could change the cover of your bowl to suit your function or mood. I had lots of help making my initial prototypes, and my gravitation towards stretch fabrics (probably from hosiery) really led me to the invention of making fabric concave in this manner. I have received numerous utility patents on this very simple idea. I would say it was a sculptural expression that didn't "turn into," but that I made into, a saleable product/concept.

As an artist, what kind personal changes did you go through to become a designer/businessperson?

I have absolutely no conflict . . . There is no turmoil for me about not being an artist and instead being a designer/businessperson. I adore what I do, and I am enormously proud of my accomplishments.

Do you develop, produce, and market for a specific audience, or is your work to be accepted as is by whomever?

At first, in the design process, it is all about the integrity of the design, but very shortly into it, I am thinking . . . Will this sell? I am interested, not in "mass," exactly, but being accessibly priced to a large audience, and I gravitate towards materials that lend themselves to that price point. I, myself, am a consumer of some exquisite and pricey objects, but this is not what drives me in my designing.

What is your "invention frequency"? At what pace do you strive to create a new product line?

I am "inventing" continually . . . and have ideas every day. I am passionate and driven, and I am gluing, stapling, cutting, and tearing all the time. It takes a tremendous amount of effort, capital, and discipline to bring something to market and sustain it successfully, however. Many ideas stay on the "back burner." Creating something that hasn't been done before, figuring out how to produce it at a target price, etc., can be exhausting. I am currently in the throes of figuring out how to make my vinyl floor covering technically viable for commercial applications, and it is like giving birth.

As the creator of aesthetically pleasing utilitarian products, what are your standards? What is quintessentially good design?

Criteria for "good design" . . . such a hard question. I am so unintellectual about this. Things can be good or bad for so many reasons. It depends so much on intent. I might think something is great because it is inspirational, but it might be a failure because it was intended to be comfortable and it is not.

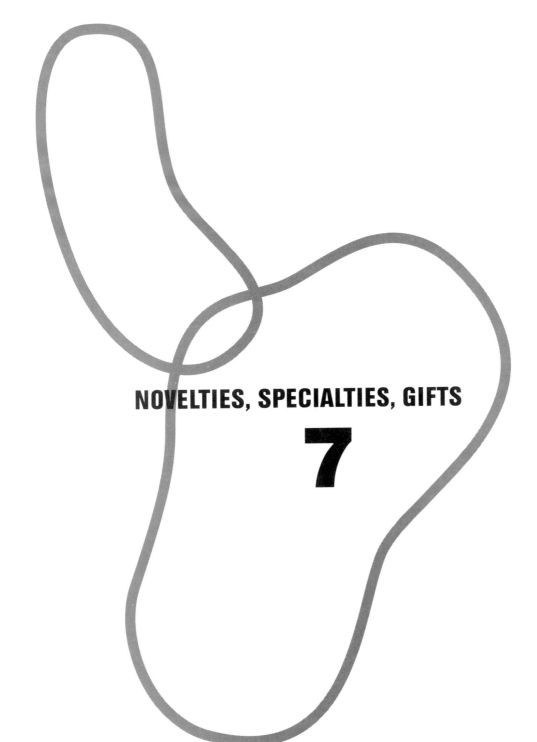

NOVELTIES, SPECIALTIES, GIFTS

7

CANDY MAN

with Seymour CHWAST,
Cofounder of Push Pin Studios

SEYMOUR CHWAST is the cofounder and director of Push Pin Studios, the groundbreaking graphic design firm. As a designer and illustrator, he has authored over thirty children's books and a score of others. His unique graphic style has been applied to publications, packaging, posters, advertising, and corporate communications. He is a member of the Art Director's Hall of Fame, and his work is included in the permanent collections of the Museum of Modern Art and the Louvre. In the late 1970s and 1980s, he produced the Pushpinoff line of specialty candies.

Do you consider yourself a design entrepreneur?

Generating work, when the phone didn't ring, fit with my thirties depression mentality. The answer is yes, but I had no choice.

Describe how the Pushpinoff line of products came about.

Pushpinoff came about as an extension of an idea we had for a Christmas gift, called *Pushpinoff Caviar on Ice*, a glass soufflé dish filled with rock candy and topped with a three-inch layer of black "caviar" mints. This was the idea of Phyllis Flood (now Phyllis Feder), who handled Push Pin's business at the time. Roger Horchow (The Horchow Collection) ordered the item for his catalogue. It was a big success, although the fragility of the glass container made it expensive to pack and ship. So, Phyllis came up with the idea to package it in tins, they way "real" caviar is sold. This allowed for a lower price point, which translated into a terrific increase in volume.

From this point the line developed into a total of eighteen items, all of which were in decorative tins, except for the Pushpinoff Ultimate Chocolate Bar—at the time, the "world's largest chocolate bar." It was five pounds of chocolate with an exquisite Rolls Royce–illustrated label, which I designed.

Was Pushpinoff a lark or a truly serious attempt to make a profit?

The Pushpinoff business was a lark in that it was fun, but a business in that it was the goal to create an income stream so that the design studio could take on projects, not so much for money as for love.

Pushpinoff began in the 1970s, before the torrent of specialty and boutique foods and confections began. What kind of success or failure did you have being ahead of the curve?

Being ahead of the curve was not a new position for Push Pin. It was what we expected of ourselves, and it was gratifying for us when companies doing terrific packaging, like Crabtree & Evelyn, sent us notes of congratulations (and bought our candies). The negative aspect of this was that as a start-up, we had terrific acceptance in the marketplace, but not sufficient capitalization to have sufficient funds available to both develop product and show a profit. We added to our line as funds allowed, but the real problem was not having a sufficient margin to hire distributors or a sales force. Ultimately, collections on accounts and manufacturing issues became too difficult for our "team" of two to continue.

What did you learn about this business that you did not already know?

We learned that without vast distribution and corresponding sales, the unit costs were too high. Therefore, the retail prices for the stuff was high, even for these discretionary products.

Producing food, even candy, requires certain safeguards for yourself and the customer. What did you have to do that you never expected to do?

The Feds make the rules, and we followed them. The safeguard for me was avoiding nausea from the aroma when entering a chocolate factory.

Why did you stop producing Pushpinoff products?

Without a manufacturer for a partner, our price points did not allow us to have the customary three-tier relationships of wholesaler/distributor/retailer. Maybe if we had been Pushpinoff Sweets.com, we'd have been able to go public!

What other entrepreneurial ventures have you attempted over the years? How did these turn out?

We produced a half dozen designs for shower curtains. They were sold in Bloomingdale's. Before we were Push Pin, Milton Glaser, Reynold Ruffins, and I produced a gross (funny, I remember the number) of place mats. It was Reynold's art that we showed to Wanamaker's, a now-defunct New York department store. They gave us an order, and we filled our loft studio with drying, silk-screened cork mats. That was the only order. I consider the packaged children's books as entrepreneurial. We sell manufactured books to publishers, while owning the art.

Do you think a designer needs a special talent or acumen to engage in a product-based business? And what are the differences between running a design firm and this other entrepreneurial pursuit?

Designers market their talents to corporations and the media. To be entrepreneurial, they have to have great ideas and be motivated by desire or need to engage in a totally different business activity. Talent and commitment and good business practices are important. Timing is critical. They would have to consider those things—the market, for instance—that they usually leave up to their clients. When successful, it is immensely satisfying. "We made something!"

If you had to do it all over again, how would you design your business?

It's too hard and personal to contemplate. All in all, I consider myself lucky to have been able to do good stuff while working with good friends.

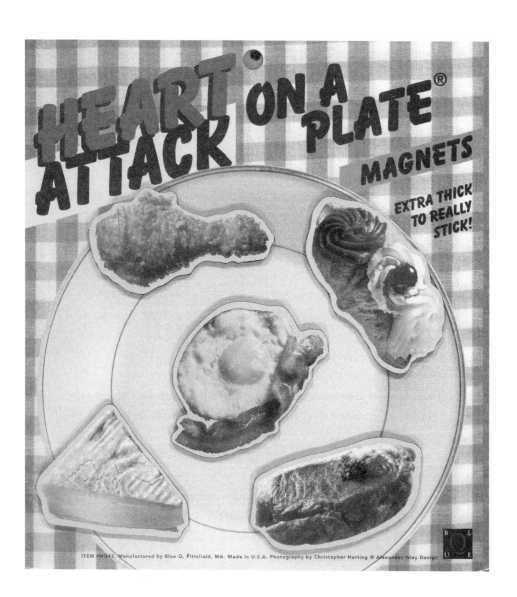

HEART ATTACK ON A PLATE® MAGNETS

EXTRA THICK TO REALLY STICK!

ITEM #MG42, Manufactured by Blue Q, Pittsfield, MA. Made in U.S.A. Photography by Christopher Harting © Alexander Isley Design

ANIMAL MAGNETISM

with Alexander ISLEY,
Principal of Isley Design

ALEXANDER ISLEY, principal of Alexander Isley Inc., was a senior designer at Tibor Kalman's M&Co. and served as the first art director of *Spy* magazine, for which he was awarded gold and silver medals from the Society of Publication Designers. He has been an adjunct professor at The Cooper Union and at the School of Visual Arts in New York City, teaching courses in design and typography, and was elected to the executive committee of the New York Chapter of the American Institute of Graphic Arts. He is presently a visiting critic at the Yale University Graduate School of Art.

What influenced you to start a side business designing "novelty" magnets?

We were originally approached by a company, Blue Q, to create a line of greeting cards. Michael Mabry had recommended us to them. Blue Q is run by two entrepreneurial bothers, Mitch and Seth Nash, out of an old factory in Pittsfield, Massachusetts. Some years before, they had created the "flat cat," which is an easel-backed cardboard cat for those who live in "no-pets" apartments. It sold like crazy, and they followed up with a dog and a baby. They also created stationery sets, note cards, and a lot of other things. They appreciate good design and have a good eye. I was impressed with what they'd done.

Anyway, they thought we might do a nice job with greeting cards, but I looked around and saw how many people were doing these. I wanted to do something a bit different, something that could be a gift item. Between us, we came up with the idea of doing magnets, and not just individual magnets but assortments of five or six shrink-wrapped onto slip sheets. The idea was to have something with a $10 to $12 price point that could be a good gift item with an unusual theme. They would be created, to use Mitch's phrase, "guerilla-style," with us putting the artwork together rather quickly. The slip sheet would sell the idea, and the magnets would be a mix of fun, elegant, quirky, etc., to sell in a variety of stores. Blue Q would handle the manufacture, sales, and distribution. We would receive a royalty on sales. This suited me fine, as I have no interest in going to trade shows and having to sell things, or dealing with fulfillment or returns.

How many did you create?

Originally, we did twenty or so sets. They were a big hit, and we soon found ourselves continually having to make more sets, as retailers always want new product, even if the old ones are selling. This was the biggest surprise to me; I thought we'd be able to do a few sets and then sit back and watch the checks come in. After a while, the magnets started to take over our office, and we'd have four or five people working on them at once. We also found that we were spending more and more time on creating the artwork. If you look at some of the early ones, they were really rough-and-tumble. The biggest seller of all was and continues to be the "White Trash" magnets, which to my eye is pretty horribly put together. It just goes to show that for these items, the idea is more important than the execution.

What was your investment? Did you put in money and time, or just time and imagination?

We put some cash into them, but mostly a great deal of time and labor cost. We took a lot of the photos and illustrations, but on occasion, we'd commission photography.

You worked for Tibor Kalman at M&Co. Did you get the idea of doing quirky products from his M&Co. Labs?

When I was at M&Co., I was involved in a lot of the products, working with Tibor on the design of their first set of several watches. I also created a ruler with a case that they sold and created the architectural blueprint paperweight (the building on that was designed by my father; it's the press box at Duke University's football stadium). Doing products is something I always wanted to do, and from working at M&Co. I took the notion that an efficient way of creating products is to work on something where you can incorporate a graphic element within an existing structure. By putting graphics on a stock watch, ruler, or sheet of plastic, you can create a custom design. This is different from industrial design in that you aren't making molds, tooling, etc.

What was the result? How many did you do?

We eventually did between sixty and eighty magnet sets. I've honestly lost count. Some (usually the ones with campy themes) did well. Others, like my favorite, "The Worst Vice Presidents," tanked. (Did you know that Andrew Johnson was drunk at his inauguration? That Elbridge Gerry refused to sign the U.S. Constitution?) We did some pretty ones (flowers, bugs, fruits) and some that had art themes. We also experimented with selling the same magnets, but using different slip sheets to change the theme. A set of Old Master nudes was also sold as "Naked Chicks in Art." Different stores bought different sets.

And how did they do for you?

Overall, it was worthwhile. It was fun to see the magnets sold around the country. I saw them in a store in Australia, and they were sold in Japan as well. They made more money for us than we would have charged to design them on a per-project basis, so in that respect it was a successful enterprise as well. We still get our quarterly royalty checks, two years after doing our last set, although the payments have diminished sharply. The most fun part about it is seeing the quarterly sales reports, just to get an immediate response to what's selling. It's the kind of factual, tangible result that I don't usually see from our typical graphic design projects.

How did you conceive them? Was it your private cottage industry, or did you shanghai studio members to come up with ideas?

Originally, most of the ideas came from me. I would brainstorm lists of ideas, pass them to the guys at Blue Q, and they'd come back with some more. We'd pick our favorites and go from there. I still have files with hundreds of ideas. Maybe I'll get a second wind and do some more.

From a distribution standpoint, did you have any say in how these were marketed? Did you devote yourself to their production and marketing?

I did not have much involvement. We did some trade show items for Blue Q, but mostly, the guys from Blue Q handled that aspect of the business. I think they did a terrific job.

Why did you stop producing the magnets? You weren't stuck on them any more?

After a while, I found it was taking over our studio. I didn't want to be a magnet magnate (sorry). Also, we found that there was a big market for licensed magnets—Babar, Felix the Cat, Pez dispensers, etc. While this was a lucrative market for Blue Q, I was not as interested in doing those; I had more desire to work on our own ideas.

Do you want to continue producing independent, entrepreneurial products?

I definitely want to do some more; we have prototype designs created for a range of other products and are exploring manufacturing options. Most of these require custom tooling, however, so there is an investment required. Unfortunately, my paying clients come first.

Has this activity changed your relationship to your primary work as a designer who runs a studio?

Not much. It started off as a hobby and has served as a fun diversion. I am still shocked at how popular refrigerator magnets are. Who knew?

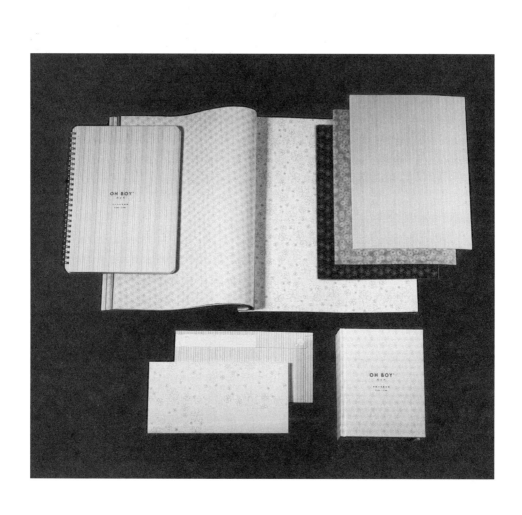

THE ROLE OF TASTEMAKER

with David SALANITRO, Principal
of Oh Boy, A Design Company

DAVID SALANITRO is the principal and creative director of Oh Boy, A Design Company. His experience lies in the fields of fine art exhibition, architecture, and theatrical and graphic design. Within two years, Salanitro grew Oh Boy from a two-person shop to a ten-person studio with a client base that includes Andersen Consulting, Cadence Design Systems, Charles Schwab & Company, Gap Inc., and Mohawk Fine Papers. In addition to design, Salaniro has appeared on stage, to the delight of audiences, as Pish Tush in Gilbert and Sullivan's *The Mikado*, as Richie in *Bleacher Bums*, and in the title role in *Fiddler on the Roof*. Additional stage credits include *Annie, Funny Girl, The Sound of Music,* and Sandy Wilson's *The Boyfriend*.

Do you define Oh Boy as an entrepreneurial firm?

Sure, in two ways.

One, in that I personally assume the primary risk for the business.

Two, we're conducting business from a unique perspective: mine. We're trying not to be slaves to committees, rigid corporate hierarchies, or exhaustive and overanalyzed market research. Certainly, for many businesses, there is an advantage to being market-driven. But there is something truly entrepreneurial in bringing your personal philosophies to the market and seeing the market adopt them. Maybe more so than financial reward, here's the true perk to entrepreneurship: All of us who were told that we didn't conform as we were growing up, that our ideas were odd and that was bad, have the opportunity to prove our detractors wrong.

What motivated you to integrate design and product creation and development?

I've long been troubled by the lack of respect for design in culture. Certainly, I am heartened to see design gain more respect recently, especially in the press. Still, we have a long way to go with the general populace. Where designers were once regarded as tastemakers, as people to be admired for their talent, innovation, and studied eye, we now often find ourselves in situations where we are designing not out of necessity or for beauty, but rather to package commodities for the same corporations that make our movies, form our bands, and devise and print sentiments on greeting cards. In fact, those most in need of design help have instead become de facto arbiters of taste.

I was looking for an outlet that would allow Oh Boy to move more actively into the role of tastemaker. I want to evolve the studio to a place where we take on clients that we can help—and who want to be helped—and at the same time, find ways to create things that inspire each of us individually. The artifacts idea is that each line is made up of projects devised by designers for people who appreciate good design. We're not pandering to a lowest common denominator here. Oh Boy's designers bring to the table projects that interest them, and the entire studio collaborates. We're offering designers an outlet free from corporate constraints. At the same time, we're enabling them to explore new, influential ideas that, if we have our way, will change the way people think about design.

What was your first product, and how did it develop?

Necessity is the mother of invention. Designers keep sketchbooks. We couldn't find any notebooks that we liked, so we made our own. We paid special attention to the details, choosing paper that was suited to our needs (thicker and with a nice tooth), employing a spiral binding so the book would lie flat or fold back on itself, rounding the corners so they would not curl or be so easily damaged and laminating the cover for durability. We produced about three thousand books and quickly realized that we had more than we could ever use internally, so we began to give them away to prospects and clients as gifts. Everyone loved them. It was heartening because the aesthetic was simple—people were responding to the practical aspects of the design.

Now, we're working to take that practical aspect further and to be more ingenious. Our gift-wrap book is a great example: forty-eight sheets of two-sided gift wrap that can be stored in limited space, easily accessed, and not so easily damaged. Or, how about the idea of gift wrap as a gift?

Sounds sound to me.

Still, the paper products we've designed so far are really just the tip of the iceberg. Oh Boy, Artifacts are essentially comprised of products in two categories: disposables and covetables. We're looking at other utilitarian objects, everyday disposable objects that might be made of paper, our credo being that utility or temporary needn't be ugly or half-assed. We're also moving forward to create artifacts that are meant to be kept: chronicles of designed objects, trends, even prose—these will comprise the covetable side of the line.

What role does design play in the conception of your work? By this I mean, is it focal or incidental? And by this I mean, do you build off a design idea, or is design applied to a larger idea?

Well, I'm still not sure what you mean exactly. But how about this:

Design is everything.

No detail goes unaccounted for. Everything is considered.

The entire "experience" of the line is designed to merge art and utility, to raise awareness about the difference between poorly designed objects and well-designed objects. Consider the lost art of gift giving. People have forgotten that half (or more) of the fun of and much of the good will generated by gift giving is in the presentation. So often, I receive gifts handed to me in a shopping bag accompanied by the bearer's apologies for not having time to wrap it properly. Or, perhaps worse, I receive gifts emblazoned with a store's logo. People have become less in tune to the art of gift giving, to its personal nature. Now, we've taken the phrase, "it's the thought that counts," and turned gift giving into an apologetic anticlimax. I believe that this is due in large part to gift-wrap products that inspire nothing. Our products let people dress a gift with the same pride they might take in dressing themselves. We have six patterns and six solid colors applied to gift wrap, gift cards, tissue, sealing tape, and ribbon. You can match, clash, layer. It's fun. And it's less of a chore. You can wrap a gift and be proud of the outcome. This is not by accident. This is planned. This is designed.

What is your most successful product? And why do you think it works as well as it does?

The gift cards are our best seller (but it's all a very close race). Again, the ingenuity of thirty-six cards being bound into a book so attractive that you might keep it *on* your desk instead of *in* your desk really appeals to people.

As a designer, how did you develop the mindset for business? And do you feel that your strengths lie in both areas?

I have always been hyper-organized. I would spend hours organizing closets as a very small child. I had paper files at nine years of age. Prior to Oh Boy, I worked as an architect. Here, I saw my own organizational abilities reflected back to me tenfold. Architects are very persnickety people. Out of this intense attention to detail comes amazing discipline, and out of discipline comes some extraordinary work. A consideration for details and discipline, plus some decent problem-solving abilities, are really all business is about. If you have these traits, there is little you can't learn by asking the right questions or picking up a book.

After leaving architecture, I worked briefly for *Publish* magazine, whose designers

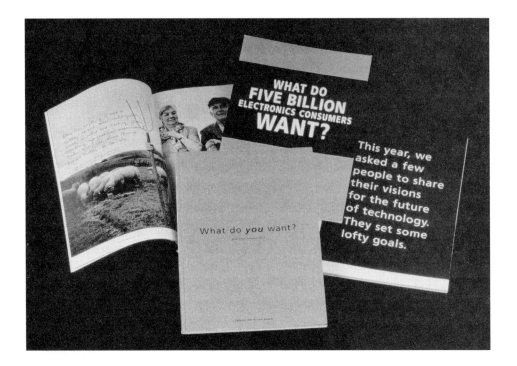

were embarrassingly disorganized and made me seriously question why anybody would want to be saddled with the moniker "Graphic Designer." I wanted desperately to bring business acumen to design. Not just to the business of design, but to design itself.

So, yes, my talents do lie very strongly in both areas.

How much of your work is self- (or company-) motivated versus client-based?

Most studios are 100 percent client-dependent. We're working to get away from that.

Not that there's anything wrong with clients. I don't think I'm ever going to want to move entirely away from client work. Problem-solving is an integral part of what keeps me vital. And I only have a limited number of problems to solve for myself.

Still, Oh Boy, Artifacts allows us to make the stuff that we want to make entirely as we envision it. And so far, people want to buy the stuff we make. As long as that continues, I imagine we'll divide our revenues equally between client-based work and product development.

How do you develop your ideas? What determines what will be put in the marketplace?

It's all about what we would want to buy. Again, it's the tastemaker thing. When I recognize potential in the market—an opportunity for product development that appeals to me—I act on it. I'm lucky to be the sort of person who trusts his instincts. And it doesn't hurt that I have a high threshold for risk.

We're not at all into utilizing focus groups or anything like that to develop product. I'm not sure why so many place so much emphasis on them [focus groups]. They are an entirely manufactured environment. They're not at all reflective of the way people shop. In cases where consumers might naturally respond very positively to something within the retail environment, within the controlled environment of the focus group, their response would be entirely different. They would feel compelled to offer some bit of "constructive criticism." In my opinion, It's uniquely American that we communicate through criticism.

What have you learned from Oh Boy that is unique to the experience of running this company?

Perhaps a little humility. Some might say not much, but really, I have. Being in a business where you are constantly critiqued, it's inevitable that your ego will take a few blows. I've learned not to simply disregard criticism, and not to take it all to heart either, but simply to put my ego aside for a moment and listen. Often, the most helpful criticism is found in the subtext anyway.

You obviously have an ambitious promotional component. How else do you expect to grow your company in the future?

Word-of-mouth generation. Many companies have mistaken impressions of the power of print. They rely on print to inform and other media to inspire. I believe all media should do both. A brochure, for instance, that lives on a desk as opposed to in a desk will be seen by a greater audience, and a brochure that is passed on will be seen by even more. A brochure that inspires people to talk will have a reach well beyond its physical lifespan. With the Artifacts line, and with the agency, we're in the business of creating a virus, a buzz. Talk is the best promotional component you can generate.

What have you not done that you would like to do with Oh Boy? What is on the horizon?

We've opened an office in New York. Next, perhaps, we'll try Europe. I don't want to become a very large company, but I do want to have a vast presence. Maybe more than money, I'm seduced by the component of fame.

I'm also very interested in writing more. The covetables side of Artifacts is going to afford me that opportunity.

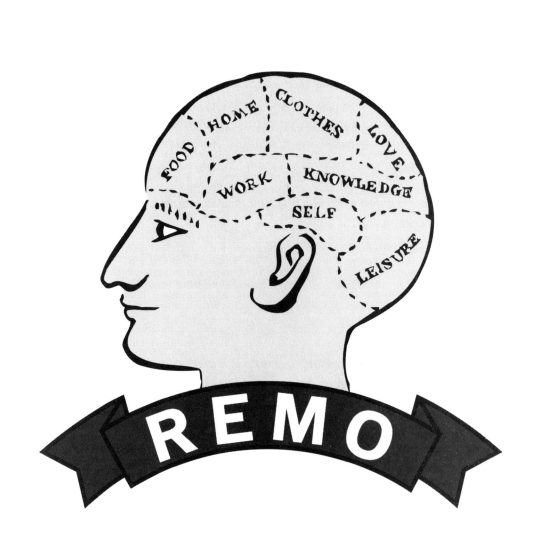

MAKING LOTS OF PEOPLE HAPPY

with Remo GIUFFRÉ, Cofounder
of General Thinking, Inc.

REMO GUIFFRÉ is cofounder, chairman, and CEO of General Thinking, which is the sponsor of an ongoing initiative to gather online a global Network of Thinkers, something akin to a "guild" of high-quality and like-minded people—drivers of excellence. General Thinking was initially conceived as a fresh demonstration of a unique and empirically developed Network Branding & Communications Model that has been a central focus and obsession for many years. He has been responsible since the launch of the General Thinking Network for envisioning the experience, architecting the information, planning the interactive development, and driving the overall business vision.

How has design played a role in your business life?

Design has played a big role in my business life. As an attorney in Sydney [Australia], I was best known for founding, designing, and editing the firm's internal weekly newsletter. In those days my passions (design, communications, and people) were at cross-purposes to my "career path" (corporations and business). Then, years later, I stumbled upon the idea for the REMO General Store. For the first time, my passions were in alignment with what I did for a living. I was now, more or less, where I wanted to be . . . deep in the Business of Design. That could be why REMO developed so much momentum so quickly. Within a year of our opening in Sydney, we were being lauded within retail and design circles all over the world. In one 1991 article Tibor Kalman (whose brand we represented in Australia) even went so far as to call REMO "the best store in the world. By far."

Descriptions of you have included "design guru" and "style merchant." What do these signify?

These labels tend to imply that I was the source from whom all the light radiated. This was not the case. My role was/is/will be that of the editorial director and orchestral conductor. Initially, it was my vision and intuition that played the dominant role. However, this was quickly complemented and bolstered by the network of people (customers, designers, etc.) who clustered around THE IDEA = SPQR: Senatus Populesque REMO?

The REMO General Store is a designed entity. Can you define your standard of or requirement for what makes good, successful, and popular design?

These words from one of our catalogs, written in reference to product design, apply equally at the more holistic and enterprise level: "The development emphasis is on simple, smart, enduring, value-for-money products. Forgotten quality. Not luxuries. Useful and intelligent things. Authentic items from the real world. The flavor of the brand is the result of an intuitive and iterative 'recipe'—a unique and delicate combination of ingredients: function, passion, classicism, intelligence, serendipity, and wit."

To answer the question another way . . . I feel now that REMO was/is a *process* brand more than it was a product or even an experience brand. The process invited/utilized/celebrated the involvement of the customer community in the process of the development of the merchandise for themselves. I actually think that, properly led, this might be the absolute best way to ensure "good, successful, and popular design."

You have worked in the area of branding for some time. How did you become a branding expert?

For reasons of necessity. To move to the United States required a visa sponsor, which meant needing a job. Being a merchant and an entrepreneur for ten years (even if you are being widely described as the best there is) doesn't necessarily qualify you for anything else! So, I had to figure out ex post facto the theory underlying the success of the REMO General Store.

I am not a theorist by nature, but in order to become marketable to others, I had to take ten years of visceral/intuitive experience and turn it into notions and thinking that would travel and scale to the benefit of much larger businesses and brands. This is what ultimately led to what I feel are the breakthrough branding ideas manifest in what we've referred to as the "Network Branding & Communications Model."

What does the title Director of Strategic Development mean?

That was just a fancy title for someone whose job it was to evaluate various new business opportunities and make recommendations to the CEO.

How did your various experiences in retail and brand management, and with such a variety of media businesses, as well as your work as an "associate attorney" for the large law firm Baker & McKenzie, prepare you for an entrepreneurial life?

I guess everything contributes to the preparation. The interesting thing for me is how little the graduate degrees prepared me for the sheer terror and messiness of new venture

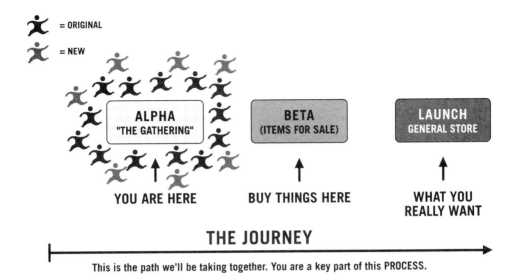

= ORIGINAL

= NEW

ALPHA
"THE GATHERING"

BETA
(ITEMS FOR SALE)

LAUNCH
GENERAL STORE

YOU ARE HERE

BUY THINGS HERE

WHAT YOU
REALLY WANT

THE JOURNEY

This is the path we'll be taking together. You are a key part of this PROCESS.

development and management. Going into Chapter 11 with REMO (and the ensuing three year of turmoil and torture) taught me more lessons than anything else and has made me a much better entrepreneur.

Why did REMO General Store go into bankruptcy?

The business was inappropriately and inadequately capitalized. We grew too fast (50 percent compounded per annum), ran out of cash, and got into structural trouble. Then, we couldn't find anyone with both the desire *and* resources to help us through. Access to capital and smart money is difficult in Australia at the best of times. Also, at that time in Australia, it was very hard to find the depth of senior management talent required to execute and administer the back end. Although a good leader and demand generator, I personally fell short as an operator and controller. Too much yin, not enough yang. Hard lessons got learnt. All in all, and with what I know now, I think that the original version of twentieth-century REMO was somewhat naive and flawed from the outset. Bottom line is, raise enough money to meet anticipated demand. Don't take follow-on funding for granted. Don't assume that hitting the milestones will be enough. Capital markets are not always rational.

How would you define an entrepreneur?

Someone who seeks to create something where there was nothing. Someone whose vision is clear and readily communicable to others.

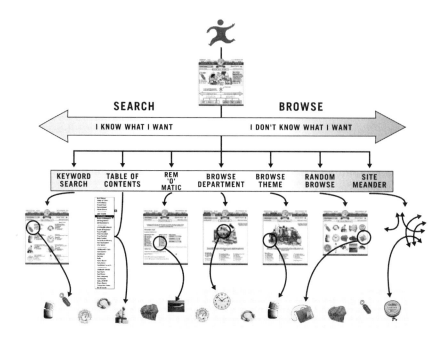

How has the Internet changed or concretized your attitudes about business?

REMO was an online brand even before there was an online. Communications technology (and specifically the Internet) solves a couple of major and long-standing issues that I was perpetually obsessed about with REMO, namely: (1) how to scale globally; and (2) how to more elegantly involve the customer community in the expression and development of the brand.

For a communicating guy such as myself, the Internet is a dream come true. Therefore, the Internet has dramatically changed not so much my attitudes re: business . . . but my expectations re: the scalability of my/our vision.

Why did you cofound the Web site General Thinking and what is the goal of this site?

REMO is a great idea that will someday make lots of people very happy and some people very wealthy. Even so, the capital markets are super-unfriendly to anything that even smells like retail. Therefore, the relaunch is on hold until things turn around or someone smart enough comes along to see that our community-driven business model is actually the elegant solution that people are seeking. Meanwhile, what do I do? Where do I focus my energies? How do I support my family? Spend another five years scratching around for lone-wolf consulting gigs as I pitch for money?

The idea for General Thinking came along as a parallel way to demonstrate our REMO-developed Network Model without the need for large amounts of inventory and working capital. Like REMO, General Thinking is a very tribal idea . . . except that this tribe will be very much smaller. (The universe of people who can generate certain qualities is a tiny fraction of the number who have the capacity to appreciate those qualities.)

And lately, I see General Thinking as much more than another way to skin the REMO cat. In fact, I feel very excited about the potential for General Thinking to become a global cultural phenomenon and a force of good. Like REMO, it's a very intuitive and simple idea that, for whatever reason, others have missed.

Do you see this venture as potentially a viable business model for future endeavors?

Yes, very much so. See my thought starters in the Thinker Forum under these subject headings: General Thinking Development and General Thinking Business Model (FYI).

Think TED Conferences . . . but bigger, better, and perpetual.

Think media brand—e.g., General Thinking Magazine.

Everything boils down to the quality of the network and the management of the network brand. (For these tasks I am qualified.) If we get that right, all else will follow.

What role does design play in the General Thinking philosophy?

As you can see . . . there's a modernist sensibility at play here. Functionality is paramount. Also (and this links back to my REMO biases), good design is as much about knowing what to leave out as it is knowing what to put in. To Decide Not to Design is to Design (with apologies to Sartre).

Do you have as yet unrealized plans?

They are all 90 percent unrealized. Most of the good stuff lies ahead. The endeavors are perpetual.

HOUSE OF CARDS

with Margaret and John MARTINEZ,
Founders of J&M Martinez

MARGARET MARTINEZ is a graphic designer and brand development specialist. She began her career as an art director in advertising and publications; however, much of her work has focused on branding and product positioning for many different markets. In addition to books and periodicals, she has worked on projects in the food and drug industry, film and television, and retail merchandising. As the president and co-owner of J&M Martinez, Limited, she is responsible for the company's gift and stationery business. JOHN MARTINEZ, a former advertising art director, has been responsible for projects that include major national advertising accounts, brand development, book design and illustration, and product development. His body of work includes film, television, and print. His work has been selected for the permanent collections of the Library of Congress and the Museum of Modern Art, which has honored him in its broadcast advertising shows. His opera images have been collected in a book published by Harry N. Abrams, and his original art is exhibited at The Gallery at Lincoln Center in New York and at Storyopolis in Los Angeles. For advertising, production, and publishing clients, J&M Martinez, Limited provides creative direction, design, and illustration for print and television, as well as product design and development for wall art, home accessories, fashion accessories, stationery, and other paper products.

How and why did you start your "paper" business?

Margaret: John had been doing pieces based on operas just for himself. That brought him to the attention of City Opera and then the Met. Opera Guild. At the time, I had a small studio to work on corporate brand development projects. The Met asked us to produce prints and stationery based on John's images to be sold through its retail operations. The program was successful and kept growing, but it was such a special market that it was going to be hard to keep that going. I decided to add a broader line of stationery based on the production we were already using and see if the whole thing together could be large enough to be viable. That was the J&M line of boxed stationery, and it went well enough that before our first trade show opened, I was arranging to drop everything else and just develop the stationery business.

John, you were in advertising and also did illustrations and prints. How was the transition from the grind to the cottage industry accomplished?

John: I was a creative director in advertising, and leaving that was a gradual process. I had been very fortunate in the kind of work I was able to do, collaborating with very talented people on nice image accounts, but there's a lot of responsibility and very little flexibility in those positions. My partner and I decided to leave the agency and do free-lance together. Right off, I had to get used to not having a lot of staff and other sup-port, not to mention a regular paycheck, but I liked it. I had regular opportunities to choose what kind of work I wanted to pursue. Eventually, I focused more on illustra-tion, something I'd never been able to do before. I did a book of the opera pictures with had a show of the originals. I got back to doing book covers, had more gallery shows, and started working with Margaret on some of the development projects that were coming up. I haven't worked on an actual advertising project in over a year.

What are the vicissitudes of this kind of business? By this I mean, do you have to cater to public taste or your own?

Margaret: In terms of the business, the public taste in a given segment at a given time is of much more interest to us than our personal preferences (which change radically on a regular basis anyway). We want our business to support us and a bunch of other people. We have to come up with something that a sufficiently large pool of customers will find so appealing that they'll gladly spend their money on it and then be so happy with it that they'll look for us the next time. The job, and the thrill, is engineering the whole thing: identifying a pool of customers, interpreting their preferences in an item, and then figuring out how to produce that at the right price—and, the real challenge, get-ting it in front of them. You can't feel bad about having a lot of wonderful ideas that just won't work in the market you're dealing with at the time. In any case, in the areas we're in, it would be hard to do work that you couldn't be reasonably happy with.

It is my understanding that you began on your own steam and then sold the company to a larger concern. How did this work?

Margaret: You're referring to the J&M stationery line. I did the start-up, with so little capital, went through several rapid growth phases, and was still facing a serious expan-sion. We were considering taking in a financial partner and a couple of other options, when a publisher that had done John's posters in the past contacted us. The company had expanded into stationery, had been watching the line get around, and they licensed it. That was six or seven years ago. Our company retains ownership and approval, and we design the line. The publisher produces and distributes and pays us a royalty on sales. The arrangement allowed the line to grow significantly and freed us to do other

things. We don't have to pitch in packing boxes or picking up skids of envelopes any-more, so we can develop for several companies now, including an entertainment pro-duction company. Nothing could replace the benefits we got from experiencing the start-up, but this is better for the long run. It's a far more efficient way to work.

How does the business run? How are the creative aspects reconciled to the operational?

Margaret: With sales and production jobbed out, operations are really streamlined. Everyone still has to be willing to do whatever, but there's a limit to what that entails now. With so many threads, schedules are largely uncontrollable (we probably couldn't have done this when our children were younger), and negotiating and contract issues are constant. Some of that is covered by agents or attorneys, but we have to keep up with it. We had to learn not to duplicate each other. I like selling, so I do most of the presenting and the meetings on my own now. John's work is by nature more intense and time consuming, so he only shows up for special occasions.

On creative, we rarely work on the same project, or at least the same aspect of a project. We both have backgrounds in brand development, and that helped us get into a loose routine of sitting down together, brainstorming, going back for quick reviews, and settling on a direction. Then, it's just interrupting each other to look and consult.

What are some of the pitfalls in creating products that aim at an impulse market?

Margaret: The big one is probably the temptation to do something that you really, really love and can't explain in any other terms. Overpricing is the other big issue in discretionary goods, and we're fortunate that our manufacturers are all very smart about that.

Do you try to appeal to a loyal following? Is this possible?

Margaret: Absolutely and yes, to an amazing degree. It's the reorders that really count. Our part in building loyalty is keeping each line branded, to an extent, distinct and consistent so that customers (retailers, but especially end customers) can identify it immediately and will be pleased every time they encounter the product.

Do you foresee a need to grow the business, or are you content with the operation as it is?

Margaret: The great thing about this kind of business is that there's always growth to be had if you want it. The J&M line is something very different and much larger than the original line; the original niche is a big segment now. The line is big and solid enough that we can start to spin off smaller sublines now, which is a real opportunity. Our relationships with other manufacturers have multiplied, and those projects are all growing. Every time we get a project off the ground, it frees us up to some degree to move on to the next thing, so yes, we're always looking for growth in that sense. Now that we're getting into projects that are much more involved and long-term, the cycles may get longer.

What does having a business afford you that the staff or freelance life did not?

Margaret: What we do now is strictly development, and working this way, without having constraints of geography and being able to do only the part of the job that we really do well, has been great for us. We work really hard and long in phases, but there is always something new (good that we respond well to change), and we actually like all the work. Almost. Most of the staff we rely on are under someone else's roof, so we don't spend as much time meeting or supervising as we used to. And as long as we're on top of everything, there's no reason we can't go for a beach walk whenever the time is right.

TYPE, GRAPHICS, DESIGN

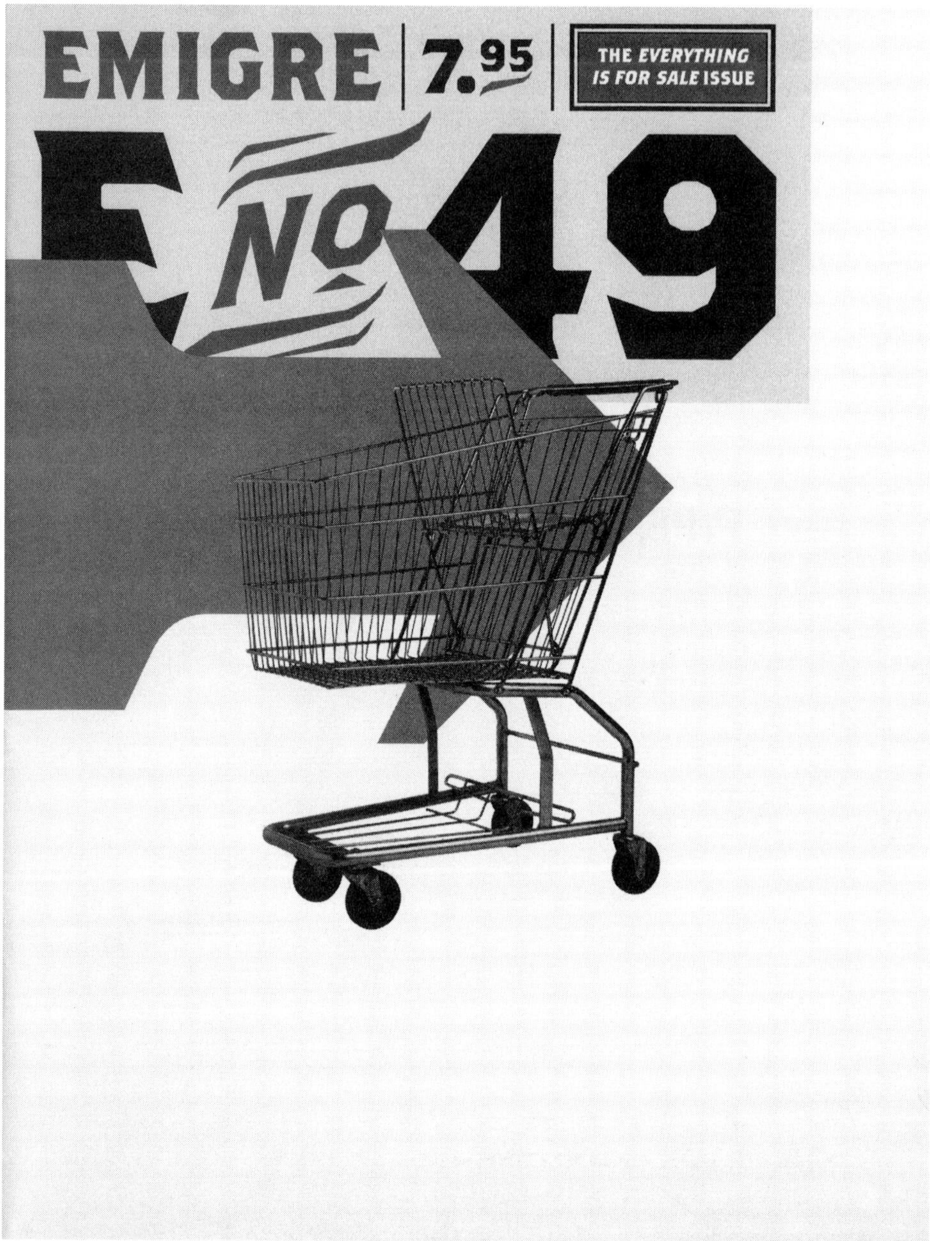
EMIGRE
7.95
THE EVERYTHING IS FOR SALE ISSUE
E NO 49

REVOLUTIONARY TYPES

with Rudy VANDERLANS,
Cofounder of *Emigre*

RUDY VANDERLANS is the editor and designer of the quarterly design journal, Emigre, and the cofounder, with Zuzana Licko, of the digital typefoundry of the same name. After studying graphic design and working as a newspaper designer, he started a business that became the lynchpin of the digital revolution in graphics and typography. His magazine has been a clarion of the postmodern aesthetic, and the foundry has issued some of the most emblematic faces of the digital age.

What prompted you and Zuzana Licko to shift from being staff designers to starting your own design, type, and magazine business?

It occurred gradually. We went from being full-time employed as designers, to being freelance, to creating our own products, with a lot of overlapping in between, such as working full-time during the day and freelancing at night and on the weekend. We were able to try out a little bit of everything. In the end we simply realized that neither of us is a great team player, that neither of us enjoys working for other people, and that we do our best work and derive most satisfaction from creating our own projects.

It was pretty shrewd to publish a magazine that would showcase your type wares. In fact, what came first, the magazine or the type?

The magazine came first. It was started when I was still a graduate student at UC Berkeley. I remember working on the original logo as far back as 1983. We didn't realize the magazine's use as a showcase for our typefaces until issue #2 or #3, when people started showing interest in Zuzana's low-resolution typefaces. Of course, today, showcasing typefaces is one of the main purposes of *Emigre*, much like *U&lc* was for ITC and the *Monotype Recorder* was for Monotype.

It is something of a gamble to start any venture, but starting a digital type foundry was truly breaking new ground. How did you establish yourself in the early stages?

That, too, was a gradual development. Zuzana initially designed typefaces to satisfy her curiosity with the low-resolution capabilities of the Macintosh, which was released in 1984–85, and I used these fonts in *Emigre* magazine. It was a way to circumvent the cost of an outside typesetter setting galleys, which was how most magazines were made in those days. Then, seeing these fonts in *Emigre*, designers asked if we could set type for them. As a result, we even placed some ads in very early issues of *Emigre* offering typesetting services. Before too long, as designers started buying their own Macintosh computers, we would sell them the fonts on disk, and we started advertising the fonts for sale in our magazine. As the Mac became more popular, we sold more fonts. We didn't really set out to start a digital type foundry. We created a demand without intending to, and when we realized there was a market, we exploited it as best we could.

At the time, as far as I know, we were the only company creating low-resolution fonts for the Macintosh and selling them. Then, when Adobe developed PostScript, much more sophisticated font design became possible, and more people became involved in designing fonts on the Macintosh. But it took a while before this explosion of small type foundries happened. That didn't happen until the early nineties. Meanwhile, it seemed like everybody who had tried designing a new font on a Macintosh came to us, or we found them—Jeffery Keedy, Barry Deck, Jonathan Barnbrook, John Downer, to name but a few. We all got to know them through our mutual interest in type and this new machine. The big foundries like Adobe and Bitstream were concentrating on digitizing the classics, so there was almost no competition in the area of experimental typefaces.

Emigre, the magazine, began as a "culture tab" and ultimately shifted gears when it became a design magazine. What was the impetus for this editorial switcheroo?

By around the sixth or seventh issue, two of the original founding members, Menno Meyjes and Marc Susan, had each moved on to bigger and better things. Menno received an Oscar for writing the screenplay adaptation for *The Color Purple* and then wrote the third Indiana Jones movie, and Marc moved to Los Angeles to pursue various writing projects. They left Zuzana and me with this publication that really had no direction whatsoever. Graphic design was our true passion, and at the time, the world of graphic design, type design, printing, and pre-press were being turned upside down by the introduction of the Macintosh. It was a very exciting period, so we thought it was an opportune time to focus the magazine on graphic design. It made everything easier when the magazine became focused on one topic. And the topic turned out to be inexhaustible.

What has required the most acumen and energy on your parts, the magazine or the type business?

Actually, it's all the other stuff that takes the most acumen. All the mundane things required to run a business. It just takes an enormous amount of really hard work.

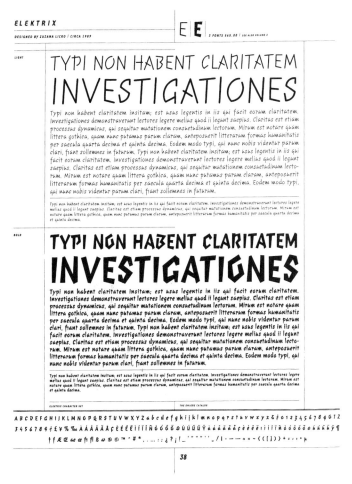

Designed by Zuzana Licko.

People ask us, "Who transcribes your interview tapes? Who kerns your fonts? Who writes your advertising copy?" Truth of the matter is, we are a five-person company, and we do almost everything ourselves. For instance, when we get a delivery of 30,000 catalogs at our office, we all chip in and unload those suckers ourselves, by hand, because we don't have a loading dock. Up until issue #19 or #20, I distributed *Emigre* magazine myself within the Bay Area. I used to pack as many copies in my car as would fit and visit bookstores and newsstands and try to sell the magazine on consignment. That was a real lesson in humility.

Have you considered growing your staff and building a larger business?

There were plenty of opportunities to grow, but we've kept it small on purpose. Over the years, we have turned down hundreds of typefaces that have been submitted to us.

We could have been much less selective and released more, but it would have required hiring additional people to handle the production, advertising, contract negotiations, etc. We have also turned down dozens of clients who approached us to work for them on various design projects, but this, too, would have meant hiring additional staff and overseeing them. We're not interested in the role of manager or art director; we still enjoy doing hands-on design. Instead of growing a larger business, we try to grow a more stable business where we enjoy what we do and hopefully provide something of value to others without killing ourselves in the process.

Emigre Fonts is not simply a type business—you are not simply vendors—it is a wellspring of an au courant sensibility. How do you reconcile "art" and "business"?

For us, it's a natural combination. We find great satisfaction in "making" things, but we equally enjoy creating methods of "selling" them. It's an exciting challenge to take a project from its inception all the way through production, marketing, and then distribution and sales, and be very much in control of the entire process. But ultimately, in order to do all this properly, we were really lucky when we hired Tim Starback in 1992. He is the *Emigre* who is rarely mentioned. Tim is our office manager, and he's taken on a great deal of the day-to-day operations of the "business" side of *Emigre*. He developed the infrastructure of our Web site and sales, distribution, and accounting systems, and how these elements interrelate. These systems have become crucial elements to the success of our business, and it has freed up time for Zuzana and me to concentrate more on the creative side. The three of us meet weekly to discuss business-related issues such as accounting, legal matters, distribution, sales, insurance, payroll, those sorts of things. We rarely discuss design at the office.

When you started, did you ever think you would have weekly meetings of this kind? It is, well, so grown-up.

No. We never even imagined that we would run our own business. That was the furthest from our minds when we started out. But I also never imagined I'd ever use a computer to design, or run a type foundry. Or sell our products over the Internet! I went to art school because I wanted to become an illustrator. Zuzana started out studying architecture. But once you start your own business and produce your own products, now, you are the one paying all the production, distribution, and advertising bills, as opposed to a client, and that changes your relationship to the work. Anybody can publish a magazine or release a font. There's not much too it. But we wanted to make a living doing this, which meant getting involved in all these other aspects of running a business.

Have you been able to stick to your initial mission? Or have the demands of business altered your course in any way?

I feel we have taken great risks creatively over the years, but we have never overextended ourselves financially. *Emigre* has never operated in the red. As much as we like to push the envelope in design, we are very conservative businesspeople. And we're proud of what we have accomplished in that area. There was never a mission statement or manifesto. No business plan. No five-year projection. No long-term plan. And there still isn't. There's always six or seven major projects in the works, which we will work on over the next year or so, but that's the extent of our outlook. We're still driven by our creative impulses. We still allow ourselves to explore unknown territory. Recently, Zuzana involved herself with producing pajamas and ceramics; I'm doing photography and releasing music. But whatever we do, it must somehow fit within our financial framework. Again, we aspire to make a living doing this and pay the rent and pay wages and provide health insurance and a pension plan to ourselves and our employees. The demands of the business have made us more efficient, perhaps, or a bit more conservative in how we spend money, and perhaps that has altered our course, but in a very positive way. More is possible now than before.

In terms of the magazine, you are in complete control of its direction; you are not a slave to marketing departments and other overseers. How have you maintained balance and at the same time created new challenges that keep the publication fresh?

The magazine is at times a huge pain in the ass to create. Like pulling teeth. At other times it's the best thing I imagine anybody can do for a living. It has always been a big challenge to keep it fresh and exciting. To maintain that has been a struggle from day one. But that is the essence of making a magazine. And the balance is pretty spotty, which is visible in the issues we've published over the years. The great thing about publishing a magazine, though, is that there's always the next issue to try it all over again.

Regarding the font business, have you developed rules and formulas for yourselves? Or is instinct still the most operative force?

In terms of font selection, I'd say instinct is still the operative force. But when it comes to commercially releasing a font, there is a definitive method to the madness. It's become increasingly expensive to release a font properly, so we've become very selective. We used to release up to ten font families a year, now we release maybe one or two. We're keen on keeping our library at a manageable size, where you can still see the trees for the forest, so to speak. We have a pretty intense process that each font goes through in terms of its production, and we invest a fair amount of money in marketing and advertising each font. Obviously, none of the fonts we release comes with any guarantee that it will sell, but we try to give them all a fair chance to prove themselves.

Emigre *is a veteran. What was new is now history. How do you see the company moving in the future? What will (or does) keep this exciting for you?*

Actually *Emigre* is pushing two decades, and people keep reminding us of that. They say that *Emigre* is not anymore what it used to be. But I think that's a good thing. The early work had a lot of youthful exuberance, and when I look back at it, I wish I could retain some of it. But I can't. The work is now produced under very different circumstances. There's more money. It has become more reflective. It takes us much longer now to create anything we're pleased with. We're also less inclined to constantly follow new technology. There's not the same kind of urgency to figure out the latest gadgets in our design work. The computer is crowding out everything. There seems to be no other future but the future of the computer, and after fifteen years of that, we're trying to push the technology to the background a bit and focus more on content.

Also, our interests are shifting. People want us to continue publishing "cool" new design work and "cool" new fonts, but I'm less interested in that now. I feel disconnected from that. Plus, there's a small cottage industry of book publishing that has sprung up showcasing that type of work. I had imagined that, by now, somebody would have been publishing a magazine to cover new design trends to extend what *Emigre* did in the late eighties and early nineties. I'm really surprised that hasn't happened. But we're working on all sorts of projects to keep things exciting for ourselves. For instance, we're using our distribution channels to help other designers distribute their productions. That's been very satisfying. And we're starting to publish our own artist books. Who knows, maybe twenty years from now, you'll be asking me questions about how *Emigre* became an art-book publisher and distributor.

What aspects of being an entrepreneur are the most pleasurable, and the most displeasing?

The most pleasurable is that you have a great deal of control over your life. I really can't see any drawbacks in that.

THE HEYDAY OF COMMERCIAL ART

with Rich ROAT, Principal
of House Industries

RICH ROAT and partner Andy Cruz founded House Industries in 1993 as a graphic design/illustration studio. In early 1994, the company entered the typography marketplace with twelve "questionable" fonts and some very effective marketing materials. House has since grown into a studio that sells theme-based font kits, illustration and design services, and clothing and accessories. Roat is a 1987 graduate of the University of Delaware, with a degree in communications. Before forming House Industries in 1993, he worked as a writer and public relations specialist at several small organizations. At House Industries, Roat helps develop ideas, assemble fonts, sweep the sidewalk, and take out the trash.

What caused you and your colleagues found House Industries?

We had drawn a bunch of custom type for various design projects and thought that it would be interesting to complete the character sets and sell them as fonts. We bummed some paper from a client and did a little 6" × 9" card, which we mailed to addresses from the back of the *Communication Arts* design annual. We called it House Industries so that if it was a miserable failure, nobody would relate it to Brand Design Co. (That's what we called ourselves back then.)

Did you know from the outset the kind of business you wanted to build, or was it a catch-as-catch-can operation?

It was definitely a seat-of-the-pants operation. When we did the card mentioned above, we only had enough characters to spell the name of each font. That put us in a bit of a jam when someone actually wanted to order them. It really wasn't until sometime in early 1998 that we really started to see the font thing as something with which we could earn a living.

You entered the type business at a propitious time, but also at a fairly early stage in digital type founding. Is there anything you would do differently today?

We probably would have tried to at least do some more-conservative type early on, because that's what sells. I don't know, though, because so many of the mistakes we made actually improved us in the long run.

At what pace did the business grow? And were you ready for this?

The font business started to grow rapidly in 1995, and we definitely weren't ready. We suddenly had a customer base who thought we knew what we were doing when we really didn't.

Do you now have a business plan?

Business plans are great if you're going to build cars or starter motors. Having a business plan would make us become fiscally responsible rather than aesthetically responsible, and that would probably be the end of House Industries.

What or who were some of your business models?

We've really always done our own thing, but if I had to pick a model I'd say Emigre. They really gave us lots of advice, and they're the one company that seems to profit from selling retail type.

Does this imply that you are not making a profit?

For the past two years, we started showing some black ink. It's expensive to keep a full-time painter, line illustrator, and typographer on staff . . . plus Andy and I have to pay ourselves something. We joke sometimes that nobody does things quite like House Industries. Why would they, there's no money in it.

House is clearly rooted in a sense of pop culture and irony. What determined the tone of your collective work?

We're rooted in our reference materials. We became enamored with the way advertising materials and collateral were produced in the heyday of commercial art. We like the fact that a company doing a quarter-page black-and-white ad in the back of a 1969 *Car Craft* would use a piece of professionally drawn custom type for a headline. Regardless of what we're working on, we try to apply the fundamental commercial art techniques used in the reference materials. Trader Vic's used custom-painted illustrations on their menus, so we did our own paintings for the mailer and packaging. The Custom Papers Group materials and the Street Van collection definitely gave us a label as "those guys who do the retro seventies stuff," but the type and color selections were deeply rooted in the sixties. The cars threw everyone off, I guess. Anyway, the common denominator was that the images were drawn by hand in pen and ink, and the type was all custom, just as they would have been done by an artist of that era.

The funky faces are your stock and trade. Do you ever think about more conservative or conventional faces now? Do you see the funky as having a limited currency?

The funky and eclectic definitely have a limited currency. We built a customer base on "funky," but now we're trying to give them something they can use every day.

There is a performance quality to House Industries. You are not simply vendors, you are entertainers. Was this deliberate, or something that eventually came with the territory?

If you're referring to our music shtick, that was a result of our becoming tired of doing boring lectures with a bunch of slides. Also, when you're trying to sell a product, a certain "show business" frame of mind takes over . . . it's effective marketing. Plus, we live in Wilmington, Delaware, and don't get out much.

You are a partnership of many talents. How do you manage and reconcile your individual abilities, and egos?

That's simple. We try to work together, and everybody has their own input, but Andy makes all of the final aesthetic decisions. There's a lot of collaboration, but there's really only one guy who "pulls the trigger." I think that makes things easier.

So, what does each of you do?

Andy Cruz is the art director. He makes all executive aesthetic decisions and cooks up most of the ideas. Ken Barber draws most of the type and directs commissioned typography. Chris Gardner sits at a drawing table all day and does most if the line illustrations. Adam Cruz just paints. I run the company, make sure the bills get paid, and help Andy cook up the next big thing. We have two other staff members, Luong Ngyuen, who administers retail font sales, builds Street Vans and Space Ships, and generally makes sure everything ships out every night. Lynn Barber is in charge of magazine distribution, advertising sales, public relations, and being the token female.

Now that you've established yourselves, what keeps House challenging for you?

I don't know if we all would consider ourselves established. Yeah, we have a nice office and sit in nice chairs, but this is still a hand-to-mouth operation. It comes from turning down a lot of work that we don't find interesting, taking way too long to bring products to market, and blowing loads of money on our magazine. The challenge is to keep doing what we want while keeping food on the table.

LAYERS

MEMORY

ONEDOLLAR

Silver Certificates

MONEY

VOID

Obligations & Stocks

Mortgage Rates

Last Will And Testiment

The Gazette

The Weekly Rocket

NOVUS · ORDO · SECLORUM

UNION

·BIG REWARD·

$10.000

TOP SECRET

ELECTION DAY

Vote For Some Guy In A Suit!

TYPECAST BUSINESS

Erik VAN BLOKLAND, Type Designer
and Coproprietor of LettError

ERIK VAN BLOKLAND and Just van Rossum started LettError in Berlin in 1989. Now, more than twelve years later, the duo works separately together on various projects. That means that there is no LettError office, but still, typefaces (Instant Types, Trixie, Advert, Kosmik, Federal), typography, graphic design, sites, and movies get produced. LettError clients include the Dutch PTT, for which they've made two series of stamps, MTV Europe, KPN (the Dutch telecom), GAK (a branch of privatized government), the province of South Holland (a branch of nonprivatized government), Apple Computer, and many others. LettError hosts the *TypoMan and Crocodile* show, featuring a typographic superhero and his coldblooded sidekick, who protect the world against big words, flying arrows, and hopping lamps.

Why did you start LettError?

We quickly discovered that starting a new firm was going to be more interesting than working in someone else's.

How old were you when you made this momentous decision?

I was just twenty-three.

As type designers, you serve a very specific clientele. Does this allow you to retain the integrity of your creations?

It depends on the project and the client. Most clients are aware that if they try to micromanage type design, they're going to get something that's only as good as they are—if that's enough, why bother hiring an expert? We've told some clients to do it themselves, and usually, they come back. We'll do our job so they can do theirs. Luckily, it goes smoothly most of the time. This doesn't mean that our "creativity" has to rule everything else. It's important to listen and find out what they're trying to solve—but it's possible that even the client isn't fully aware of the issues that need to be addressed. We are, and that's what we do, but sometimes it takes an effort to get all the faces pointing the same way.

You have created type design that is distributed through type shops, but LettError seems to be a hybrid of a type shop, custom type house, and retail environment. How would you define the company?

We have a great relationship with FontShop. Our typefaces are doing very well in the FontFont library. But for a couple of specialty designs, the shaded Federal and NewCritter for broadcast design, we're experimenting with other kinds of marketing. The LTR Type Company is somewhat closer to the customer than the FontFont typefaces are. They're different things; they can be marketed in different ways.

What do you mean by closer to the customer? Does LTR market your quirkier faces?

The Federal faces are for Mac OS only at the moment. The application that supports the shading, LayerPlayer, is a Mac application, and we don't have any experience of porting it to PC. Maintaining the same application on multiple platforms is a challenge to large corporations. The fact that a small company such as ours can develop applications at all is an exception. FontShop International has a policy that their library is available for Mac OS and Windows, rightly so. But it makes Federal incompatible with the library, so we're floating it on our own. Apart from that, it's an interesting experience to sell fonts ourselves and see where the orders come from.

Do you spend much time thinking about business issues?

Too much and not enough. Business is a different game from creating stuff, building projects and products from the ground up. Business is multiplication: making more out of stuff that's already there. But it is no use if you have nothing to begin with (multiply by zero). Development is addition: making something out of nothing. It's slower, but necessary. I find development infinitely more interesting; unfortunately, that means that we won't be rich. But looking back at the dot.com boom and subsequent bang, we're all right. We're making a profit, we're not laying off, and we're not blasting through someone else's venture capital. It's all paid for. I guess that's conservative for today's business practices.

Your Web site is entertainment, information, and showcase. What are the key concerns in developing this site?

Maintenance needs to be low, and adding content should be as easy as possible. When there's a threshold for new content to get online, it won't get there, or it will get there too late. The new system (currently being renamed) does that. It takes care of all tedious referencing, linking, copying. What's left is almost pure content. A source file contains the things you want to say, a couple of very rough pointers what the system should do with it, and that's it. Tuning the HTML is possible, of course, but it should be done in a central place where every change reflects all pages at once. Thus, a fix for a problem is site-wide rather than one page at a time. The system is countering the full-Flash approach: Everything looks great in Flash, but it is impossible to maintain, change, edit. All changes need to be made manually: some guy opening a file, making the change. Then, on to the next. Life is too short and working hours too expensive to keep coming back to old HTML and SWF to fix it up. We just patch the engine, and everything's up to speed, like an F1 pit stop. The new engine powering the site is humming—we can concentrate on our work again. That's reflected in the no-frills layout and design of the pages. Rough-pixeled imagery comes with super-small files—incredibly fast, a rarity these days.

What has been the most challenging aspect of getting your products—typefaces—into the marketplace?

Getting things finished—to build a great idea into a rounded-off, complete package. For instance, for Federal, that meant not only building the digital engraver and the master fonts, but also coming up with a useful selection of styles and an application that helps the user with assembling. During design and production of a typeface, we discover how it can be used best. It makes sense to transfer that experience to the user by giving examples and tools.

How many new types do you create in a year, let's say? What do you feel is necessary to keep up with the market, with the demand?

Our development work is quite detached from the current fashion. If anything, we look for vacant lots in the scenery. Judging by how often the designs get copied, both in concept and as piracy, we're not doing so bad.

Do you consider yourself entrepreneurs?

I think so. We're fending for ourselves, making new things, building products from scratch.

After all these years creating and producing, what would you like to do as an encore?

A really big book (fodder for the book engine we've built) or some movie-title sequence or something (for the Robotfonts) or some new Web project; we've got some great tools.

AN ELEMENTAL BUSINESS

with Mies HORA, Founder of Hora
Associates and Ultimate Symbol

After graduating from Parsons School of Design and completing a three-year apprenticeship with Art Director's Club Hall of Fame member Cipe Pineles Burtin, MIES HORA worked for several corporate design firms in the late seventies before realizing that he wanted to run his own multidiscipline design firm, Hora Associates. Starting in 1979, Mies coauthored four design reference books with his father, package designer, architect, and artist extraordinaire, Richard Hora. That "Design Elements" series became the basis, more than twelve years later, for Ultimate Symbol Inc., which publishes books and CDs of electronic art. Although Mies still provides corporate identity services to several organizations, Ultimate Symbol is his obsession.

How would you define "design entrepreneur"?

A designer who organizes, operates, and assumes the risk for a business venture. Also, a person who finds the courage to locate his/her unique "voice" and puts his/her ass on the line.

So then, what line did you put your ass on?

In the beginning, my wife and I solicited funds from the "three F's": friends, family, and fools. We raised more than $150,000 in start-up capital. We were forced to take out a second mortgage on our house to keep the company going after we hit the critical three-to-five year "death ground." That is a period when all start-ups eventually have to "face the music" and either trend towards profitability or simply run out of cash and fold. Fortunately, we prevailed by retooling our cost of goods and cutting other costs by, for example, printing our promo mailers in Hong Kong instead of in the United States. Basically, as an entrepreneur, you either wise up or wash out.

How and why did you begin publishing books and CDs of graphic symbols?

It became evident in the late eighties, as design professionals began to turn to the Apple Macintosh as a serious tool, that they would need a visual dictionary of symbols in electronic format. Digitizing the print version of *Design Elements* was a logical next step. The prospect of learning a new language of computing and selling a product of my own was quite exciting and *very* enticing. I also knew that if I didn't do the digitizing myself, someone else would try, with or without my permission, and with uncertain quality.

Did you have any previous business experience?

Aside from running a service-oriented graphic design/advertising firm for twelve years, I had never had to raise large sums of capital, hire computer illustrators, create, package, and market a product of my own before.

Did you foresee that this would indeed become a full-time business?

Although I dreamed, as every green entrepreneur must, of being independently wealthy within a few years, I didn't necessarily expect the business to become full-time nor my life's work.

You started with books and moved on to CDs, but your company is very focused. Have you had the impulse to expand with additional products?

We have extended our product line with fonts derived from our CD products. We are also currently developing an expanded Web site that will allow real-time, single-image searching and downloading of all of our symbols, as well as illustrations by the renowned designer Seymour Chwast. We have also been successful in licensing our visual materials to other firms in various OEM arrangements for different industries such as 3-D modeling and sign making. However, I have been very disciplined about not allowing our energies to become diffused by interesting sidelines to the core business.

How do you produce this material? Do you have a large staff? Do you do most of the work yourself?

Each of our products requires from one-and-a-half to two years of intensive collection, organization, and labor to complete before being marketed. I have a modest in-house staff of four and a virtual staff of many. In-house, I have a junior designer, a production assistant, and an office manager who handles business administration duties.

My wife, who began as a full-time founder/vice president of Ultimate Symbol, now consults part-time as strategist/financial advisor. In addition, I contract four or more freelance designer/illustrators to actually render and create new symbol sets/illustrations for new products by the project. Of course, most of the product development/writing falls on my shoulders, which is what I enjoy most. For example, I had a ball collecting actual leaf samples by taking forest walks and visiting nurseries for our CD *Nature Icons*.

There is art, and then, there is business. Do you find that you've been successful in marrying the two?

Yes, by working for myself and developing my own products, I feel intensely gratified by the flow between art and business. I've given the parts I don't enjoy or am not good at to others and retained the aspects that provide me the most pleasure. The result is a seamless web of activity that is aimed at obtaining my long-term goal: global domination (just kidding).

How much time do you spend on each of these two parts of the whole?
Forty percent art and 60 percent business.

Do you feel that you've created a niche that is entirely your own?
Yes, our products reside at the peak of the market triangle in both quality and price. What makes them unique is the level of creativity/taste/care expended in producing them and the personal service provided in selling them. All of which results in a doggedly loyal and growing customer base.

How do you keep that customer base coming back for more?
We have an aggressive upgrade strategy for our customers who do not own all of our products, and we mail to them on a regular basis, at least once a year. We also upgrade our existing products, to address problems that become apparent and to add new material that has, in many cases, been requested by our clients. They really appreciate our attention to their needs.

How do you address competition in the field?
We have found that we have no real competition in our chosen area of electronic art. Companies that produce similar materials are usually more "commercial" and tend not to cater to discerning professional designers, who form our core constituency. That is because I am a practicing designer and I understand my clientele. . . . I am basically selling to myself.

Is there anything you have not accomplished that you hope to in the future?
I have enough unpublished material for at least another five to six CD/book products, which should all make their way to market over the next few years. I intend to begin selling our library of images as hardcover books, with or without the CDs, to reach an even broader book-buying public. Another goal is to build a broad system of international symbols, including hotel and hospital sets, to take up where the AIGA DOT Symbol Sign System left off twenty years ago.

AT HOME IN VIRTUAL SPACE

with Marlene MCCARTY,
Cofounder of vBureau

MARLENE MCCARTY and Donald Moffet started the design firm Bureau in 1989
after having met in an AIDS activist group called Gran Fury. McCarty's experience with design had been predominately involved with making people's commercial ventures look appealing. But through Gran Fury, which produced various campaigns in the fight against AIDS, she was able to see her design work
have an effect on the environment. McCarty and Moffet set up Bureau to do a
variety of projects, including some art projects, as well as more commercial
work to support their social efforts. In 1999 the company's name became
vBureau.

**Bureau has made inroads into the motion design realm. At what point did
you engage with other than 2-D media?**

Well, I have a history that actually goes way back into "other media." I studied design
at the old-fashioned "*Allgemeine Kunstgewerbeschule Basel.*" I say old-fashioned because
this was before it had "*hochschule*" status. In the "*grafiker abbildung*" (the five-year Swiss
program, not the American two-year program), you had to do this weird thing. You had
to "major," or I guess, more appropriately, "have an emphasis," in either illustration or
film animation. Well, I chose film animation, simply because I thought it was more
"modern." (Which, by the way, is why, my freshman year at University of Cincinnati, I
chose design as a major, not painting.) We had to do all these labor-intensive exercises,
like: paint an arrow out of black-and-white plaka, then animate it using an Oxberry
animation camera and stand, so the arrow would move across the screen. In typical
Swiss style, this took months to do. Anyway, after two years of these exercises, film animation was burned into my brain. I also did a lot of video work in the beginning of the
Basel video program (1983).

When I moved to New York in 1983, I was very interested in film and video, but I
had no contacts and I was very poor, so I didn't think I would ever be able to afford to do
any work in that field. Because so many of the Swiss exercises involved typography, I guess
I always was looking for an opportunity to "move type." That chance came in 1990, when
Tom Kalin (also a Gran Fury member) did a movie called *Swoon*. I asked him if we
(Bureau) could do the film titles. To be quite honest, at that point I actually had no idea
what that entailed. I had never produced any kind of film "thing" professionally.

Your movie title sequences are much admired. Once you entered this realm, did your turn away from print?

No! In fact, it made print seem really cheap and easy. Film titles are hard. Remember, in 1990 Bureau didn't even have a computer! So, to conceptualize titles, convince your director they would be good, and figure out how to produce them was a bit like pulling a rabbit from a hat. Also, in the beginning we were working on such tight budgets that we only got to shoot the titles once! We couldn't afford to have the animation reshot if we weren't happy. This made it very intense.

Bureau is a unique mix of political and commercial work that emphasizes direct communication and provocative ideas. How do you balance the two? In the classic sense, do you rob Peter to pay Paul?

Well, the first thing I have to say before we address the Peter and Paul issue (is this a direct biblical reference?) is that we have *never* done any pro-bono work. Even when we work with small organizations, we charge for our services. We have found this creates a better environment of respect for both us and the client. So . . . no, it has not always been taking on commercial clients to pay for the noncommercial jobs. Yes, of course, many of the commercial jobs leave a little extra money in comparison to the nonprofit jobs, but one doesn't pay for the other.

Okay, now the big question: What made you decide to develop a virtual studio, to my knowledge the first such studio?

We wanted freedom. We wanted liberation. We wanted more flexibility. We have many interests at Bureau, and we just started feeling bound in by the requirements of a traditional studio. There was a time only a decade ago when you needed a whole studio of people to get things done—to do the mechanicals, to do the stats, to spec the type, to have a place for all the photos and type galleys to be delivered . . . and so on. We don't need all that anymore. Things can be sent via e-mail. And all that production is now in our laps, so we just kept asking ourselves why we needed to run an old-fashioned studio.

Old-fashioned. That smarts. I'm sure many people will ask whether the future has really come, or is vBureau just a portent of what might come? What was physically and technically involved? Did you literally close your doors, fire your staff, turn off your phone?

Yup, that was pretty much it. We set up a Web site, fired our staff, moved the phone line to our secret holding place, along with all those pesky real archives, and went about our business.

written and directed by todd Haynes

Describe where you work and how you work now.

Now, I work anywhere I have access to a computer. Usually, I need a pretty decent Internet connection, so that can be a bit hindering. I work in my art studio, at home, in hotel rooms, and my goal is to do it on the beach. I work in my underwear if I want to. The weirdest thing, though, is how time has changed. There is a completely different way of being in the world when you are not tied to office hours. Also, the constant interruption of an office is gone. Concentration is much more intense. For the most part, it's really great. There are just some details, like, "Oh, now I don't have anybody to send out for stamps, or to return those phone calls I don't want to deal with . . ."

Today, design firms spend huge sums of capital in designing their spaces, both for fetishistic and public-relations reasons. How has this shift from the norm affected the way you work and your clients' relationship with you?

Well, I guess considering we started in a basement behind a super's storage room, we've never really had clients who come to us for our office space. We have dropped some clients that we didn't really want to work with anymore, and we have kept mostly clients that we like and who like us. I have found that, in fact, my contact with my clients has been enriched by not having to constantly be dealing with the office. Most of my clients and I keep in touch via e-mail.

When I first heard that Bureau had become vBureau, I found it very mysterious—indeed I still do, to some extent. In my fantasy, you exist as an entity, but you are kind of invisible. Do you feel less involved in the politics of the design business in this state?

What do you mean by the politics of design? If you mean the whole, "Guess who did this fabulous project . . . Did you read what so-and-so said in such-and-such design rag? . . . Did you see who won what prize . . . blah blah blah . . . ," if that's what you mean, we've always been a little outside that anyway. We never participate in competitions, and our work isn't reproduced that often in the normative design magazines. So, that doesn't feel any different . . . However, if by politics you mean the politics of what we do, I think we have greater potential to engage in "meaty" projects now.

By putting all your eggs in the Internet basket, are you able to focus more on the quality of your work? Are you in a position to truly limit your client base? Or are you still consumed by the needs of making a studio work (i.e., profitable)?

Yes and no. I wouldn't say I am consumed by making this be profitable. Part of the goal is to only have to achieve the profitability level (amount of money) that we need, not massive profits.

What work are you doing now that you did not do when you were just Bureau?

Drawings!!! Yes, it is true, but more in the graphic world. I personally have been doing some Web design for an Eastern European news site . . . I would have never taken this on for myself at Bureau because I wouldn't have had the time or concentration to figure out how to do it.

Many design firms have Web site extensions. Must vBureau put more into its site than other firms?

Well, we should. At this point, both Donald and myself are restless with our site. It is, at the moment, just acting as a "portfolio" in the front part that the public can see. Once things have settled a bit more (you know we are still figuring this out day to day), we must decide if one of our priorities is to make the site more vibrant and alive (which I think it is). Perhaps we will do more direct, self-generated projects or hook up with more Web sites or have part of the site be more like a forum. All this is in our hip pocket, but we are not there yet.

Do you think the virtual world will be the "next big thing," or is this something of an anomaly?

I do think the virtual world will change the world as we know it. I do not think it is an anomaly. I also do not think it will replace human contact, but I think our working relationships will change. Huge companies cannot allow themselves the kind of lawlessness. And by lawlessness, I mean, lack of control over the people who are working for (or, as I prefer, with) you. We are working with various people, and we can no longer control how they use our name or how they describe their affiliation to us. Also, their use of our materials and assets is no longer as easy to control. We are willing to take those risks, but a huge company might not feel quite so "free" with their assets.

I think the effect the Web will have on language worldwide is interesting . . . My main clients at the moment reside in Russia and Mongolia. We all use English to communicate but refer to German or French for help. We do all our work over the Web . . . presentations and delivery of mechanicals.

Suddenly, Mongolia seems very near and accessible.

MAKING MAGIC

with David LAI, CEO of Hello Design

DAVID LAI is the CEO of Hello Design (*www.hellodesign.com*), which he cofounded in January 1999. Clients include Sony Pictures, The Smithsonian Institution, Neutrogena, Disney, Columbia TriStar, National Geographic, and Adobe Systems. A graduate of Cornell University, David has worked for several top-tier firms, including Studio Archetype and cow. David has won numerous awards for his work, and his designs have been featured in *Critique, Communication Arts, How Design, The Web Design Wow! Book*, and *New Design: Los Angeles*. As a faculty member at the Art Center College of Design in Pasadena, David teaches and lectures on Web design.

How would you define entrepreneurism?

The ability to find opportunity and seize it. I think an entrepreneur is someone who sees possibilities where others usually don't. They have to be willing to take risks and be willing to make mistakes—often. At the heart of it, they have to have a passion for what they are doing. Without passion, I don't think the word "entrepreneur" can exist.

As the principal of Hello Design, do you feel that you work for others or for yourself?

When I started this company I wanted to create a place where I would want to work. In doing that, I think I've always felt that I work for myself. As the company grows, I am now beginning to feel that I work *with* others. I firmly believe you can do more when you surround yourself with smart people. They inspire you, and their strengths, hopefully, complement your weaknesses. So, in the end, I feel it's not so much about who you're working for but rather what you're working towards.

On your Web site you exhibit your work for clients and experimental work. Is there a nexus of the two? Does one nourish the other?

Absolutely. It's funny, because I remember a couple years ago, when a few studios put out experimental work and then others followed. It seemed like everyone had an experimental section in their site, but when I clicked in, it was always a "coming soon." Here at Hello, we enjoy coming up with new experiments all the time. It keeps the thought process going and allows us to explore combining design and technology. Sometimes, our client work will give us ideas for a new experiment, but inspiration can come from anywhere. For the holidays, we created a Wish Genie that lets people make wishes and share them with others. We created it just for fun, but in doing so we learned a lot about Flash, databases, and DHTML. It's sort of like being in school; the learning never stops.

Is "Wish Genie" a potential product?

Ha ha, I never thought about that. The Wish Genie is actually a powerful little site and comes with its own admin tool, so I guess it could be! It's quite fun to see what people from around the world want. You can make three wishes and send them to five of your friends. Your friends then get a custom e-mail and URL that takes them to your wishes. The cool thing, though, is that if your friends make wishes, their wish lists are linked to yours. So, you can go from friend to friend seeing what they've all wished for.

What are some of your entrepreneurial projects, and how have they come about?

I think that I always somehow seem to stumble onto them, but I guess it all started in high school. A few of my friends saw these icons on my computer and wondered how I had made them. They, too, wanted to customize their computers and asked me to teach them. I realized a lot of people probably wanted to do this, and I thought I'd put together a little pamphlet. To make a long story short, that idea became the first book I wrote, titled "Icons for the Masses." Then, in college, I wanted to learn Photoshop and thought the best way to learn would be to write a book on it. I approached the book from a user's point of view in that I wanted to write something I would really want and use. There was a need, because if that book existed I would have just bought it. That book was titled *Photoshop Type Magic* and was the first "recipe" computer book. It was step-by-step, so you couldn't mess up even if you knew nothing about Photoshop. That book became a bestseller, and a whole series of Magic books came out after that.

Do you believe entrepreneurialism can be taught to designers today?

I'm not sure how to answer this one, because I've never thought about teaching it. You can teach business and marketing, but I think part of being an entrepreneur has to come from the heart. You have to have a passion and a belief that is yours. I think you'll run into a lot of doubters along the way and probably a lot of failure, but if you have the passion and the patience, you will succeed. One thing for sure is that I think entrepreneurs help each other. A lot of what I've learned has come from other entrepreneurs, mentors. We seem to find each other like magnets.

Should this notion of entrepreneurialism be key to what the "new graphic designer" is all about?

I think it's important that graphic designers realize there is more to design than design. What I mean is that we're problem solvers, and sometimes, companies might not believe they have a problem. I think there are many opportunities for better design and better solutions, and I think it will take resourceful entrepreneurs to help companies realize what they are missing. Someone has to communicate and convey these challenges, and that takes more than just a solid portfolio.

Once you become an entrepreneur with a marketable product, do you become less of a hands-on designer. Does one interest eclipse the other?

No, I don't think so. I think that's a personal choice. I started this company with Hiro Niwa, and we both wanted to be hands on. We could have grown this into a much larger studio, and I'm glad we didn't. I think it's important to have clear responsibilities and roles, but they can overlap. Hiro and I are comfortable mixing together business, design, and technology. Actually, I think you have to as an entrepreneur.

How has your life and work changed from your time as an employee to now, as your own boss?

I think my perception of time has changed. I mean, it feels like I started the company yesterday, but in reality it's been two years now. It's been a lot harder to separate my work life from my personal life, since I work in the company of friends. There is a great sense of freedom, but with the good comes the bad. There are many responsibilities, and others are depending on me, so it can be quite stressful.

If you asked me if I'd do it all over again—it would be big "yes." I think I've learned more in these two years than I would have as an "employee" working for some big company. I started thinking Hello was a big experiment, and, well, it continues . . .

PLAZM²⁴

scary
nightmare

USA $6 CDN/MEX $7.5
Printed in the USA

I do not care
earth is nothing
go to hell

LABORATORY OF POP

with Joshua BERGER,
Principal of Plazm Media

JOSHUA BERGER is founder and one of three principals of Plazm Media, a graphic design firm that builds complete brands, advertising, and retail marketing plans using custom typography. Its clients include Lucasfilm, MTV, and Nike. Founded in 1991 by artists as a creative resource, Plazm Media also publishes _Plazm Magazine_, an eclectic design magazine with worldwide distribution, and operates an innovative digital type foundry. Berger has been recognized by numerous design publications and award shows.

What caused you and your colleagues to found Plazm?

The process was very organic. Originally, we had open-ended meetings discussing topics like media accountability and artistic representation. There were people of many disciplines involved: writers, designers, photographers, filmmakers. The most common theme was a general dissatisfaction with avenues of expression available. The evolution of this discourse was the creation of _Plazm Magazine_. None of us knew anything about publishing, and all of us had "real" jobs. The magazine was completely self-published.

Did you know from the outset what kind of business you wanted to build, or was the process more intuitive?

The evolution has always been a very fluid process based on contributors' varied interests. As the organization has grown, many decisions have become more businesslike. The integrity of the collective creative process, however, remains separate from many of the business decisions.

Did Plazm Magazine _come first, or your type and design business?_

Plazm Magazine launched in 1991, Plazm Fonts in 1993, and Plazm Design in 1995.

You entered the type business at a propitious time. Was this motivated by art or commerce?

Plazm Fonts launched in 1993 and grew out of the design experimentation happening in _Plazm Magazine_, Pete McCracken's personal interest in developing typefaces, and submissions from a number of talented young typographers, most notably Marcus

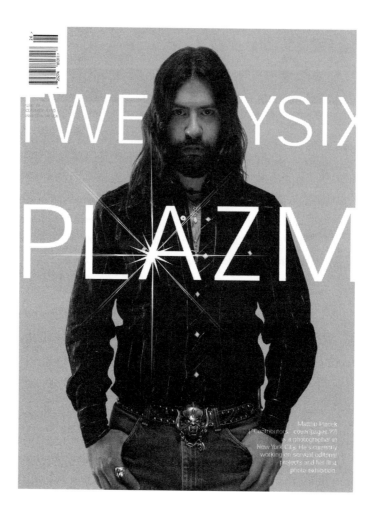

Burlile and Christian Küsters. The financial model for selling type is much better than for publishing a magazine, and we thought this might support our magazine habit.

Who or what were some of your business models?

Early inspiration for the magazine came from *Mondo 2000, Utne Reader*, and *Anarchy*. *Emigre* was also inspiring when we launched Plazm Fonts. I remember reading an issue where Rudy VanderLans was talking about *Emigre* magazine never making any money, but their font sales always paying the bills.

Plazm is clearly rooted in a sense of pop culture. What determined the tone of your collective work?

Contributors view themselves as artists. We view our magazine as a printed laboratory, where we experiment with form, process, and content. Popular culture, the age of information, the hegemony of global corporations are refracted through the lens of our contributors.

At what pace did the business grow, and were you ready for this?

The magazine grew at a shoestring level and a snail-mail pace, always run as a labor of love on a strictly volunteer basis. When we launched Plazm Design in 1995, the business expanded rapidly, about 600 percent in each of the first two years. The growth since then has been more modest, about 20 to 25 percent each year. During 1996 and 1997 we were going crazy trying to keep up.

You are a partnership of many talents. How do you manage and reconcile your individual abilities and egos?

We have an open-business model; partners are able to pursue their own interests, bringing experience to the collective. Each of us, at one time or another, has been full- or part-time, or off the map entirely. Pete McCracken, for instance, is on his way to graduate school to study music. Certain projects arise that suit one partner's talents more than another's. This is the way projects are funneled.

Do you have a business plan? Can you predict where Plazm will be in, say, ten years?

There are many areas we are pursuing: film titling, motion graphics, sound design, fashion. We are reinventing *Plazm Magazine* as a tenth-anniversary project, and we are launching Plazm East in New York City. I would like to personally retire in ten years, but all bets are off.

Now that you have been around for a while, have you shed some of your earlier edginess?

We have often found a perception that Plazm is about a specific style. We approach all of our problem-solving in a conceptual manner; the style of the solutions are as varied as the projects we take on. If we have shed any edginess, it is only through the vernacular of experience. That said, we regularly take on interns and employees with little or no experience and assign them difficult and complex projects. These contributors temper our experience with an infusion of energy.

What keeps Plazm challenging?

Simply existing is a challenge.

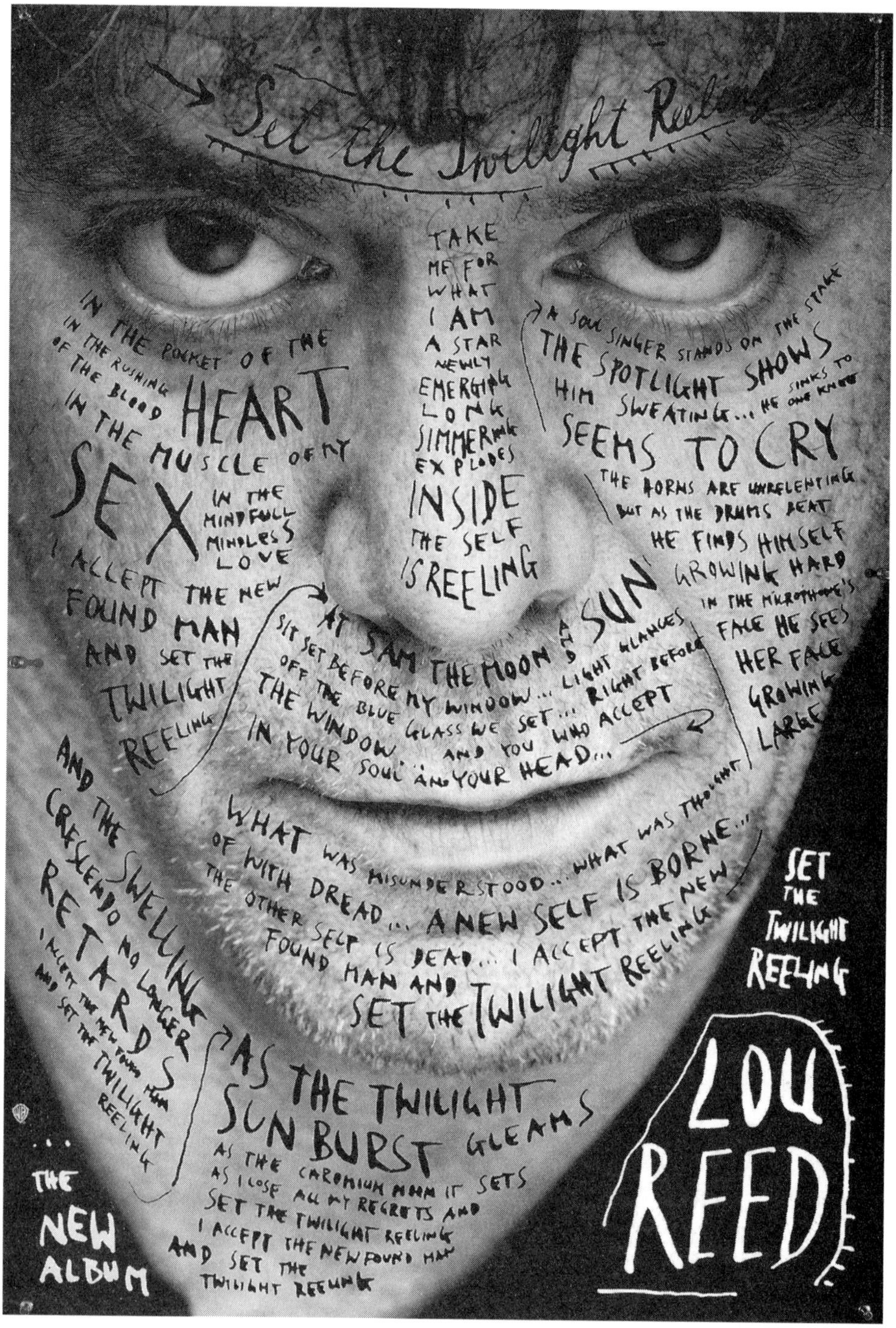

Set the Twilight Reeling
TAKE ME FOR WHAT I AM A STAR NEWLY EMERGING LONG SIMMERING EXPLODES INSIDE THE SELF IS REELING
IN THE POCKET OF THE HEART
IN THE RUSHING OF THE BLOOD
IN THE MUSCLE OF MY SEX
IN THE MINDFULL MINDLESS LOVE
I ACCEPT THE NEW FOUND MAN AND SET THE TWILIGHT REELING
A SOUL SINGER STANDS ON THE STAGE THE SPOTLIGHT SHOWS HIM SWEATING... HE SINKS TO HIS KNEES SEEMS TO CRY
THE HORNS ARE UNRELENTING BUT AS THE DRUMS BEAT HE FINDS HIMSELF GROWING HARD
IN THE MICROPHONE'S FACE HE SEES HER FACE GROWING LARGE
AT 5AM THE MOON AND SUN SIT SET BEFORE MY WINDOW... LIGHT GLANCES OFF THE BLUE GLASS WE SET... RIGHT BEFORE THE WINDOW AND YOU WHO ACCEPT IN YOUR SOUL AND YOUR HEAD...
WHAT WAS MISUNDERSTOOD... WHAT WAS THOUGHT OF WITH DREAD... A NEW SELF IS BORNE... THE OTHER SELF IS DEAD... I ACCEPT THE NEW FOUND MAN AND SET THE TWILIGHT REELING
AND THE SWELLING CRESCENDO NO LONGER RETARDS
I ACCEPT THE NEW FOUND MAN AND SET THE TWILIGHT REELING
AS THE TWILIGHT SUN BURST GLEAMS
AS THE CHROMIUM MOON IT SETS
AS I LOSE ALL MY REGRETS AND
SET THE TWILIGHT REELING
I ACCEPT THE NEW FOUND MAN
AND SET THE TWILIGHT REELING
SET THE TWILIGHT REELING
... THE NEW ALBUM
LOU REED

HAPPY EXPERIMENTS

with Stefan SAGMEISTER,
Proprietor of Sagmeister

Following stints at M&Co. in New York and as creative director at the Hong
Kong office of the advertising agency Leo Burnett, Austrian native STEFAN
SAGMEISTER formed the New York–based Sagmeister Inc. in 1993. He has
designed graphics and packaging for the Rolling Stones, David Byrne, Lou
Reed, Aerosmith, and Pat Metheny. His work has been nominated four times for
the Grammies and has won most international design awards.

How would you define yourself? Are you a graphic designer or "author"?

I'm a designer. I like this well-worn term; it is wide and large and covers whatever I'm
doing well. If I'd call myself an author, I'd feel obligated to author all the time, and I'd
feel confined rather than liberated.

**The traditional definition of an author is one who authors (often in print),
but as a designer, you are authoring ideas. How far do you go to maintain
the integrity of your ideas?**

Like most people in my profession, I work with clients, with other designers here in the
studio, with photographers and illustrators, with color separators and printers. All
pieces are collaborations. How far do I go keep a project intact? I scream, I yell, and I
beg. I cry inwardly. I promise big rewards. I look at it from their point of view. The
difficult part is to know which battles to fight and on which to compromise.

**How do you feel about collaboration? At what point in a collaboration is an
idea still your own? Conversely, at what point does it become something
else?**

I normally have a very tight idea from the start how the end result should look like. We
all work until that conceived end result is achieved. When it's all done, I can say, this
was my idea, executed in collaboration. Recently, I sometimes have been trying to leave
this way of working, because it does not take advantage of occurrences happening along
the way (nor does it take much input from my collaborators). I would hope to work
both ways in the future.

In the year 2000, you closed your design practice to spend a year doing other things. What were those other things?

Happy experiments. It's a list of all the things that I felt would be worthwhile exploring, but never had the time. This includes things as simple as thinking about the whole wide world and my place within it, all the way to more concrete projects like designing fictitious CD covers under time pressure, doing them in three hours rather than my customary three months and seeing how that self-imposed restriction changes the process and the result.

In general, I try to come up with a whole slew of seed concepts that I hope to utilize for projects in collaboration with clients later on. Since my brain has a tendency to follow the well-beaten path, I think it might be helpful to start a project, not from within itself but from an outside departure point, again with the hope of arriving at a different solution.

Can you tell me what some of these are?

All over the board. There are a lot of formal ideas for CD covers; one is a food package (containing three meals for a homeless person) that doubles as a building brick for a shelter; there are sketches for furniture, glasses, playing cards, and books; an idea for a house I'd love to live in; and a concept for an airport I'd love to fly out of.

In planting seeds for when you return to "commercial" practice, you are authoring ideas. Are any of these ideas viable without the intervention of a client?

The ideas themselves are nothing but thoughts brought down on paper in my sketchbook and, as such, of little value to me. I will only like them after their execution. It is valuable to start the thinking process without a specific project in mind. This allows for the production of concepts, for which I can then go out and look for a client.

By taking this hiatus, you showed yourself to be in control of your destiny, at least to a certain extent. What lessons have you learned about how to conduct your business and, as important, make your design?

It turned out that some of the anger I had towards the day-to-day dealings with clients had nothing to do with them and was within me (i.e., the anger was still there when the clients were not). Most importantly, I learned (again) how much I love being a designer.

Could you see yourself becoming either an artist, on the one hand, or an entrepreneur, on the other, and entirely giving up your design business?

No. I have no interest in becoming a fine artist. Despite the fact that an incredible amount of fantastic work is being produced in the art worlds right now (I am touched more by art of the last decade than of any other in the twentieth century), I find the art world itself a ghetto and its distribution within the gallery system not very compelling. I have little interest in becoming an entrepreneur: If I would have wanted to become a manager, I would have gone to business school.

INDEX

A

Absolut Vodka advertising campaign, 6

Access Guide series, 43–45

accuracy, ensuring, 49–50

Adobe, 222

adolescent male power fantasies, 74

advertising. *See also* marketing

    credit for design in, 6

    restricting ads, 114–115

    storehouse of advertisers (magazine), 133

    targeting special interests, 10

aesthetic responsibility, 230

agreements. *See* contracts

Aldus, 25

Alphagram Learning Materials, 8, 65–70

American pop culture

    magazine design, 120, 122, 252

    tolerance for cartoony, 100

    typefaces, 230

amusement and humor, 80

Anarchy, 252

Andersen, Charles Spencer (CSA Archives), *xi*

"Animal Magnetism" (Isley), 199–201

"Animated Properties" (Girardi), 31–33

animation, 91, 100, 149–154

AOL Time Warner, 31

approaches to business, 3

Arisman, Marshall (painter and illustrator),
    157–159

Ashjaee, Javad, 60

associates, choosing work, 55

"At Home in Virtual Space" (McCarty), 241–245

authorial voice, digital environment, *xv*

authorpreneurship, *xi*

authorship, *x–xi, xiii,* 6

"Authorship in the Digital Age-You're Not Just a
    Designer Anymore, or Are You?" (Heller),
    x–xv

autonomy, 127, 183. *See also* freedom

Avedon, Richard, 6

B

Bains, Mike, 127

Baker, David C. (*Persuading* and ReCourses, Inc.),
    2–3

bankruptcy as motivation, 121

Barber, Ken, 231

Barber, Lynn, 231

Baseline, 127–129

Basel video program, 241

Baseman, Gary *(Teacher's Pet),* 149–154

Bass, Saul, 134

Batman Collected (Kidd), 165

Behar, Yves (fuseproject), 59–62

Benzel, Gary (Green Lady), 185–187

Berger, Joshua (Plazm Media), 251–253

Bernard, Nancy, 134

"Birth of an Idea: or, How I Learned to be
    Observant and Leave the Rest to Fate"

(Vogler), 12–17
Bitstream, 222
Bjorklund, Tim, 150, 151, 153
Blechman, Nicholas, 19
Blechman, R.O., 150
Van Blokland, Erik (LettError), 233–235
"Blondes Sell More Books" (Ilyn), 167–169
Blue Q (company), 199
blurring, 6, 19, 133
"Book as Performance" (Lehrer), 141–147
book-jacket designing, 163–164, 216
books
    children's, 89–90, 197
    desire to write, 161
    merchandising characters, 90, 104
    performance of text, 142
    specific audience, 89–91
boundaries between art and commerce, 6. See
        also blurring
Boym, Constantin (Boym Studio), 107–110
brand, defining a, 177, 210
bringing products to market, 82, 109, 191, 231
Burlile, Marcus, 251–252
business. See also profitability
    bankruptcy as motivation, 121
    commitment required, 110, 222–223
    compared to a passion, 125, 209, 247, 248
    "creative control" clause, 81
    "death ground," 237
    of design vs. design of business, 24, 29, 41,
        197
    focus, inappropriate, 132–133
    good instincts, bad acumen, 105
    growth, 28, 69, 178, 196, 218, 223–224, 230,
        238, 244, 249, 253
    measuring success, 7, 234
    mission statement, 225
    models, 37, 50, 135, 178, 179, 212–213, 230,
        252, 253
    multitasking, 67
    problem-solving by designers, 132
    pro-bono compared to nonprofit, 242
    prostitution of, 3
    separation from personal needs, 3, 27
    side business, complimentary, 128
    thinking ability, 10
    understanding budgets and economics, 94, 242

    visual junk, 159
    working with others mindset, 247
business plans
    logical, but no relation, 132
    not always desirable, 230
    as prediction tool, 253
    proposals, 19, 68–69, 127
    purpose of, 10
Byars, Mel (author and Webzine publisher),
        137–139

C

Cablevision, 31
"Candy Man," 195–197
cardboard pets, 199
Carson, Carol, 164
cartography, 49–53
cartoons, 150. See also animation
Castro, Alex, 113
challenges
    breaking into field, 95
    circulation development, 132
    content-heavy Web site, 137
    dealing with authors, 128
    developing entrepreneurialism, 29
    of entrepreneurial pursuits, 69
    existing, 253
    finances, 128, 231
    finishing projects, 235
    in game design, 74, 75
    no experience, 113, 114
    in positioning product, 146, 186
characters, models and development, 152
Chiasso (company), 86
Chicago Museum of Science and Industry project,
        37
children, 89–91, 104. See also toys and games
Chilewich, Sandy (Chilewich), 189–191
Chinese shoes, cotton, 189
chocolate, 195
Chu, Chris, 134
"church and state, blurring," 133
Chwast, Seymour (Push Pin Studios), 195–197,
        238
circulation development, 132
clients. See also consumers; customers

affecting, 8, 53

bringing discipline to work, 37

client-driven projects, 36

interference of, 135, 233

lack of experimentation, 185

learning from, 57

pinpointing users, 52–53

problem-solving for, 174, 177, 206, 249

promoting self to, 41

relationship with, 32, 40, 50, 55, 68, 134, 182

sensitivity to needs of, 175

useful perspective of, 178

virtual studio impact on, 243

"Clothes For the Street" (Benzel and St. John), 185–187

clothing. *See also* fashion industry

black (for children), 104

Green Lady, 185–187

HUE legwear, 189–190

Walking Man, 177–179

Clowes, Dan, 164

CMCD company, 25, 26

Cole, Jack, 165

collaboration. *See also* partnerships

artistic, 125

authorship issue, *xi*

compared to individuality, 121

creative freedom, 32

delegation and division of duties, 51, 115, 121, 124, 127, 153, 183, 217, 224, 231, 238–239

digital environment impact, *x–xi*

final decision, 231

integrity of idea, 255

team, 39, 151, 204

"total user experience" focus, 60

trend of, 135

color stereotyping, 82

commercial success, designing for, 3

Commodity (Glenn), 120, 121

"Communicating with Every Person on Earth" (Kalman), 103–105

communication

with customers, 178, 212

impact on design, 128

poor, 86, 94

with public, 159

through criticism, 207

compact discs (CDs)

covers for, 256–257

Nature Icons CD, 238

photo CD technology, 25

competitions, participation in, 243

complimentary side business, 128

compromise. *See* selling out

computer, as material, 173

conference management, 46–47

confidence in product, building, 49–50

consistency, 14

consumers, 56, 177. *See also* clients; customers

content

assets and commodities, 31

selling compared to, 133

structural and formal, 32

by writing, 6–7

contracts, 81, 82. *See also* proposals

control

business decisions, 125

clause in contract, 81

losing, 2, 146, 183, 244

maintaining, 65

over personal life, 227, 257

of work life, 55

convergence, model of (Eames), 27

conversation, graphic design of, 143

core values, 81, 82

corporate funding, 36

costs. *See also* funding; money

bringing product to market, 82, 109, 191

games, to produce, 76

overpricing pitfall, 216

pricing formula, 88

as stricture, 82

cottage industries, 80, 99, 216

cotton Chinese shoes, 189

covetables, 204

Cox, Paul, 19

creativity

American pop culture, 100, 120, 122, 230, 252

amusement and humor, 80

clause in contract, 81

developing solutions, 59

driven by, 115, 225

expressing through writing, 6–7

freedom, 31, 80–81, 125

future projects, 51
    heart and soul, 80
    losing, 2
    mass market idea generators, 12
    rebellion, 15
    relation to making money, 3
    separate from business decisions, 251
    small groups, 57
    time limitations, recognizing, 59
credit for works, 6
criteria for materials used, 99
criticism, handling, 207
Critique (Neumeier), 131–135
Cronan, Michael Patrick (Walking Man), 177–179
Crossing the Boulevard (Lehrer and Sloan), 144, 147
Cruz, Adam, 231
Cruz, Andy, 231
CSA Archives, *xi*
customers, 178, 212, 218. *See also* clients; consumers
"cute meter," 100

D

Van Dam, Stephan (mapmaker), 49–53
Danielewski, Mark, 147
David Vogler Design, 17
"death ground" for business, 237
deconstruction, 144
delegation and division of duties, 51, 115, 121, 124, 127, 153, 183, 217, 224, 231, 238–239
delivery method, 133
design
    activity, 75
    and the business of design, 24, 29, 41, 197
    ceding expertise, 168
    as common bond, 12
    as continuum, 178
    earning the right to, 107
    lack of respect for, 203
    as mystic priesthood, 135
    problem-solving technique, 132
    tastemaker role, 203–207
"Design à Clef" (Kidd), 161–165
designed entity, 210
design entrepreneurs, becoming

Arisman, Marshall, 157
Behar, Yves, 59–60
Benzel, Gary and Todd St. John, 185
Berger, Joshua, 251
Van Blokland, Erik, 233
Boym, Constantin, 108
Byars, Mel, 137
Chilewich, Sandy, 189
Van Dam, Stephan, 49
Freymann, Saxton, 97
Girardi, Peter, 31
Glaser, Byron and Sandra Higashi, 79
Glenn, Josh and Anthony Leone, 119
Guiffré, Remo, 210–211
Holzman, Joseph, 113
Hora, Miles, 237
Ilyin, Natalia, 167
Isley, Alexander, 199
Kalman, Maira, 103, 104
Kelley, David, 55
Lehrer, Warren, 141
Licko, Zuzana, 221
Martinez, Margaret and John, 215–216
McCarty, Marlene, 241
McGuire, Robert, 89
Mok, Clement, 23
Neumeier, Martin, 131
Richardson, Forrest, 93
Richert, Hans Dieter, 127
Roat, Rich, 229
Schlossberg, Edwin, 39
Shapiro, Ellen, 66
Small, David, 35
Vanderlans, Rudy, 221
Vignon, Jay, 181
Wurman, Richard S., 43
Zimmerman, Eric, 73
"Desktop Monuments" (Boym), 107–110
development
    cottage industry, 99
    creative solutions, 59
    entrepreneuralism, 29
    magazines, 120, 122
    new mediums, 36, 52
    product selection for, 82, 115, 144, 182, 206–207
diaries, *Baseline*, 128

dictionary of symbols, 237
digital environment, *x–xi, xv,* 24. *See also* technology
diminished returns on ideas, 99–100
discipline, 37, 205
dishonesty, 178–179
Disney Company, 14–15, 31, 32
disposables, 98, 204
Distributed Art Publishers (DAP), 19
distribution
    handled by agent company, 201
    importance of, 18–19, 196
    limitations, 44
    selling rights, 26
downsizing, 4
dynamic systems, functioning of, 74

ethnic diversity of Queens (NY), 144–145
eToys.com, 10
experience
    designers, 95
    enhancers, 60
    planned design, 205
    understanding, 40
"Experiencing Experience" (Schlossberg), 39–41
experimental work
    prototypes, 61
    restricted by clients, 185
    typefaces, 222
    at Web sites, 234–235, 247–248
expertise, ceding design, 168
exploitation, 120–121
"An Expressive Journal" (Richert), 127–129

E

Eames, Charles (model of convergence), 27
editorial and advertising intentions, 133
"The Education of a Design 'Entremetteur'"
    (Vienne), 4–7
Edwin Schlossberg, Inc., 39–41
eeBoo Corporation, 97–100
"An Elemental Business" (Hora), 237–239
Elffers, Joost, 97–98, 100
Ellen Shapiro Design, 8–11
Emigre, 221–227, 230, 252
"entertainment," 163
entremetteurs, 5
"Entrepreneur by Circumstance" (Mok), 23–29
entrepreneurialism, 23, 36–37, 60
entrepreneur(ship)
    business models, 37, 50, 135, 178, 179,
        212–213, 230, 252, 253
    client relationships, 43, 55
    entremetteurs comparison, 5
    experiencing the process, 11
    fulfilling results, 69
    helping each other, 248
    previous experience, 43
    reasons for becoming an, 22, 31, 39, 43, 49,
        55
    self-initiated projects, 147
    state of being *vs.* approach, 23, 60
    stewing pot of mediums, 20

F

"factors" (fashion industry), 178–179
failure
    based on intent, 191
    compared to creative success, 132–133
    due to success, 196, 211
    emotional toll, 133
    future entrepreneurial efforts, 134
    success-to-failure ratio, 56–57
    understanding, 46
fashion industry, 178–179, 182. *See also* clothing
Feder, Phyllis Flood, 195
feedback, influence of, 80, 145
Fili, Louise, 19
film and motion design, 241–245
Filth (Welsh), 147
Finklestein, Louie, 141
Flash approach, Web sites, 235
Fleming, Shawn, 153
Fletcher, Alan, 134
Flood (Feder), Phyllis, 195
focus, inappropriate, 132
fonts. *See* typefaces
FontShop, 234
food, 97–100, 195–197
Le Food Frenzy: The Rugrats in Paris Game (multiplayer game), 15
"Food That Does Not Spoil" (Freymann), 97–100
formula for pricing products, 88

Fortunato, John, 97
fortune cards, 83
forward thinking, 24
Frank, Can, 164
freedom
    autonomy and responsibility, 127
    creative, 31, 80–81, 125
    from traditional studio, 242
French Fries (Lehrer), 141
Freymann, Saxton (eeBoo Corporation), 97–100
"From a Long Line of Merchants" (Chilewich),
    189–191
Fulbrook, John, 163
functionality, 83, 213
functional-speculative divide, 37
funding. *See also* costs; money
    corporate, 36
    credit cards, 121–122
    family, 237
    follow-on, 211
    fools, 237
    friends, 237
    for future growth, 125, 183, 211
    garment industry comparison, 186
    grants, 146
    investor, 44
    for online games, 75
    self-funding, 121, 138
    subscriber base, 132
    "three F's," 237
    venture capitalists, 49, 234
funky and eclectic limitations, 231
Funny Garbage, *xi*, 31–33
furniture, 173–175, 182, 190
fuseproject, 59–60
future directions
    animation, 91, 100
    design and business collaboration, 41
    elaboration of articles, 128
    expanding product lines, 70, 187, 239
    fashion, 253
    film and movies, 37, 53, 159, 235, 253
    financial health, 116, 125
    fortune cards, 83
    game culture change, 76–77
    home furnishings, 91
    interactive museum exhibits, 53

multimedia platforms, 91
publishing, 46–47, 235
raising perceived value of designers, 57
reevaluation of goals, 227
retirement, 253
ridiculous, communicative, humanistic proj-
    ects, 105
service-to-product transition, 33, 135
sound design, 253
TED conferences, 46–47
vast presence, 207
Web experiences, 91, 139, 235
writing, 165, 207
fuzzy function, 108–109

G

gag-oriented design, 98
Gak, 12–14
gameLab, 73–77
games. *See* toys and games
Ganzfeld (annual book), 18–20
Gardner, Chris, 231
Garland, Ken, 128
garment industry. *See* clothing; fashion industry
General Thinking, Inc., 209–213
genetics project (Chicago Museum), 37
"get a life" approach, 3
gifts, 204–205
Girardi, Peter (Funny Garbage), 31–33
Giuffré, Remo (General Thinking, Inc.), 209–213
"giving birth" (bringing products to market), 191
Glaser, Byron (Zolo), 79–83, 85
Glaser, Milton, 23, 134
Glenn, Josh *(Hermenaut),* 119–125
Goldman, Harvey, 147
golf course design, 93–95
Graham, Nick, 179
Graves, Michael, 6
Greenburg, Al, 11
Green Lady, 185–187
Grimwade, John, 50
Grooms, Red, 19
"Group Think" (Kelley), 55–57
GRRRHHHH: A Study of Social Patterns (Lehrer),
    143
Guarnaccia, Steven, 85

H

"Happy Experiments" (Sagmeister), 255–257

Haring, Keith, 159

heart and soul, 80

Heller, Steven

    appreciation expressed for, 134

    "Authorship in the Digital Age-You're Not Just a Designer Anymore, or Are You?" (Heller), *x–xv*

    "So You Want to be Your Own Boss," *viii–ix*

Hello Design, 247–249

Hermenaut, 119–125

hiatus for experimental work, 256

Hibma, Karin (Walking Man), 177–179

Higashi, Sandra (Zolo), 79–83, 85

Hinrichs, Kit, 134

"hit-driven" industries (Hollywood), 76

holiday gifts, 103

Holmes, Nigel, 50

Holzman, Joseph *(Nest, A Quarterly of Interiors),* 113–116

Hora, Mies, (Hora Associates and Ultimate Symbol), 237–239

Horchow, Roger, 195

House Industries, 229–231

"House of Cards" (Martinez), 215–218

House of Leaves (Danielewski), 147

housewares, 182

How Are You Peeling? (Freymann), 98

"How Hard Can This Be, You Ask?" (Baker), 2–3

"How to Teach Entrepreneuralism (Not)" (Shapiro), 8–11

HUE legwear, 189–190

human genome project (Chicago Museum), 37

I

"Icons for the Masses" (Lai), 248

ideas. *See also* inspiration

    authoring, 255, 257

    basis of design, 50

    design character and personality, 60

    diminished returns, 99–100

    experimental projects, 50, 61, 222, 234–235, 247–248

    giving form to, 24, 55–56

    from group, 57

    mass market tools, 12

    serendipity, 14

    taking risks on, 107, 203, 221

IDEO, 55–57

Ilyin, Natalia (author and designer), 167–169

images, store for, 181–183

imperfect forms, 99

importation problems, 87

"Improving Everyday Life" (Behar), 59–62

individuality, work style, 114, 121

influence, 36, 113

"Information is My Game" (Wurman), 43–47

information visualization, 32

inspiration. *See also* ideas

    from consumers, 56

    from locations, 144

    mistaken impressions, 207

    from objects, 90, 190

    from personal experience, 44, 66–67, 104, 150

integration of life and work, 83, 104, 186, 217, 243, 249

intellectual property, 6, 76, 153

intentions, blurring, 133

interactive museum exhibits, 53

International Trade Council, 87

Internet. *See* Web (World Wide Web)

intimidation as motivation, 167

invention frequency, 191

inventory, 26

investor funding, 44, 83

Isley, Alexander (Isley Design), 199–201

Ives, Norman, 141–142

J

Japanese aesthetics, 99, 186

J&M Martinez, 215–218

K

Kalin, Tom, 241

Kalman, Maira and Tibor (M&Co.), 6, 23, 103–105, 200, 209, *xi*

Kelley, David M. (IDEO), 55–57

Kidd, Chip (author and designer), 161–165

"Kinko's Law," *xiii*
Kodak company, 25
Küsters, Christine, 252

L

"Laboratory of Pop" (Berger), 251–253
Lai, David (Hello Design), 247–249
Lane, Nathan, 153
LayerPlayer, 234
learning, personal growth, 24
Lee, Peter, 75
Lehrer, Warren (writer and designer), 141–147
Leone, Anthony *(Hermenaut),* 119–125
Letraset, 127
LettError, 233–235
Lewy, Michael, 124
licensing, 80
Liden, Johan, 61
life and work integration, 83, 104, 186, 217, 243,
    249
limitations, recognizing, 62
limited editions, 109, 128
limits
    business growth, 28, 196, 223–224, 230, 249
    pushing, 29
literature, visual, 147. *See also* "Book as
    Performance" (Lehrer)
living, making a, 105, 147, 153, 181, 230
living theater (McDonald's restaurant), 144
location, one (over time), 90
logo work, 181–183
longevity of work, 95
loyalty, customer, 218, 239
LTR Type Company, 234
Luvboat Earth, 119

M

Macintosh computer, 222, 234, 237
Maeda, John (MIT Media Lab), 172–175
"A Magazine of His Own" (Neumeier), 131–135
magazines. *See also* specific magazine
    experiences with starting, 113–114, 119–120
    as objects, 124
    opportunity for improvement, 226
    pop culture design, 120, 122, 252

as printed laboratory, 252
    reader comments, 133
    showcase of product, 221
    storehouse of advertisers, 133
magnets, 199–201
Magritte, René, 159
"Making Hay from Play" (Zimmerman), 73–77
"Making Lots of People Happy" (Guiffré), 209–213
"Making Magic" (Lai), 247–249
"Making My Own Magazine" (Nadel), 18–20
managing, 5, 94, 110
"Mapmaker, Make Me a Map" (Van Dam), 49–53
maps, 49–53
marketing. *See also* advertising
    capital required, 26
    distribution, 18–19, 26, 44, 196, 201
    in game industry, 76
    pricing, 76, 88, 218
    problem with self as seller, 26
    products, 10, 62, 85–86, 158
    "show business" frame of mind, 231
    strategic alliances, 41
    student projects, 35
    word-of-mouth promotion, 207
marketplace
    bringing product to, 82, 109, 191, 231
    campiness sells, 200
    designing for, 3, 35–36, 175, 186, 190–191,
        216, 229
    exploring, 67
    niches, 12, 18, 216, 239
Martinez, Margaret and John (J&M Martinez),
    215–218
materials
    losing confidence in, 173
    relationship to mind and body, 174
    switching from planned, 108
    used in products, 99
"Materials and the Body" (Maeda), 173–175
Mattel, 12–14
*Maus (*Spiegelman), 164
"Mavericks in the Rag Trade" (Cronan and
    Hibma), 177–179
Maximum Rocknroll, 121
McCarty, Marlene (vBureau), 241–245
McCracken, Pete, 251, 253
McGahan, Dustin, 134

McGuire, Richard (Work Is Play), 20, 85–91

McKnight Kauffer cotton labels, 128

M&Co. (Kalman), *xi,* 103–105

mediums

appropriateness, 33

blur between lines, 19

connections, 143, 145, 147

development of new, 36, 52

game designing, 74, 77

scrolls, 141

meetings, weekly, 224

merchandising characters, 104

metamorphic food, 97

Metaphors (Garland), 128

Mills, Mike, 144

mindset of working *with* others, 247

"Missing Monuments" product line, 108

MIT Media Laboratory, 135, 136, 172

model of convergence (Eames), 27

Mok, Clement (interactive guru), 23–29

Mondo 2000, 252

money. *See also* costs; funding

distinction with creative time, 75

making a living, 105, 147, 153, 181, 230

unrelated to creative life, 3

monitor saddle, 60

monuments, desktop, 107–110

Moskal, Kathy, 189

"mother of invention," 26

motion design (film), 241–245

motivation, 121, 135, 167

MULAN (Mutation Labs), 15–17

multidimensional view of time, 90

multiple platforms, computer, 234

multitasking in business, 67

multiuser games, 15–17

mystic priesthood, design as, 135

N

Nadel, Daniel (*Ganzfeld* coeditor), 18–20

Naef (company), 86

Nahas, Margo, 181

"Name on the Marquee" (Vigon), 181–183

narrative design, 98

Nash, Mitch and Seth, 199

Nature Icons CD, 238

navigation, 32

Nest, A Quarterly of Interiors, 113–116

"Nesting Magazines" (Holzman), 113–116

NetObjects software, 26

network cartoon series, 150

Neumeier, Martin *(Critique),* 131–135

Newgarden, Mark, 89

newsstand sales decrease, 133

Newton, Helmut, 6

New Yorkistan, 102

Ngyuen, Luong, 231

niches

finding and filling, 12, 40

pinpointing users, 52–53, 216, 239

problems with generalizing, 18

Nickelodeon, 12–14, 15, 149

Night Becomes Day (McGuire), 89–90

Nimkin, Maggie, 98

Niwa, Hiro, 249

"Not Just a Magazine Anymore" (Glenn and Leone), 119–125

novelty magnets, 199–201

numbered editions, 109

O

obsolescence, 29, 98, 108

Oh Boy, A Design Company (Salanitro), 203–207

old-fashioned studio, 242

online multiuser gaming (MULAN), 15–17

The Orange Book (McGuire), 90

organization skills, 205

ownership, maintaining, 36

"Ownership Above All," 35–37

P

painting compared to game designing, 73

paper, 203–207, 215–218

Parrinello, Ed, 98

Parsons School of Design, 50

partnerships, 125, 182, 183, 216–217. *See also* business; collaboration

passion compared to business, 125, 209, 247, 248

patterns, 24

PDAs, part of exhibits, 40

peeves, incorporating in authoring, 162

Penn, Irving, 6
PeoplePC, 60
performance, text as, 141–147
permanence of design, 93
personalizing mainstream items, 59
personal pursuits, 3
Persuading journal, 3
pets, cardboard, 199
Pets.com, 10
Philou (hair products), 62
photo CD technology, 25
photocopied zines, 120
Photoshop Type Magic (Lai), 248
place mats, 197
PlasticMan (Cole), 165
play, viewpoint of, 75
Play With Your Food (Freymann), 98
Plazm (Berger), 251–253
politics of design, 243–244
pop culture. *See* American pop culture
POPX, 16
portable communication tools, part of exhibits, 40
portfolios, Mass Art, 121
"Powered by the Light" (McGuire), 85–91
power fantasies, adolescent male, 74
pricing, 76, 88, 216
print, 123–124, 207
problem-solving
    for clients, 174, 177, 206, 249
    designers technique to business problems, 132
    due to poor communication, 86, 94
    entrepreneurial trait, 205
    experimental projects, 61
    for humanity, 174
    importation complications, 87
    material changes, 108
    registration marks, 88
    for self first, 142, 158, 206
    through creativity, 59
    through need, 66–67
pro-bono work, 242
products
    brand loyalty and recognition, 218, 239
    bringing to market, 82, 109, 191, 231
    delivery method, 133

distribution, 18–19, 26, 44, 196, 201
expanding line of, 182
ideas and other intangibles, 10–11, 40
imperfect form, 99
magazine showcase, 221
marketing, 10, 62, 85–86, 158
personalizing mainstream items, 59
positioning, 80, 146, 186
pricing, 76, 88, 216
quality control, 52
refining, 50
selection for development, 82, 115, 144, 182, 206–207
as solutions, 66–67
time devoted to new, 52
"Products of Need" (Shapiro), 65–70
profitability. *See also* business
    act of love, 129, 195, 230
    benefits of low profit products, 36
    just enough, 244
    merchandising of product, 121
    "old economy" standards, 138
    product selection, 82
    too much success, 196, 211
    venture capitalists expectations, 49, 234
programmers compared to game designers, 74
proposals, 19, 68–69, 127. *See also* contracts
prostitution of business, 3, 5–6
prototypes, experimental work, 61
public, reaching and communicating with, 159
pulp sci-fi genre format, 122–123
punctuation, graphic design of, 143
Push Pin Studios, 195–197
push scooters, 61
Puzzlehead, 85–86

Q

Q-cards, 83
quality
    controlling, 52, 83, 150–151
    inappropriate focus, 132
    losing control of, 146
    visibility of, 68
Queens (NY), ethnic diversity of, 144–145

R

Rand, Paul, 6, 134, 174, 175

RayBowls, 190

reader comments, 133

"recipe" computer books, 248

ReCourses, Inc., 3

refrigerator magnets, 199–201

Rege, Ron, Jr., 19

registration mark problems, 88

reinvention, 46

Remo General Store, 209–213

"repurposing," 134

reputation, as promotion, 41

responsibility, 127, 230

"Revolutionary Types" (Vanderlans), 221–227

Richardson, Forrest (Richardson or Richardson),
   85–91

Richert, Hans Dieter *(Baseline),* 127–129

Roat, Rich (House Industries), 229–231

roles
   delegation and division of duties, 51, 115, 121,
      124, 127, 153, 183, 217, 224, 231, 238–239
   redefinition, *xii*
   supporting, 2

royalties
   on sales, 199, 200, 216
   during thesis project, *xiii*

Rupp, Debra Jo, 153

S

sabbatical. *See* hiatus for experimental work

Sagmeister, Stefan (Sagmeister), 255–257

Salanitro, David (Oh Boy, A Design Company),
   203–207

Salen, Katie, 75

Sapient, 27–29

Scharf, Kenny, 159

Scher, Paul, 134

Schlossberg, Edwin (Edwin Schlossberg, Inc.),
   39–41

School of Visual Arts, M.F.A. Design program,
   9–10, *xi–xiv*

Scoot (city-commuting), 61

scrolls as medium, 141

sculptural expression, 190

The Search for IT and Other Pronouns (Lerer and
Goldman), 147

Sedelmaier, J.J., 150

self as seller, problems with, 110

self-initiated projects, 147. *See also*
   entrepreneur(ship)

selling compared to content, 133

selling out, 7, 158

Sephora (retailer), 62

"Serious Play" (Glaser and Higashi), 79–83

service-to-product transition, 33, 135

Shapiro, Ellen (graphic designer, writer, Ellen
   Shapiro Design), 8–11, 65–70

Shawn, Wallace, 153

shoes, cotton Chinese, 189

"show business" frame of mind, marketing, 231

shower curtains, 197

side business, complimentary, 128

signature on works, 6

silk-screen edition prints, 182

sketchbooks, specialized, 204

skills, *xi,* 74, 152

Sloan, Judith, 141, 144–145

Small, David (Small Design Firm, Inc.), 35–37

smile to grimace, emotional toll, 133

Smith, Peter Buchanan, 18

social relationships, game design, 73

social stigma, games, 77

software, NetObjects, 26

solutions. *See* problem-solving

souvenirs, 108

Souvenirs for the End of the Century, 109

"So You Want to be Your Own Boss" (Heller),
   viii–ix

Space (company), 61–62

speculative-functional divide, 37

Spiegelman, Art, 89, 164

"Spiritual, Obsessive, and Sacred" (Arisman),
   157–159

St. John, Todd (Green Lady), 185–187

stability, regaining, 134

Stanton, Frank, 44

Starck, Philippe, 23

startup capital. *See* funding

stationary, 215–218

Staying Up Late (Talking Heads), 104

Steinkellner, Bill and Cheri, 150, 153

stereotyping, color, 82

Stewart, Martha, 36, 93–94

Stiers, David Ogden, 153

Stiller, Jerry, 153

storehouse of advertisers, 133

storytelling, 142, 145, 161. *See also* animation

"Storytelling is Everything" (Baseman), 149–154

Stradler, Matthew, 114

strategic alliances, 41

Stuart, David, 134

Studio Archtype, 27–28

styles, recognizable, 40

subscribers, estimating, 132

success

    designing for commercial, 3

    failure compared to creative, 132–133

    measuring, 7, 200–201, 253

    success-to-failure ratio, 56–57

    too much, 196, 211

symbols, dictionary of, 237

T

Talking Heads, 104

Talmud Project, 35–36

Target store promotion, 6

Teacher's Pet (Baseman), 149–154

teams. *See* collaboration

technology. *See also* digital environment; Web

    (World Wide Web)

    agnostic liability, 28

    collision with design, 31

    forward thinking, 24

    influencing development of new mediums, 36

    photo CD, 25

TED (Technology, Entertainment, and Design)

    conferences, 45–47

"The Biggest Game" (Richardson), 93–95

"The Heyday of Commercial Art" (Roat), 229–231

"The Role of Tasternaker" (Salanitro), 203–207

thesis project, *xii–xv*

time limitations, recognizing, 62

Tordjman, Philippe, 62

toymaker, becoming a, 85

toys and games. *See also* children

    cost to produce, 76

    D-Toys, 14–15

    EO, 88

Gak, 12–14

gameLab, 73–77

"Go Fish"-type cards, 86–88

MULAN, 15–17

multiuser games, 15–17

Puzzlehead, 85–86

Q-cards (fortune cards), 83

solar-powered, 88

Trader Vic's, 230

transitioning

    from cottage industry, 80

    to furniture and art, 173–175

    service-to-product, 33, 135

trust, 178–179

"T-shirt" test, 182

"Typecast Business" (Van Blokland), 233–235

typefaces

    despondency over, 168

    digital type foundry, 221–227

    Emigre, 221–227

    fitting design, 123

    House industries, 229–231

    LettError, 233–235

    Ultimate Symbol, 237

typography as metaphor, 144

U

Ultimate Symbol, 237–239

UNFOLDS maps, 49–53

upfront story area, 115

upgrade strategy, 239

user interfaces, 32

Utne Reader, 252

V

values, core, 81, 82

Vanderlans, Rudy (Emigre), 221–227, 252

vBureau, 241–245

vendor experience, 8–9

Viacom, 31

Vienne, Véronique (author), 4–7

Vigon, Jay (graphic and fashion designer),

    181–183

virtual studio, 242–245

vision, design character and personality, 60